Transport Law in South Korea

Transport Law in South Korea

Fourth Edition

In Hyeon Kim

This book was originally published as a monograph in the International Encyclopaedia of Laws/Transport Law.

Founding Editor: Roger Blanpain
General Editor: Frank Hendrickx
Volume Editor: Eric Van Hooydonk

Wolters Kluwer

Published by:
Kluwer Law International B.V.
PO Box 316
2400 AH Alphen aan den Rijn
The Netherlands
E-mail: lrs-sales@wolterskluwer.com
Website: www.wolterskluwer.com/en/solutions/kluwerlawinternational

Sold and distributed by:
Wolters Kluwer Legal & Regulatory U.S.
920 Links Avenue
Landisville, PA 17538
United States of America
E-mail: customer.service@wolterskluwer.com

ISBN 978-94-035-2459-7

e-Book: ISBN 978-94-035-2469-6
web-PDF: ISBN 978-94-035-2479-5

This title is available on www.kluwerlawonline.com

The Author

In Hyeon Kim (captainihkim@korea.ac.kr), born in 1959, is a full-time professor of Maritime Law and Marine Insurance Law and the director of the Maritime Law Center at the School of Law, Korea University in Korea. He was a former master of Sanko Steamship Co., Ltd, and he is a holder of a valid master's license until 2029. He studied Nautical Science at the Korea Maritime University and Law at Korea University. He obtained LLD from Korea University and LLM from the University of Texas at Austin. He studied Maritime Law at the National University of Singapore as a visiting professor. He was the chairman of the Korea Maritime Law Association. He acted as legal adviser for the Korean government to the International Convention on the Establishment of an International Fund for Compensation for Oil Pollution Damage (IOPC FUNDS), UNCITRAL Transport Law Project (Rotterdam Rules) and Legal Committee of the International Maritime Organization (IMO). He was also a member of revision committee for the Korean Commercial Code (KCC) Maritime Law Section. He is the director of the Maritime Law Research Center at Korea University.

The Author

Table of Contents

List of Abbreviations

ABS	American Bureau of Shipping
B/L	Bill of Lading
BBC	Boat Charter Party
BBCHP	Bareboat Charter Party Hire Purchase
C/O	Chief Officer
CLC	International Convention on Civil Liability for Oil Pollution Damage
CMI	Comite Maritime International
COA	Contract of Affreightment
COGSA	Carriage of Goods by Sea Act
D/O	Delivery Order
E-B/L	Electronic Bill of Lading
EEZ	Exclusive Economic Zone
F/F	Freight Forwarder
FIO	Free In and Out
FOB	Free on Board
FOC	Flag of Convenience
IACIA	Industrial Accident Compensation Insurance Act
IACS	International Association of Classification Society
IMO	International Maritime Organization
IOPC FUND	International Convention on the Establishment of an International Fund for Compensation for Oil Pollution Damage
KAVELP	The Korean Act for Vessel's Entering and Leaving Port
KCAB	Korea Commercial Arbitration Board
KCC	Korean Commercial Code
KCEA	Korean Civil Procedural Act and Korean Civil Execution Act
KIPL	Korean International Private Law
KMLA	Korea Maritime Law Association
KMST	Korea Maritime Safety Tribunal
KMTSA	Korean Maritime Traffic Safety Act

List of Abbreviations

KOPCA	Korean Oil Pollution Compensation Act
KOPOA	Korean Open Port Ordinance Act
KORAIL	Korean Railway Corporation
KOREA	Republic of Korea
KR	Korean Register of Shipping
KSA	Korea Shipping Association
KSLLPA	Shipowner's Limitation of Liability Procedural Act
KSSA	Korean Ship Safety Act
L/C	Letter of Credit
L/I	Letter of Indemnity
LLMC	International Convention on Limitation of Liability for Maritime Claims
LNG	Liquefied Natural Gas
M/R	Mate's Receipt
MIA	Marine Insurance Act
MLTM	Ministry of Land, Transport and Maritime Affairs
MOF	Ministry of Ocean and Fisheries
MSA	Maritime Safety Act
NVOCC	Non-Vessel Operating Common Carrier
P&I	Protection and Indemnity
SDR	Special Drawing Right
SLLPA	Shipowner's Limitation of Liability Procedural Act
U.K.	United Kingdom
UNCLOS	UN Convention on the Law of the Sea
U.S.	United States of America
YAR	York-Antwerp Rules

Preface

I am much honored to have written about transport law for the prestigious International Encyclopedia of Law. Transport law has international characteristics and thus persons who happen to get involved in international transshipment should know the applicable law to the shipment. As a result, a comparative study of transport law of different countries is required. In order to start the comparative study, we should, in advance, collect information regarding the law applicable to each country.

Because Korea is the sixth largest ship-owning country and the eleventh largest trading country, the transport law in Korea is very important domestically and internationally.

I tried to introduce the Korean transport law to the readers as easily as possible. Court rulings do not form part of law in Korea. However, the judgment of the Korean Supreme Court has, in practice, a binding effect on the lower courts. Accordingly, several important precedents by the Korean Supreme Court were introduced in this monograph.

Transport law is basically codified in the same way as the other parts of laws in Korea. To alleviate the burden for the reader to consult with Korean law, I tried to put the pertinent provisions in the main body or as a footnote as much as possible.

The Korean government launched a program to modernize transport law in Korea. The Maritime Law section in the KCC was revised in 2008, and the Land Transport Law section was revised in 2010. The draft of the Air Transportation Law was passed by the parliament in May 2011, and the law governing multimodal transportation is now under drafting by a committee.

I would like to express thanks to Prof. Lee Sik Chai (former chairman of IMO Legal Committee) from Korea University and Mr. B.S. Chung from Kim & Chang for their valuable comments on maritime law.

General Introduction

§1. Geography and Demography

1. The Republic of Korea (hereinafter "Korea or South Korea") is located in East Asia. The Korean Peninsula is divided into two parts. One is called South Korea, while the other is North Korea. South Korea is a shortened name of the Republic of Korea. The Korean Peninsula is connected to the northeastern part of mainland China, while it is surrounded by oceans along the east, west, and south coast; the northern part of the Korean Peninsula faces the northeastern part of mainland China. The east coast of the Korean Peninsula faces the west coast of Japan, while the west coast of the Korean Peninsula faces the east coast of China.

2. As of the end of 2023, Korea had a population of about 51,400,000, among which Seoul, as the capital city, had a population of 9,500,000. Almost all people have a single origin, the Korean.

§2. History

3. Korea was established by unification of three countries about 2,000 years ago in the Korean Peninsula and the current northern part of mainland China. The Koguryo Dynasty, the Paekche Dynasty, and the Silla Dynasty were those countries. The Silla Dynasty unified other dynasties in the seventh century. The Silla Dynasty was the first united kingdom in the Korean Peninsula. The Goryeo Dynasty existed in Korea from the tenth century to the fifteenth century. The capital city was Gaesong, which is in the middle of the Korean Peninsula (currently a part of North Korea). The Goryeo Dynasty was succeeded by the Chosun Dynasty. The name Korea originates from the Goryeo Dynasty. Historically, the Goryeo Dynasty engaged heavily in trading with neighboring China and Japan. The Chosun Dynasty had continuously existed in the Korean Peninsula for about 500 years until it was occupied by Japan in 1910. After being ruled for thirty-six years by Japan, Korea became independent from the Japanese ruling in 1945. The Republic of Korea (South Korea) was born in 1948. Due to the Korean war, which occurred in 1950, the Korean Peninsula was divided into two: South Korea, supported by the United States of America (U.S.), and the Democratic People's Republic of Korea (North Korea), supported by Russia. The Korean Demilitarized Zone serves as the buffer zone between South Korea and North Korea.

4. Historically, the Korean government maintained a closed-door policy, and thus, the shipping business did not develop. Traditionally, due to the influence of Confucianism, shipping business and trade were regarded as a job for lower-class people. Thus, Korea has never been a sea-power nation except for the Silla Dynasty in the eighth century. In the late nineteenth century, Western countries requested the Chosun Dynasty to open the door for trading; however, the government rejected it and maintained a closed-door policy. Three ports, Pusan, Incheon, and Wonsan, were opened for trading with foreign countries as the result of establishing an official diplomatic relationship with Japan in 1876.

5. When Korea started modernization and industrialization under the rule of President J.H. Park in the 1960s, the importance of the shipping business was recognized. He understood that without a strong shipping industry business, trading could not happen. In line with Korea's development toward becoming a modern industrial nation, shipping industry grew rapidly. Along with the growing trade volume, the shipping industry of Korea became large enough to be reckoned with other countries.

§3. Political, Legal, and Administrative System

6. Kings and emperors ruled the Korean Peninsula and its people. When Korea became independent from Japan in 1948, Korean people chose an American-style presidential system rather than restoring the previous kingdom system. This political system was codified in the Korean Constitution in 1948. The President is the head of government and represents the Republic of Korea. Two hundred and ninety-nine representatives elected by general election every four years comprise the Parliament. According to the Korean Constitution, the Korean Supreme Court and lower courts were set up. The administration, the legislature and the judicature are separate and independent in Korea.

7. A former government body in charge of shipping business was the Ministry of Maritime Affairs and Fisheries (MOMAF), which was the successor of the former Maritime & Port Administration Agency, but it was merged with another body and became the Ministry of Land, Transport and Maritime Affairs (MLTM) in 2008. The MLTM was in charge of ships' safety, logistics, transportation, shipping policy, and crew matters. The MOMAF was revived in 2013 and took over its former function from the MLTM. The Ministry of Commerce is in charge of trade and shipbuilding. The Marine Police controls safety and the prevention of oil pollution at sea.

8. The Ministry of Justice is in charge of the enactment, maintenance, and revision of laws such as the Civil Code and Commercial Code. However, MOMAF is in charge of special acts, such as the Ship Safety Act, Seaman's Act, and Oil Pollution Compensation Act.

§4. Legal Education System

9. The Korean government selects judges, prosecutors, and lawyers through bar examinations supervised by the government (Ministry of Justice). Almost all of the successful candidates graduate from the Faculty of Law. Seoul National University and Korea University are the two most prestigious Law Faculties in Korea. Successful candidates are educated for two years by the Judicial Training Institute operated by the Korean government. In 2007, the Korean government passed a law to reform legal experts' training system. Under the new system, the candidates for legal experts should attend the School of Laws for three years after graduating with a bachelor's course. The schools of law, as the successor of the Judicial Training Institute, takes charge of training of legal experts. Korea University School of Law, Pusan National University School of Law, and Inha University School of Law are operating special programs to educate future maritime lawyers. Among them, Korea University is the most active school. It offers four maritime-related courses to the students.

§5. General Information Relating to Transportation

I. General

10. Owing to the above geographic characteristics, Korea boasts several good harbors along the east, west, and south coast.

11. Pusan, located on the southeast coast of the Korean Peninsula, is the largest port in Korea and the closest port to Japan. Pusan is the sixth largest container cargo-handling port in the world. Inchon, located on the west coast of the Korean Peninsula, is the second largest port in Korea. It is the nearest port to Seoul, the capital city of Korea, and a very important port for trading with mainland China.

12. Kwangyang, as a newly built port in the middle of the south coast, is famous for a port dealing with container shipping. The Korean government launched a program to make Kwangyang the second largest port after Pusan port for container trading in Korea.

13. Pohang is located on the east coast of the Korean Peninsula. It is famous for the headquarters of Pohang Steel Company. Many raw materials, such as iron ores and coals for making steel, are imported through Pohang, and steel products are also exported through Pohang. Ulsan, located in the southeastern part of the Korean Peninsula, is a very important port for oil storage and refinery.

II. Shipping Business

14. South Korea is known as the sixth largest ship-owning country in terms of beneficial ownership. Until the early 1980s, Korean shipping fleets were not noticeable. In line with the economic development, Korean shipping companies enlarged the numbers of their fleet. Several conglomerates, such as the Hyundai Group and the Hanjin Group, joined the shipping business as the owners of vessels and subsequently established the Hyundai Shipping Co., Ltd and the Hanjin Shipping Co., Ltd, respectively.

15. Korean shipping companies can be divided into two categories. One is tramper-oriented companies, and the other is liner-oriented companies. The Hanjin Shipping Co., Ltd, the Hyundai Shipping Co., Ltd, and the Korea Marine Transport Co., Ltd are good examples of liner-oriented companies, while the Pan Ocean Co., Ltd, the Korea Line Corporation, Sinokor Merchant Marine Co., Ltd, and the SK Shipping Co., Ltd are good examples of the tramper-oriented companies.

16. The Korea Shipowner's Association had 33 members in 2000 and 181 members as of September 2010. Due to bad economic situation in Korea, the numbers of members were reduced during 2011 and 2012. However, it had a 188-member shipping company as of the end of July 2016. Korean shipowners varied from large shipping companies such as the Hyundai Shipping, the Hanjin Shipping, and the Pan Ocean to small shipping companies which own only one ship.

17. During 2009, 2010, 2011, and 2012, the Korean shipping company had been heavily affected by the worldwide economic recession. Several prestigious shipping companies, such as Korea Line, went for rehabilitation procedure. In 2014, STX Pan Ocean was rehabilitated through the court's rehabilitation process, and the name of the company has been changed to Pan Ocean from STX Pan Ocean. In September 2016, the Hanjin Shipping applied for rehabilitation proceeding due to bad financial status and was finally liquidated.

18. The Korean Shipping Association had 1120 member shipping companies as of the end of July 2016, which operate within Korean territorial waters. Several companies which operate the business within China and Japan are also members of the association.

19. It is a usual practice in Korea that conventional shipping companies operate vessels as owners as well as charterers. Because there is no restriction to becoming a carrier under the KCC, a person without possession of a vessel is also entitled to enter into a contract for the carriage of goods by sea with the shipper and can become a carrier. Accordingly, it is not surprising in Korea that many Freight Forwarders (F/F) act as contracting carriers in liner service in addition to acting as an intermediary.

20. During recession period of 2015 in shipping business, Hanjin Shipping had to apply for the rehabilitation proceeding in 2016. Finally, it was bankrupted in 2017. Korean government tried to revitalize the HMM, the only liner company in Korea at that time. It established Korea Ocean Business Corporation(KOBC),

KOBC in 2018. The KOBC supported the HMM's building of twenty container vessels. Owing to the increased demand for transportation during COVID-19 from 2020 to 2022, its shipping business was very much successful. The HMM became stabilized.

21. During COVID-19 period, almost all Korean shipping companies recorded a surplus. They tried to pay debts which were borrowed from the bank when it was built by accumulated money. They are now in good shape from the viewpoint of financial condition.

III. Aviation Business

22. Korean Airline Co., Ltd and Asiana Airline Inc. are two prominent airline companies in Korea. Both airline companies are engaged in transporting passengers and air cargo domestically and internationally. Almost all famous international airline companies run business with regular flight schedules in Korea. Several other small-size Korean airlines, such as JINAIR Co., Ltd and JEJU AIR Inc., started operations for domestic and neighbor countries in 2008.

23. International express air-cargo service companies such as FedEx and DHL are carrying out their business in Korea.

24. Inchon International Airport, which started its operation in March 2001, is the largest airport in Korea. It boasts of the status of being the second largest airport for handling international air cargo. Gimpo International Airport, located in the Seoul City area, was opened as early as 1958 and had been used as the main international airport in Korea, but it handed over the status to Inchon International Airport in 2001. However, it was reopened for the flight schedule from/to Japan in November 2003 and China in October 2007.

IV. Road and Railway Business

25. The first railway between Seoul and Inchon was opened as early as 1899. Korean government had directly operated Korean railways until 2005. The Korean Railway Corporation (KORAIL), established by the Korean government, took over the functions of operating the Korean railway system. There is no private railway company in Korea. It is because the railway system has been controlled by the government, reflecting the public function of the railway system. KORAIL transports passengers and cargoes as well.

26. Many private bus companies, such as Chunil Express Co., Ltd and Hanjin Express Co., Ltd, are engaged in transporting passengers.

27. Many private companies called Taekbae provide door-to-door transportation service for goods by trucks. Taekbae is a kind of common carriage. The owner of a small package requests the carrier to transport the package, and the carrier undertakes to transport the package. The owner of the goods, in return, promises to pay freight to the carrier. The other way of transportation of goods by truck is called Yongdal. It is very similar to the voyage charter party. The owner of large volumes of goods borrows trucks from the owner of the truck and pays charterage to it.

Part I. Introduction

Chapter 1. General

§1. History of Shipping Business in Korea

28. The Silla Dynasty unified the Korean Peninsula around the seventh century. Mr. Bogo Jang controlled trade among China, Korea, and Japan during the ninth century.[1]

29. During the Goryeo Dynasty, which succeeded the Silla Dynasty, the name of Corea (Korea) became known to Western countries through Arabian merchants. Byuckran Islands, which is located in the middle of the western coast, was a very famous port for trading during the Goryeo Dynasty. Excavations of many wrecked trading vessels off the west coast of the Korean Peninsula show that there was plenty of trading between Korea and China around that time.

30. Rice, which was collected from farmers as tax by the king, had to have been transported to the capital city. Transportation of rice during the Goryeo Dynasty and the subsequent Chosun Dynasty were carried out by ship. It was one of the early types of shipping in Korea.

31. The Chosun Dynasty maintained, as a whole, a closed-door policy for several centuries. However, the Japanese and other superpowers forced the dynasty to open the door to Western civilization at the end of the nineteenth century.

32. The modern-style shipping business was started with the Chosun Dynasty's adoption of the open-door policy in 1876. Shipping companies started to operate vessels as the owners or charterers. Vessels were engaged in trading for the governmental purpose. In 1882, the Chosun Dynasty allowed a private person to purchase a foreign vessel. The modern type of charter party appeared as early as the 1880s.[2]

1. The story of Mr. Bogo, Chang is evidenced by Ennin's Diary (Enin's Travels in Tang, China written by Edwin Reichauer). Tae Hyun Son, *the History of Korean Shipping Business* 59 (Asung Press, 1982).
2. Tae Hyun Son, *ibid.*, 113.

33. After Korea was liberalized from Japanese control in 1945, Korea started to participate in the international shipping business. The government played an important role in the Korean shipping business. Immediately after its independence from Japan, the Korean government established a shipping company named as Korean Shipping Corporation in 1950, but it was privatized in 1968. Hanjin Shipping Co., Ltd merged it in 1988. Currently, there is no shipping company owned or subsidized by the Korean government.

§2. Overview of Korean Law

34. Korean law is based on continental law like Japan and China. The origin of Korean law is German and French law. The Korean laws relating to transportation are codified in the Korean Civil Code and KCC. Theoretically, the precedents rendered by the Korean Supreme Courts do not bind the lower courts. In this sense, the judgments by the court are not regarded as the source of the law. However, the precedents, in practice, affect the decision of the lower courts.

Chapter 2. Main Source of Transport Law

§1. Korean Commercial Code

I. Overall Structure of the KCC

35. Transport law comprises of four different kinds of transportation: maritime transportation, land transportation, air transportation, and combined (multimodal) transportation. Currently, the KCC deals with only land transportation, maritime transportation, and air transportation.

36. Land transportation is regulated by the provisions in Book II (Commercial Business Activities), whereas maritime transportation is regulated by those in Book V (Maritime Business Activities). Transportation in the lake and within port area falls within land transportation (Article 125). Transportation by rail and road are all regulated by the KCC Book II.

37. Combined (multimodal) transportation had not been regulated by the KCC until 2008, when the Korean government inserted a provision regulating liability issues in multimodal transportation in the KCC. Article 816 in the KCC is intended to designate laws to be applied for the legal issues involved in combined transportation. It follows a network liability system. Because Article 816 regulates only combined transportation, necessarily including maritime leg, and thus there is no regulation addressing transportation covering both land and air leg, the Korean government is now drafting a new combined transportation law.

II. Maritime Law

38. When the KCC was adopted for the first time in 1962, it was based on the Japanese Commercial Code, which had been modeled on German and French Commercial Codes. Marine insurance law is not a part of the maritime law section, but it is contained in the insurance law section, which is the major difference between the KCC and Japanese Commercial Code and the Chinese Maritime Law Act.

39. The private maritime business activities are regulated by the maritime law section (Book V) in the KCC. Since the initial codification of commercial law in 1962, the maritime law section in the KCC has been revised twice. The first revision was done in 1991, and the second revision was done in 2007.

40. Since its initial codification in 1962, it contains relevant provisions for the ship, crew, shipowner's limitation of liability, carriage of goods by sea, charter party, ship collision, salvage, general average, and maritime lien.

41. At the first revision in 1991, the KCC adopted the most provisions in the Visby amendments, such as the increased package limitation amounts. At the second revision in 2007, the KCC was modernized in accordance with the development of maritime transportation. The provisions, such as the sea waybill, electronic Bill of Lading (B/L), and multimodal transportation, were codified in the KCC. However, the main contents of the Hamburg Rules are not adopted even in the 2007 KCC. Korea is neither a contracting state of Hague-Visby Rules nor the Hamburg Rules. The scope of ship collision has been expanded to the indirect collision in the 2007 revision.

42. Korea does not have a separate and distinctive Carriage of Goods by Sea Act (COGSA), which the U.S., the United Kingdom (U.K.), Japan, and Canada have. Provisions regulating the carriage of goods by sea are contained in one of the chapters in the maritime law section (Book V) of the KCC. The KCC maritime law section deals with the carriage of goods by sea as well as the charter party.

43. The KCC contains the marine insurance law rules in the insurance law section (Book IV), not in the maritime law section (Book V). However, Japanese Commercial Code has it in the maritime law section. China placed it in the maritime law.

III. Air Transportation

44. Korea ratified the 1955 Hague Protocol to Warsaw Convention on July 13, 1967, and it came into force in Korea on October 11, 1967. Since then, international air transportation has been regulated by the revised Warsaw Convention in Korea. In addition, Korea ratified the Convention for the Unification of Certain Rules for International Carriage by Air, 1999 (hereinafter "Montreal Convention") on September 20, 2007, and it took effect in Korea as of December 29, 2007. There was no domestic private law governing air transportation in Korea.

45. The Korean government is trying to enact a domestic law governing air transportation. The draft is based on the Montreal Convention. The draft aims to apply the law to international air transportation between Korea and a non-contracting state to the Montreal Convention and to purely domestic transportation within the Korean territory. The draft for air transportation law was passed by the Korean Parliament on May 23, 2011, which was effective as of November 24, 2011.

§2. Korean Civil Code

46. The Korean Civil Code functions as another main source of law regulating legal matters involved in the maritime business. While the Korean Civil Code has a status as a general law, the KCC is a special law. Special provisions in the KCC prevail over the general provisions in the Civil Code under the Korean law. As a result, when no provision applicable to the case in the KCC is found, one should consult with the Civil Code. The Korean Civil Code includes both the contract law and the tort law.

§3. International Private Law

47. The Korean International Private Law (hereinafter "KIPL") is one of the main sources of laws and should not be neglected. It deals with the jurisdiction and governing law issues. When a foreign factor is involved in a particular case before a court, the judge in charge of the case should decide the applicable governing law to the case based on the provisions in the KIPL.

48. The KIPL stipulates party autonomy as one of principles in Article 25. Accordingly, parties' free agreement prevails over the provisions in the KIPL.

49. In the 2003 revision, a provision on jurisdiction was inserted based on the Korean Supreme Court's judgments (Article 2). The court should take into consideration several factors, such as fairness, effectiveness, and speediness, in order to decide whether there is a substantial relationship between the case and Korea when it decides whether the Korean court has jurisdiction over the relevant case. Whether or not the Korean courts have jurisdiction pursuant to Korean Civil Procedural Law, if it is purely a Korean case without a foreign factor, plays a good factor in deciding that the Korean court has jurisdiction in case of a foreign-related case.

50. In the 2022 revision, jurisdiction issues became included in the International Private Law. The number of each provision became renumbered. The basic principles, such as the freedom of contract, still exist in the law.

§4. Special Acts for Transportation

51. Korea is a contracting state of the 1992 International Convention on Civil Liability for Oil Pollution Damage (CLC) and 1992 IOPC FUND. In order to implement them, Korean government enacted the Korean Oil Pollution Compensation Act (KOPCA) in 1992. IOPC FUND can be a valid defendant under the KOPCA. The shipowner should establish distinctive and separate limitation funds only for victims caused by oil pollution pursuant to the KOPCA. It is a good source of law for regulating oil pollution compensation in Korea. Along with ratification of the Bunker Convention, the Korean government added the relevant provisions to the KOPCA in 2009. There is no special and distinctive fund for victims caused by the bunker pollution, which is the main difference between the oil pollution case leaked from oil tanker and bunker oil pollution case.

52. Even though the substantive laws regarding the shipowner's limitation of liability are regulated by the KCC, the procedural matters are regulated by a particular and special law called the Procedural Act for Shipowners' Limitation of

Liability, codified in 1991. In a case involved in the shipowner's limitation of liability, the governing law regulating substantive matter for the case is decided by the KIPL.

53. Korea is neither a contracting party to the 1910 Collision Convention nor the 1986 Salvage Convention. The maritime law section of the KCC deals with collision and salvage. However, most of the above Conventions are reflected in the relevant provisions of the KCC.

54. Korea is neither a party to the International Convention Relating to the Arrest of Sea-Going Ships, 1952, nor to the International Convention on Arrest of Ships, 1999. Unlike China, Korea does not have any special provisions in the laws based on the convention for the arrest of a vessel. The Korean Civil Procedural Act and Korean Civil Execution Act (KCEA) are two main sources regulating ship's arrest; the relevant provisions applicable to the ship are very much different from those of the above international conventions.

55. Korea is neither a party to the 1967 International Convention for Maritime Lien and Mortgages nor the 1993 Convention. Substantive laws for maritime lien are stipulated in the KCC. Crew claims, pilot charges, port dues, salvage charges, general average expenses, and collision damages are good examples of triggering maritime lien under the KCC. When a foreign factor is involved in the relevant case, the governing law is decided by the KIPL. Therefore, a Japanese vessel is subject to a maritime lien before the Korean court, and whether the applicant has a maritime lien should be decided by the Japanese maritime law. However, procedural law, such as the execution of the arrest based on the maritime lien, is regulated by the KCEA.

56. The Pilot Act, Seamen's Act, Ship Safety Act, and Ship Registration Act are special acts for the purpose of public and administration. Newly revised 2012 Maritime Safety Act functions as a general rule for safety matters. It includes wreck removal, ISM Code, and Collision Avoidance Rules. Party's agreement based on general terms is regulated by the Act for Regulating General Terms. Party's agreement may be null and void if it is against the Act.

57. The Safety Act for Leisure Boats was also adopted to regulate the leisure boat's safety. Leisure boats less than 20 GRT is subject to the Safety Act for Leisure Boats in respect of registration for the purpose of title of the boat. There is no need to register the title to registration office operated by the court. Only the registration in a local governmental agency satisfies the requirement for the purpose of registering the title. It has special navigation rules for leisure boats and other leisure equipments.

Chapter 3. Court System and Jurisdiction

§1. Court Systems

58. Korea maintains a three-instance court system. Legal disputes are dealt with at a district court as the first instance court. Parties in disputes are entitled to make an appeal at the High Court as the second instance court (appellate-level court). The Korean Supreme Court functions as the third and final instance court.

59. The Korean Supreme Court is located in Seoul. Korea maintains five High Courts at Seoul, Pusan, Daegu, Taejon, and Kwangju. The Patent Court of Korea is an appellate-level court established in 1998.

60. There is no jury trial in Korea. The first and the second instance courts function as fact finders. The Supreme Court deals with only legal issues.

§2. Special Tribunals for Maritime Cases

61. Korea does not operate any special court for maritime law cases which the U.K., Singapore, and China have. Maritime law cases are dealt with by the general district court along with other general cases. Even though Seoul Central District Court and Pusan District Court allocate maritime law cases to the special divisions of the court named as the International Business Transaction Team, the judges in the team are not fully familiar with maritime law issues. There was a discussion about establishing a special court for maritime cases. As a result, the special divisions for the maritime cases were established in the Seoul Central District Court and Seoul High Court as of February 22, 2016.

62. However, Korea has a special agency called the Korea Maritime Safety Tribunal (KMST) to investigate the cause of maritime accident. The KMST has two functions: one is to decide the cause of maritime accident by the decisions of umpires, and the other is to punish holders of navigational officer's licenses and pilots on behalf of the MOMAF. The KMST added a function to assess the contributing ratio when multiple parties are involved in maritime accident such as a collision. The contributing ratio in the collision case decided by the KMST is presumptively accepted as the fault ratio for the assessment of liability in the damage compensation proceeding.

63. Several attempts to establish an admiralty court from 2017 to 2023 failed due to lack of demand from the end user. Pusan City, Inchon City and Korea Maritime Law Association (KMLA) are among the most active parties to the movement

§3. ARBITRATION

64. Arbitration is one of the popular dispute resolutions in Korea. However, any special and independent board for maritime arbitration does not exist in Korea, which the U.K., the U.S., Japan, Singapore, and China maintain. Instead, the Korea Commercial Arbitration Board (KCAB)[3] has a special division to provide parties involved in maritime law issues with maritime law-related arbitration. However, ad hoc arbitrations have also been selected as an alternative dispute resolution method in Korea, and they are gaining popularity these days. London Maritime Arbitration agreement is inserted in most maritime contractual agreements such as NYPE, GENCON, Lloyd's Open Form, and shipbuilding contracts executed in Korean jurisdiction.

65. The arbitral award shall have the same effect on the parties as the final and conclusive judgment of the court; according to Arbitration Act Article 35, Korea signed and ratified the UN Convention on the Recognition and Enforcement of Foreign Arbitral Awards.

§4. JURISDICTION

I. General

66. Jurisdiction issue is different from governing law issue. Jurisdiction issue is whether a certain court has the power to adjudicate a defendant to the court. Governing law issue is which law is applicable to the case.

67. When a foreign factor is involved in a case, the governing law is decided by the KIPL. Until 2002, Korea did not have a provision for international jurisdiction. International jurisdiction issues had been decided by the Korean courts rather than statutory laws. When the KIPL was revised in 2002, a provision regarding international jurisdiction was inserted in Article 2. The provision is a reflection of the famous Korean Supreme Court's decision (*2004.3.25 Docket No. 53349*).

68. Article 2 says that a Korean court has jurisdiction over the case when a party or dispute has a substantial relation with Korea. The court should follow reasonable principles reflecting ideals for international jurisdiction allocation when it ascertains the presence of a substantial relation.

69. It is one of the principles of jurisdiction in Korea that the plaintiff should follow the *lex fori* of the defendant. And thus, if a Korean shipowner suffered from damages due to collision caused by the negligence of an opposing Japanese vessel, the Korean shipowner as the plaintiff should bring about the lawsuit against the

3. The KCAB was established in 1966 and has offices in Seoul and Pusan.

Japanese owner in a Japanese court (Korean Civil Procedural Act Article 2). However, even if the plaintiff raises a lawsuit in Korea, the Korean court may have jurisdiction if the case has a substantial relationship with Korea, according to the KIPL Article 2. The address of the defendant, the place where the obligation was provided by an obligor, the place where tort was taken place, and place where a business office is located are enumerated as good examples of the substantial relationship. Accordingly, if, in the above case, tort was done within the Korean territorial waters, the case has a substantial relation with Korea, and thus, the Korean court has a jurisdiction over the case, pursuant to Article 2 of the KIPL.

In crew claims of the Korean Supreme Court case *2009.11.12. Docket No. 2009da54553,* a bereaved family of the Korean crew brought about the lawsuit against the P& I club as a liability insurer of the Japanese shipowner in a Korean court rather than the U.K. The Japanese owner of the crew entered into the P&I insurance contract with the U.K.-based P&I club. The Korean court decided that the Korean court had jurisdiction because the plaintiff was a Korean and furthermore, the P&I club had its branch office in Korea.

70. Under the KIPL Article 25, party autonomy is upheld as a principle of the law. Accordingly, if the parties agree to decide which country has jurisdiction over disputes, Korean courts admit the agreed jurisdiction.

II. Exclusive Jurisdiction Clause

71. The Hague-Visby Rules does not regulate the jurisdiction. Therefore, the validity of the exclusive jurisdiction has been left to domestic law under the Hague-Visby Rules. However, the Hamburg Rules have a jurisdiction clause. Korea is neither a contracting state for the Hague-Visby Rules nor for the Hamburg Rules. It is common for Korean shipping companies to use the B/L with the exclusive jurisdiction agreement clause. It is also common for Korean shippers to enter into a contract for the carriage of goods by sea with foreign shipping companies with the B/L, including the exclusive jurisdiction clause. Several disputes involved in the validity of the exclusive foreign jurisdiction clause in the B/L were dealt with by Korean courts.

72. In the Korean Supreme Court case *2004.3.25. Docket No. 53349*, a Korean claimant was brought into the lawsuit in a Korean court even though there was a Japanese foreign jurisdiction agreement in the B/L. The Japanese carrier as the defendant argued that the court did not have jurisdiction because there was a Japanese jurisdiction agreement in the B/L. It is the settled principle of the law by the Korean courts that if three requirements are met,[4] the foreign jurisdiction clause is

4. On Mar. 25, 2004, the Korean Supreme Court, referring to its leading case (*1997.9.9. Docket No. 96da20093*) on the validity of the exclusive jurisdiction clause of the Korean Supreme Court case, set forth the ruling: in order to exclude Korean jurisdiction and make an exclusive foreign jurisdiction clause effective, (i) the case must not be subject to the exclusive jurisdiction of Korea, (ii) the designated foreign court should have jurisdiction in accordance with the foreign law and in addition,

valid, and thus, the Korean court does not have jurisdiction to stay the action: one of the requirements is the presence of a reasonable connection between the selected foreign country's court and the case. The defendant argued that the case had a reasonable connection between the case and Japan because of the Japanese governing clause in the B/L. The Korean Supreme Court decided that the Japanese governing law clause in the B/L did not apply to the case because the cause of action in the case was not based on the breach of contract but in tort, and thus, the case did not satisfy the requirement for the foreign jurisdiction clause to be valid and accordingly the Japanese foreign jurisdiction clause was not valid.

73. In this respect, Korea can be classified as one of the countries admitting the validity of the exclusive jurisdiction clause in a contract only if certain requirements are met.

---

the case should have reasonable relationship with the foreign court, and (iii) if the exclusive jurisdiction agreement is clearly unreasonable and unfair, the agreement will be null and void because the contract is against public policy.

Chapter 4. State Immunity and Transport Law

§1. General

74. According to the 2004 UN Convention on Jurisdictional Immunities of States and Their Property, a State enjoys immunity, in respect of itself and its property, from the jurisdiction of the courts of another State subject to the provisions of the current convention (Article 5).

75. State Immunity is a theory that a State is not subject to another State's jurisdiction.

§2. State Immunity Theory in Korea

76. Unlike the U.K. and the U.S., Korea does not have any codified provision on State Immunity. However, in the Korean Supreme Court case *1975.5.23. Docket No. 74ma281*, the court accepted the State Immunity theory. The court rendered that a foreign State should not be subject to Korean jurisdiction regardless of the cause of dispute. In the Korean Supreme Court case *1998.12.17 Docket No. 97da39216*, the court upheld the relative theory of foreign sovereign immunity. The court upheld that the theory was applicable for only the public action of the foreign State in Korea, and thus, if the foreign State carried out functions as a private person rather than a public entity, the State should be subject to the Korean jurisdiction.

77. In relation to transport law, it may be supposed that a foreign State owning shipping company may become a carrier to transport cargo bound for Korea. If the shipper who suffered from damages brings about a lawsuit in Korea, whether the shipping company is eligible for rejecting the case based on the State Immunity theory or not might be dealt with by the Korean court. In the above example, the foreign government acts as a private person rather than a public entity. Therefore, the Korean court may decide that it has jurisdiction over the lawsuit.

78. When a foreign vessel laden with cargo on board tries to enter a Korean port, the master or the pilot may rely on the depth that appeared in a chart which is produced by the Korean government. If there is a rock which is not marked on the chart, the vessel may go aground and incur damages. In this case, the owner of the vessel or the shipper may make a claim against the Korean government in a foreign court. The Korean government may argue that it enjoys the State Immunity, and thus, the lawsuit should be rejected by the foreign court.

79. When a classification society carries out a safety inspection on behalf of a foreign State government and, as a result of the negligence of the classification society, the vessel or cargo on board is damaged, whether or not the owner of the vessel or the cargo is eligible to bring about a lawsuit against the classification society in Korea is a related issue in conjunction with the State Immunity theory.

80. In the Prestige oil pollution case, the local government of Spain brought about a lawsuit against the American Bureau of Shipping (ABS), which is one of world-class classification societies in a New York District Court. When the ABS made a counterclaim against the Spanish government, the New York District Court dismissed the counterclaim by the ABS on the ground that the Spanish government was entitled to sovereign immunity.[5]

5. IOPC FUND 92 FUND/EXC.38/7 5.

Chapter 5. Transport Intermediaries

§1. Freight Forwarder

I. Freight Forwarder in Korea

81. One of the good examples of transport intermediaries in Korea is the F/F. Freight forwarding business can be found in maritime transportation and air transportation as well.

82. Because most of the goods are exported and imported by sea transportation, the F/F focusing on maritime transportation is prevalent in Korea.

II. Three Functions of Freight Forwarder

83. The F/F exercises three different functions in Korea. Express provision exists only for pure F/F in the general commercial activity section of the KCC.

84. First, it acts as an agent of the carrier or the shipper. Because it acts as an agent on behalf of the principal, in this case, it is not liable for the legal consequences of its act if it was done within the scope of the delegation in the agency relationship. The agency provisions in the Civil Code are applicable for the case. In the Korean Supreme Court case *2007.4.26. Docket No. 2005da5058*, the court held that in order for the F/F to be held as the carrier, it should issue the B/L as the carrier; however, in this particular case, a different party was listed on the B/L as the carrier and, in addition, the F/F as defendant signed as the agent of the carrier; as a result, the legal requirement for the F/F to be found as the carrier has not been met. It is a good example that the F/F acted as the agent of the carrier.

85. Second, it acts as a carrier itself. Even though it carries out business in the name of an F/F, it can act as a carrier regardless of the connotation of the name as the F/F. In this case, it is liable for consequences of its act as a principal. The provisions for the carrier in the maritime law section of the KCC are applicable for the case. It is liable for the cargo damages against the shipper because it is a carrier. In a Korean Supreme Court case *2003.10.24. Docket No. 2001da72296*, the court decided that the F/F acted as the carrier. Because there is no restriction to become a carrier under the KCC, even the F/F without having title or possession of any vessel is eligible for the carrier. In this situation, the F/F is a contractual carrier. It, as the shipper, enters into another contract for the carriage with the actual carrier. The F/F as the contracting carrier issues the House B/L, which is circulated as a means for negotiation. However, the actual carrier issues the Master B/L to the F/F as the shipper. The F/F as the contracting carrier and the actual carrier are also eligible for invoking package limitation as the carrier pursuant to Article 797 of the KCC. In case it pays damages to the cargo interest, it can make recourse claims against the actual carrier, which actually incurs damages to the cargo. There are many disputes on whether the F/F acted as the contracting carrier or not. If it is regarded as the pure F/F, it can escape from the liability as the carrier.

86. Third, it acts as a pure F/F. It acts as an intermediary. It connects between the shipper as the cargo owner and the carrier. According to the KCC Article 115, the F/F as an intermediary is liable for the cargo damages unless it proves that it did exercise due diligence in receiving, delivering, storing, or selecting the carrier as requested by the shipper. One of the frequent causes of action for the plaintiff to raise to impose liability upon the F/F is that it was negligent in selecting the ocean carrier.

87. In the Korean Supreme Court case *2003.2.14. Docket No. 2002da39326,* Dodo Co., Ltd, in Korea, as a cargo owner, engaged Gio Logistics Co., Ltd, as an F/F, to transport goods which should be presented at an international exhibition in Germany. Gio selected Yang Ming Marine Transport Corporation, a very reputable shipping company, as the carrier. Yang Ming maintained a slot charter relationship with Hanjin Shipping Co., Ltd, which, in turn, chartered a vessel from unstable Choyang Shipping Co., Ltd. The cargo was loaded on board M/V Choyang Ace. At her delivery port, her berthing was refused for several days due to unpaid port charges. Consequently, the customers' goods did not arrive at their destination in due time. Alleging lost profits, Dodo sued Gio. On June 4, 2002, the Seoul High Court rendered that the defendant had selected a reputable company as the carrier, that the vessel had arrived at the destination on time, and that the vessel's berthing was delayed because her operator did not pay port charge, which was not easy for the F/F to find out in advance. The court held that the defendant did not breach its duty of care as the F/F and rejected the claims of the shipper. On February 14, 2003, the Korean Supreme Court affirmed it. The court rendered that as an F/F, the defendant had no duty to inquire about or foresee the default of the port charge of the carrier, so the defendant was not negligent.

III. Regulating Freight Forwarding Business

88. The F/F plays an important role as an intermediary or as a carrier. Too many F/F may harm a stable international transportation. The financial status of the F/F may be important when the shipper or the carrier seeks for compensation against the F/F. In this respect, the need for regulating F/F arises. The Korean government imposes several requirements upon an F/F before it obtains a license from the relevant government agency. One of the requirements is related to the financial status. It should have a surety insurance arrangement with the minimum insured amount of KRW 100 million pursuant to the Cargo Logistics Facilitation Act Article 8 and Presidential Decree Article 11.

§2. CHARTERING BROKER

I. Chartering Broker in Korea

89. Chartering brokers connect the needy charterer and the able owner of the vessel. However, parties are the shipowner and charterer, and the chartering broker is not a party.

II. Legal Nature of Chartering Broker

90. In freight forwarding business, the F/F makes a contract for the carriage of goods with the carrier. Accordingly, the F/F is a party in the contract. However, in a chartering broker, the broker cannot be a party to a contract. The broker plays a role in arranging a contract between the carrier and voyage charterer or time charterer as the cargo interest.[6]

91. There is no special provision to address legal issues in relation to chartering broker. Therefore, general provisions for brokers in the KCC may apply to the case (Articles 93–100).

6. Many shipping agents are found in Korea. Whenever a vessel visits a Korean port, a shipping agent designated by the carrier or owner arranges several matter of the particular vessel. Shipping agent is an independent merchant and an agent of the shipping company. In this respect, it is different from a servant.

Part II. Maritime Law

Chapter 1. Waterway

§1. Korean Waterway Regime

92. The Korean jurisdiction over the seawater extends beyond the territorial sea to the Exclusive Economic Zone (EEZ). The Korean territorial sea follows twelve nautical-miles regime in the UN Convention on the Law of the Sea (UNCLOS) according to the Korean Territorial Sea and Contiguous Zone Act Article 1. The sea areas inside the base line are called the internal water. Korea has exclusive jurisdiction over the water inside the territorial sea. As a party to the UNCLOS, the Korean government promulgated the EEZ Act in 1996. According to the EEZ Act Article 2(2), Korea has sovereign rights over the EEZ area for the purpose of exploring or conserving natural resources, protecting environment and safety of navigation, etc., within 200 nautical miles from the base lines. The sea areas within the EEZ are not fully implemented in the East Sea and Yellow Sea, according to Article 5, because the area is not wide enough for two countries between Korea and Japan in the East Sea and between Korea and China in the Yellow Sea to claim their own EEZ respectively.

§2. The Geographical Scope of Application of Korean Maritime Law

I. General

93. The Korean maritime law section does not stipulate its scope of geographical application. However, it is the general view that the KCC and other related acts are applicable to the maritime activities within the Korean territorial sea. Nevertheless, their scope of application extends to some maritime activities beyond the territorial sea to the EEZ according to the UNCLOS and Korean domestic law. If foreign factors are involved in the case, whether the Korean law is applicable or not depends on the KIPL.

II. Extension of the Scope of Application to the EEZ

94. Some Korean laws regulating maritime activities extend the scope of their application beyond the territorial sea to the EEZ.

95. One good example is the oil pollution case. The KOPCA applies to the oil pollution damages caused in the Korean territory, including the territorial sea and in the EEZ, according to Article 3. Accordingly, when a fisherman suffers damages in the EEZ, he is entitled to receive compensation from the IOPC FUNDS.

96. The other example is a wreck removal case. According to several Korean domestic laws, the owner or possessor of a wreck has an obligation to remove the wreck. A wreck within Korean internal waters or territorial sea is subject to Korean domestic laws, and thus, the Korean government is entitled to impose legal obligation upon the owner or the possessor. When a wreck exists in the EEZ, whether the Korean government has jurisdiction over the wreck and is thus entitled to order the owner or the possessor to remove the wreck is in question. The Public Water Management Act has a provision to the effect that the Korean government has jurisdiction over the wreck. Article 13(1) says that the administration may order the owner or the possessor of the wreck (including vessel or discarded things) to dispose of it when it regards the wreck as involving danger to impede the usefulness of the public waters or to pollute the water. The Act extends the scope of application beyond the territorial sea to the EEZ by including the EEZ in the definition of the public waters in Article 4.

97. In the Seoul Central District Court case *2007.1.18. Docket No. 2006 gahap 36580,* when about 2,000 logs were lost overboard from M/V Tyumen within the Korean EEZ on January 23, 2006, the Korean government ordered the vessel's owner to dispose of the logs drifting at sea, which were impediments to safe navigation pursuant to Article 13(1) of the Public Water Management Act. The owner did not follow the order, and thus, the Korean government spent about KRW 600 million in collecting the logs. Subsequently, the Korean government arrested the vessel by way of prejudgment attachment for the recourse claim against the owner of the vessel. The owner of the vessel argued that the arrest was done wrongfully partly because the Korean government did not have any power to regulate wrecks within the EEZ, and thus, the Act, which gave the Korean government the power to regulate foreign vessels within the EEZ, should not be applied. The court upheld that the Korean government had jurisdiction over the wreck within the EEZ, and thus, the Public Water Management Act was valid.[7]

III. Neutral Cases

98. In order to apply the KCC to a contract for sea transportation, the contract should be performed by a vessel at sea. Regardless of different sea regimes, such as the territorial sea or the EEZ, the KCC is applicable to the case. However, if the transportation is carried out within the area of a port or river or lake, it does not fall within the definition of sea transportation, and it is regarded as land transportation (Article 125).

7. For details, refer to In Hyeon Kim, *Journal of Maritime Law & Commerce* 39, No. 3, 452.

99. Only when a collision occurs: (i) between seagoing vessels; or (ii) between a seagoing vessel and a navigating vessel within internal water, the provision on the collision in the KCC is applicable to the case.

100. When any Korean seagoing vessel encounters maritime risks at any waters, the provision of the salvage is applicable to the case (Article 882). Therefore, regardless of the geographic scope of the waters, the salvage regime in the KCC is applicable to all Korean seagoing vessels.

Chapter 2. The Vessel

§1. Definition of Vessel

101. There is no official definition of a vessel in the KCC. In general, a vessel for the purpose of KCC should have a self-propulsion and thus, a barge may not be regarded as a vessel. However, t*he Korean Ship Act extends the scope of vessel, which is subject to the KCC, to the barge (Article 1bis)*.

102. Under the KCC, only a vessel is regarded as a physical facility of the shipowner. However, a container box became another very important physical facility for a liner company. There is a need to include it as another physical facility in the KCC.

103. In a Korean Supreme Court case *2014.6.26. Docket No. 2014du3945*, whether a floating dock falls within the definition of the vessel, was decided in the Korean court when the Korea Tax Agency imposed an acquisition tax upon the shipbuilding company. The Korean Supreme Court rendered that it fell within the definition of the vessel in the Local Tax Act because it was registered in the ship registration book as a vessel and had moved several times from the dock pulled by the tugboat to the sea.

104. Under Korean law, vessels are differently treated in accordance with their tonnages. Vessels over 20 tons are subject to the special provisions in the KCC regarding the title change of a vessel or mortgage. They are listed on the registration book maintained by the court, just like realty. They can be a subject of mortgage. In order for the purchaser to obtain the title of a vessel, the purchaser is not required to enter its name on the registration book and ship's Nationality Certificate (Article 743). If registered, it can be argued that it obtained the title against the subsequent purchaser who is registered (Article 743).

105. In the meantime, vessels under 20 tons are treated just the same as a general movable, and thus, in order for the purchaser to obtain the title of a vessel, it should necessarily take possession of the vessel pursuant to Civil Code Article 188. Vessels under 20 tons are not subject to the mortgage. For the purpose of offering easy access for the owner of a small pleasure boat, such as a yacht, to borrow money from a bank, the Korean government enacted a law called the Mortgage for Small Ship Act in 2007.

106. Every seagoing vessel falls under the scope of application for the KCC, and thus, the owner of even a small tugboat is entitled to invoke the limitation of liability.

107. Maritime Autonomous Surface Ships (MASS) vessel or autonomous vessel will appear soon. There are lots of discussions over the legal status of the autonomous vessel. Under the third stage of the MASS vessel, the controller at the control center at shore may be regarded as the captain on board. The controller becomes a servant or agent of the ship owner or the carrier. The negligence of the controller at shore brings about the liability of the ship owner or the carrier. By adopting a provision to the effect that the controller is regarded as the servant or agent of the Master on board, legal status and liability issues can be addressed easily.

§2. NATIONALITY

I. Korean Flag

108. According to the Korean Ship Act, only a vessel owned by a Korean citizen or entity with exceptions can be allowed to be registered in Korea. Korean-registered vessels enjoy several benefits by laws. The vessels are allowed to freely enter any port within the Korean territorial sea. In contrast, non-Korean-registered vessels are allowed to enter only open ports such as Pusan, Incheon, and Pohang in accordance with the Ship Entering and Leaving Act (Former Korean Open Port Ordinance Act). The owner of the Korean-registered vessel could receive a government loan or subsidy, but this system is no longer maintained in Korea.

109. The owner of a Korean-flagged vessel has an obligation to employ only Korean crew, with an exception, and the vessel is subject to safety inspection by the Korean government. It also has an obligation to buy liability insurance to fully compensate the crew against the injury or death on board the vessel according to the Crew Act.

110. Bareboat Charterer with Hire Purchase (BBCHP) has been treated as a Korean owner under several Korean domestic laws. In a BBCHP contract, the charterer is scheduled to obtain ownership of the chartered vessel as soon as the charter period ends. The charterer pays the divided portion of the vessel's price to the shipowner monthly. The shipowner still possesses the title of the vessel during the charter period. However, the expected ownership of the charterer against the vessel increases gradually as time passes. The charterer actually obtains the Korean title of the vessel when the charter period ends. Reflecting the expected future of the Korean ownership of the vessel, the Korean government started to regard the chartered vessel as a kind of Korean vessel. The BBCHP vessel is subject to safety inspection by the Korean government according to the Korean Ship Safety Act. However, Korean-flagged vessels are allowed to enter or leave without boarding compulsory pilot according to the Korean Pilot Act. The BBCHP vessel is regarded the same as the Korean-flagged vessel, and thus, the compulsory pilot is not required.

111. Korea is not a country to adopt bareboat registration. The bareboat chartered-in-vessel is not allowed to be registered in the Korean registration. Even though the Korean-registered vessel is chartered out to a foreign country, it still maintains the Korean flag. Only the BBCHP-in-vessel is allowed to be registered in the special Cheju Port registry, which is different from the pure bareboat registration in Germany or Singapore. The simple Boat Charter Party BBC-in-vessel is not allowed to be registered in the above registry.

II. Flag of Convenience

112. Korea does not allow a Flag of Convenience (FOC) vessel to register in Korea. Instead, many owners, in practice, would register vessels in foreign countries which allow FOC registration, such as Panama, Marshal Island, and Saints Vincent. The owner of an FOC vessel has advantages over the otherwise owner in respect of crew wages, safety regulations, and tax. In recent years, the FOC vessels are frequently engaged for the purpose of financial reasons. The bankers who lend money to the shipowner prefer to register the vessel in a foreign country such as Panama rather than Korea in order to have easy execution of the mortgaged vessel as the mortgagee.

113. In order to provide Korean-registered owners with benefits, the Korean government enacted the International Vessel Registration Act in 1997. According to the Act, the owner of the vessel, which is registered in the International Vessel Registration, is allowed to keep foreign crew or officers on board in a limited number (Article 5) and to have tax benefits. Owing to this policy, Korea enjoyed increasing the number of vessels having the Korean flag. Only Korean-flagged vessel and BBBCHP vessel with foreign flag are allowed to apply for Internation Vessel Registration. Therefore, the underlying flag of the IVG is Korean or of FOC countries.

114. The FOC vessels raise several legal issues in Korea. The registered company in the FOC country is not the real owner of the vessel. The real owner appears as the bareboat charterer or managing company. Claimants request the court to regard the bareboat charterer as the real owner and thus impose the liability upon it instead of the registered owner. It can be accomplished under the name of piercing the corporate veil. Only the property of the obligor is subject to the prejudgment attachment under the Korean law. As a result, if the vessel involved in the cargo damages against the innocent cargo owner is operated by A but the registered owner is B, the vessel is not subject to the prejudgment attachment by the cargo owner as a claimant. In this case, if there are any circumstances that the vessel is actually owned by A rather than B, the cargo claimant can apply for the attachment by way of the doctrine of piercing the corporate veil under the Korean case law. According to this doctrine, A as an actual owner could be held liable for the cargo damage instead of B, and thus, the claimant is able to arrest the vessel actually owned by A.[8]

8. Korean Supreme Court case *1988.11.22. Docket No. 87daka1671.*

§3. Registration of Vessel and Ownership

115. Korea maintains two different types of registration of vessels. First, all Korean vessels should be registered in the registration records maintained by the local port authority. It aims to provide a mechanism for the government to control vessels effectively. The other type of registration is a recording system (Registration Book) maintained by the relevant district court. It aims to provide the owner of vessels with means for title change and mortgage. In this respect, Korea maintains a system different from that of motor cars and airplanes, for which only the registration records are maintained by the local administration.

116. The port of registry plays an important role in deciding the governing law pursuant to the KIPL. For example, if the port of registry of a vessel is Panama, the governing law for the purpose of owner's limitation of liability is the Panamanian law rather than Korean law pursuant to KIPL.

117. In a Korean Supreme Court case *2014.11.27. Docket No. 12014ma1099*, a bank which lent money to the shipowner competed with the crew on board the vessel in the race to get auction sale price. The crews applied for an auction sale based on the maritime lien before a Korean court. There existed two registrations for the relevant vessel. The vessel was registered in a German court and also registered in Marshall Island as the bareboat charterer. The court decided that in case of the bareboat registration, the registered country rather than the bareboat registered country should be the basis for deciding governing law for maritime lien pursuant to KIPL. The court explained that the bareboat registration was aimed only at maritime administrative purposes, but the registration in the court was aimed at ownership and mortgage purposes and it was decided that German law should be the governing law for the case.

§4. Real Rights and Mortgages

I. Ownership and Possession

118. Under the Korean Civil Code, a vessel is regarded as a movable. In order to sell a movable, the purchaser should make an agreement to purchase the movable with the seller, and then it should obtain possession of the movable (Article 188). However, under the KCC, the purchaser could obtain the title of the vessel only with an agreement to purchase the vessel in case the vessel is over 20 tons (Article 743). The requirement of possession is not needed.

119. A vessel over 20 tons is prohibited from being subject to a pledge by the KCC (Article 789). It is because if a vessel is subject to the pledge, it should be under the possession of a creditor, and thus, the vessel cannot be employed in trades of goods.

II. Mortgages and Other Real Rights

120. Almost all vessels in Korea are mortgaged by the shipowner as a collateral for the benefit of the banker who lends money to the shipowner. The mortgage is governed by the KCC and Civil Code. The mortgage is triggered by the party's agreement. A vessel is also subject to lien under the Civil Code (Article 320) and the KCC (Article 58). The lien requires the possession of the lien holder. A ship repairer has a right to claim repair expenses against the owner of the vessel. If the owner does not pay the repair expenses, the repairer is entitled to hold the vessel until the owner pays the expenses. It is a kind of statutory lien under the Korean law, and thus, parties are not allowed to trigger it by agreement.

121. According to the KCC, the master of the vessel on behalf of the carrier has a right to retain cargoes until the consignee pays freights (Article 807). It is a kind of a statutory lien and different from the ordinary lien in that it does not necessarily require the possession of the cargo by the carrier or the ship's master.

§5. Ship's Safety

I. Laws Regulating Ship's Safety

122. Ship's safety is very important to protect passengers and cargoes on board the vessel. Safety of Life at Sea (SOLAS) is an international convention for securing ship's safety. Korea is a contracting state to SOLAS. In order to implement the SOLAS Convention, Korea enacted the Korean Ship Safety Act (KSSA).

II. Implementing the Safety Regulation

123. Under the KSSA, Korean-registered vessels are subject to safety inspection by the Korean government. However, the statutory inspection for Korean-flagged vessels is actually carried out by a recognized organization (RO) such as the Korean Register of Shipping (hereinafter "KR"). Korean-flagged vessels engaged in foreign trade are subject to the inspection of the KR, while vessels engaged in domestic trade are subject to the inspection of the Korea Ship Safety Technology Authority (<www.kst.or.kr>) established in 1977. The KR is the sole recognized organization for safety inspection on behalf of the Korean government. There has been a request from foreign classification societies to the Korean government to allow such delegation to them. BV of France was selected as another RO on behalf of the Korean government in 2016.

124. The Port State Control is also implemented by the Korean government. As a Member State of the Tokyo MOU,[9] the Korean government is an eligible party to inspect foreign-flagged vessels when they visit Korean ports, in accordance with the KSSA Article 68. This inspection is carried out by the Korean civil servant rather than the inspector by the RO.

III. Korean Register of Shipping as a Classification Society

125. The KR (<www.krs.co.kr>), established in 1960, has been a member of the International Association of Classification Society (IACS) since 1988.[10] It was located in Daejon, but it moved to Pusan in 2012. A classification society provides services for ship classification. The insurer ascertains the condition of the vessel, which will be the subject matter of the hull insurance through classification by the Classification Society. A purchaser of the vessel may rely on the condition of the vessel through the classification. The cargo insurer also has an interest in transporting the cargo as the subject matter by the safe vessel.

126. In addition to the classification function for insurance, the classification society also carries out statutory inspection on behalf of national governments. The KR represents about sixty foreign countries regarding statutory inspection in Korea. It operates sixty-three branch offices domestically and abroad. It has about 900 personnel.

127. The liability of classification society against the shipowner is limited to the amount equal to the classification charge by agreement.[11] According to the KR's general terms of classification contract, the liability of the KR is limited to the amount equal to the fees which the KR charges for the service. This arrangement deals with the legal relationship only between the shipowner and the KR. Accordingly, when third parties, such as a cargo owner, a purchaser of the vessel, or oil pollution victims, raise claims against the KR, the arrangement is not applicable to the case. Rather, tort law is applicable to the case. Under the Korean law, the classification society is allowed to enjoy the limitation of liability just like the shipowner. There is no special provision to protect the classification society except in the oil pollution case. It is not subject to the lawsuit by the third-party victims caused by the oil pollution from oil tanker pursuant to the KOPCA.

128. Classification societies successfully defended their liability against third parties, such as the cargo owner. In the Nicolas H. case, the NK successfully

9. *The Tokyo MOU <www.tokyo-mou.org> is an intergovernmental cooperative organization on Port State Control in the Asia-Pacific region. It was established to eliminate substandard shipping in the Asia-Pacific region on Dec. 1, 1993. Eighteen countries including Australia, Japan, and China are Member States.*
10. Number of vessels registered by the KR is 2,525 (42,742,855 G/T) as of Sep. 27, 2010.
11. *In the Sundance case, the ABS successfully defended claims from the ship owner. Sundance Cruises Co. and SCI Cruise, Inc. v. The American Bureau of Shipping, US Court of Appeals for the Second Circuit, [1994] 1 Lloyd's Rep, 183.*

defended the cases.[12] Currently, the ABS is under a lawsuit by the victims in the Prestige case. Fortunately, the KR has not been involved in the lawsuit by the third parties thus far.

12. The U.K. House of Lords rendered that the classification society does not owe duty of care for the safety to the cargo owner who is not a party to the classification society. *Marc Rich and Co AG v. Bishop Rock Marine Co (The Nicholas H) [1995] 2 Lloyd's Rep 299, [1996] AC 211(HL).*

Chapter 3. Maritime Lien and Mortgages

§1. MARITIME LIEN

I. Necessity of Maritime Lien

129. Vessels which are owned by the defendant in a suit are frequently subject to arrest by the claimant in the name of prejudgment attachment under the Korean law. In case the vessel is not owned by the defendant, the claimant is not entitled to arrest the vessel in Korea, since only the property owned by the defendant is subject to the attachment under the Korean Civil Procedural Rules Article 81. As a result, if the vessel was operated by the time charterer and cargo was damaged by the negligence of the time charterer, the cargo owner cannot arrest the vessel in the name of the prejudgment attachment under the Korean law. When the defendant is a foreigner, the plaintiff may experience difficulties in finding out the defendant's property located in the country of the defendant. If the defendant is allowed to arrest the vessel itself which caused the accident, it may be very useful for protecting the plaintiff. Maritime lien serves this function. The claimant is allowed to exercise maritime lien under the KCC (if a foreign factor is involved, whether maritime lien is allowed depends on the KIPL).

II. Origin of Maritime Lien under the KCC

130. Maritime lien under the KCC is modeled on the *action in rem* in common law countries such as the U.S. and the U.K. It allows the claimant to arrest the vessel involved regardless of the ownership. Maritime lien stems from the idea that the vessel itself is the obligor or defendant.[13] As a result, the vessel is subject to arrest whether or not it is owned by the obligor (Article 785). And thus, when the collision damages were caused by the vessel operated by a time charterer, the opposing vessel's owner is entitled to arrest the vessel even though the owner of the vessel is not the obligor. It was adopted when the KCC was first enacted in 1961.

III. Claims Accruing Maritime Lien

131. According to the KCC Article 777(1), the claims which accrue the maritime lien, are limited to several items. First priority is given to court-related expenses, port dues, pilotage, towing charges, and preservation expenses or survey fees for the vessel after the vessel enters the port. Second priority is given to claims resulting from the employment contract for crew or servant of the owner. Third priority is given to claims regarding salvage and general average. Fourth priority is given to claims on damages caused by collision and other maritime accidents, damages to the navigational aids, port facilities and fairway, and claims on the loss of

---

13. Byung Tae Bae, *The Annotated Maritime Law* (1982), 391; Grant Gilmore & Charles L. Black, The *Law of Admiralty* 591 (1975).

life or damages to crew or passengers. All the above claims should be incurred by the vessel itself. Therefore, if the crew served on board Vessel A, the crew is not allowed to arrest Vessel B based on the maritime lien.

132. The first prior category is related to claims for public matters such as legal expenses for the common interest of the claimant, tax imposed upon the vessel regarding navigation, pilot charge and tug charge, and preserving expense or survey fee of the vessel and its accessory after the final entering port (Article 777(1)(a)). Where a port authority has port due to a vessel, it is allowed to arrest and sell the very vessel which incurs the port due. A pilot who provides pilot service is also an eligible claimant to exercise the maritime lien against the very vessel on board which it serves. However, a claimant with a bunker charge is not allowed to exercise the maritime lien.[14] Only charge for repairing the vessel in an emergency case for safety brings about a maritime lien.

133. The second prior category is crew claims according to the employment contracts (Article 777 (1)(b)). Crews who have unpaid wages incurred on board a vessel are entitled to apply for the maritime lien against the very vessel. The compensation for crew dead is also regarded as a part of the wages subject to the maritime lien.[15] The crew's unpaid wages, which were incurred during the crew's service on board another vessel (for example, a year ago), do not trigger the maritime lien against the vessel which the crew is currently on board.

134. The third prior category is claims regarding general average and salvage charge (Article 777(1)(c)). A cargo owner who has a claim incurred by general average is also allowed to arrest the vessel on which the cargo on board was sacrificed. When a salvor provides salvage assistance in order to rescue a vessel in distress, it is entitled to exercise the maritime lien against the vessel rescued.

135. The fourth category is collision damages, damages caused by other accidents, other damages to navigational aids, port facilities and fairways, and passenger's or crew's bodily damages and loss of lives (Article 777(1)(d)). Cargo damage caused by the collision falls within this category. When the vessel (A)'s owner loses its vessel by the collision with the opposing vessel (B), it is entitled to exercise the maritime lien against the opposing vessel (B) which contributed to the collision. A passenger who suffers bodily damages is also entitled to apply for the maritime lien against the vessel on which it is on board. The port authority who suffers damages to the gantry crane in a container terminal due to the negligence of the vessel's master is allowed to arrest the vessel based on the maritime lien under the KCC Article 777.

136. The maritime lien should be allowed regardless of who was the obligor in terms of action in personam because it is an action in rem. The KCC has a provision to allow the claimant to invoke the maritime lien where the bareboat charterer

14. It was taken out from the maritime lien catalog in the 1991 revision of the KCC.
15. Jong Hyun Choi, *Maritime Law Details* p. 201 (Parkyoungsa, 2015).

accrues the same claims stated in Article 777(Article 850). As a result, whether the claims which the time charterer brings about accrue the same maritime claims or not becomes in dispute. The Korean Supreme Court regards the time charter party as one of very similar types of bareboat charter party. Therefore, it can be interpreted that the bunker supplier who supplied bunker for the time charterer has a maritime lien on the vessel based on Article 850. Pilot charges, bunker supply charges and port dues are good examples of claims incurred by the time charterer. In the Korean Supreme Court case *2019.7.24. Docket No. 2017ma1442* decision, the Court had a good opportunity to address the case. In this case, several tug boats were engaged in the escorting task for the vessel at port. The time charterer requested the tug service from the owner of the tug boat. Even when tug service was provided, it did not receive payment from the time charterer. It applied for auction sale against the vessel for which the service was made. Whether the debts incurred by the time charterer can bring about the maritime lien or not became a hot issue in Korea. In the lower court, it was denied because there was no explicit provision which allowed the claimant to invoke a maritime lien. However, the KCC admitted it, saying that even though there is no explicit provision on the maritime lien incurred by the time charterer, Article 850(2) can be borrowed by the claimant. First, the legal nature of the time charter party is very similar to that of the bareboat charter party. Second, the owner of the tug boat is not allowed to reject the requested service from ship owner. Therefore, there is a strong necessity to protect the tug owner.

137. Last priority is given to claims by oil tanker. It is allowed to victims caused by oil pollution under the KOPCA Article 51. Even though the KOPCA enacted the CLC, this kind of maritime lien cannot be found in the CLC. The effectiveness of the provision is doubtful. The claimant is protected by the liability insurance, which the owner of the oil tanker is required to enter into by the KOPCA. Furthermore, the claimant has direct action against the liability insurer according to the KCC Article 724(2). I think that there is no good reason to allow the claimant caused by oil pollution to invoke the maritime lien.

138. Cargo claim was deleted from the list of items in the 1991 revision of the KCC, and thus, the cargo owners cannot arrest the vessel by way of the maritime lien under the current KCC. In this respect, it can be said that the KCC does not protect the cargo interests reasonably and that the cargo interests under the Korean law are disadvantageous to those under the Japanese or Panamanian law, which still allows the cargo interests to invoke the maritime lien against the carrier. The author thinks that it should be restored in order to protect the cargo interests under the Korean law.

139. Basically, claims based on the contractual relations between the claimant and the shipowner do not generate the maritime lien under the Korean law. Cargo claims against the carrier, stevedoring charges against the carrier, and charterage from the shipowner against the charterer are such examples.

IV. Effect of Maritime Lien

140. The claimant with a maritime lien has the right to execute the subject matter, such as the vessel or freight or its accessories, in the public sale and satisfy its claim prior to other claimants, including even the mortgagee under the KCC (Article 777(2)). The claimant has a maritime lien on freight obtained in the voyage involved in the accident and claims derived from the vessel and freight in addition to the vessel and its accessories. Where the vessel accrued a maritime lien becomes a total loss, and thus, the owner of the vessel as the insured obtains the insurance proceeds from the insurer, the claimant is not allowed to execute the maritime lien on the proceeds (Article 780). The claimant no longer exercises the maritime lien unless he exercises it within a year from the date when it occurred (Article 786). It aims to protect the interest of the mortgagee.

141. The claimants are allowed to get compensation from the proceeds of the vessel according to the priority orders in Article 777. Where the vessel is sold at the price of only KRW 1000 million, and the crews, victims by collision accident and the mortgagee have claims against the vessel in the amount of KRW 500 million, KRW 1000 million, and KRW 500 million, respectively, the crew is allowed to get full amount of the claim of KRW 500 million and the victims by the collision only KRW 500 million, and the mortgagee get nothing.

142. Even if the owner of the vessel involved in the accident was changed to the new owner and thus the obligor no longer owns the vessel, the claimant who falls within the scope of the application under the KCC Article 777 is entitled to arrest the vessel (Article 785). It functions as a means of protecting the claimant. The claimant is not allowed to exercise the prejudgment attachment against the above scenario because the obligor is no longer the owner of the vessel. Article 777 fills the gap for the benefit of the claimant.

143. The maritime lien can be invoked by the claimant without "title for executing claim," which can be obtained only after the claimant wins the lawsuit in merit against the owner of the vessel. By submitting a document verifying that the claimant has a maritime lien, the claimant is allowed to arrest the vessel and go ahead with the public auction sale. It is one of advantage for the claimant compared with the claimants with non- maritime claims.

144. Where a foreign factor is involved in the maritime lien-related matter, the Korean court should consult with the KIPL to address the matter. According to KIPL Article 60, whether the event brings about the maritime lien or not and what the effect of the maritime lien is should be decided by the law of the flag of the vessel subject to the maritime lien. For example, where a Korean crew applies for auction sale against a Panamanian vessel based on the maritime lien in a Korean court because its wage has not been paid by the shipowner, the Korean court will consult with the Panamanian maritime lien law to decide whether crew wage claim triggers the maritime lien.

V. Maritime Lien and Mortgage

145. As far as the legal effect is concerned, a maritime lien prevails over a mortgage in accordance with the KCC Article 788. The holder of a maritime lien has priority over mortgagee. When a bank as the lender has a mortgage right on the vessel over the vessel's owner and the vessel is simultaneously involved in the ship's collision, the owner of the damaged opposite vessel may apply for the public sale based on the maritime lien. The owner is entitled to take sales proceeds in advance over the bank as the mortgagee. There is a danger that the mortgagee may be put in a disfavored place without any prior notice because the maritime lien under the Korean law is not recorded in the registration book, unlike the mortgage. This mechanism has been under heavy criticism because it makes the bank reluctant to lend money to the owner. In order to ease this disadvantage, the maritime lien holder no longer exercises it if one year has passed after the underlying related claim arose (The KCC Article 786). There is a suggestion that one-year time bar should be lessened to six months.

§2. Mortgage

I. General

146. Mortgage is allowed as one of real rights under the Korean law. A borrower provides a lender with realty as a security for the purpose of safeguarding the payment of the borrowed money. Even though a vessel is not realty, it is regarded as a realty and subject to the mortgage rules. A mortgagee has a priority over a lien holder or pledge holder (The Civil Code Article 356). A mortgagee is entitled to realize its claim against the mortgagor by executing it against the vessel as a security.

II. Mortgage on the Vessel

147. Korean shipping companies utilize mortgage as a means of purchasing vessels. They borrow money to purchase a vessel from banks and, in return, provide the lender with the vessel as a security. The fact that the vessel is under a mortgage is recorded in the ship registration book, which is administered by several local courts.

148. When the owner of the vessel does not pay the borrowed money on the due date, the claimant as the mortgagee applies for the auction sale to the court. The mortgagee gets payment from the money of auctioned vessel in advance over other claimants except the maritime lien holder.

149. According to the KCC Article 787(1), only the vessel registered in the registration book is subject to the mortgage. A vessel over 20 tons is allowed to be registered in the Book (Ship Registration Act Article 2). Therefore, vessels less than 20 tons are not subject to the mortgage (The Korean Ship Act Article 8). However, the Korean government enacted a law named as the Mortgage Act for Small Ships in 2007 for the purpose of enabling the owner of a small ship of less than 20 tons to borrow money from the lender such as banks by providing the ship as a security without handing over the possession of the ship to the lender even though the small vessel is not allowed to be registered in the registration book.

150. Container box also constitutes a physical facility of the shipping company, especially the liner shipping company. The liner shipping company is required to stow cargo into the container box. Therefore, the liner shipping company should possess container boxes. It may own the container box or borrow the box from the owner. Container box is a kind of movable, and thus, it is not subject to the mortgage. If the container box is handed over to the lender as the security for the borrowed money, it will not be used for its own purpose of transportation. The Korean government launched an Act for the owner of the container box to put it into the lender as security without delivering it to the lender. The container box is not the accessory of the vessel, and thus, it is not subject to the maritime lien under the KCC Article 777. However, the claimant against the owner of the vessel as the obligor is entitled to apply the prejudgment attachment in order to secure its claim regardless of the nature of the claim.

Chapter 4. Master and Crew

§1. General

151. Masters and crews in Korea are educated in universities or special-purposed high schools. Korea Maritime University (<www.hhu.ac.kr>) and Mokpo National Maritime University (<www.mmu.ac.kr>) are two high educational institutes to train young officers and engineers in Korea. Low-ranking officers and engineers are educated by specially established maritime high schools located in Inchon and Pusan.

152. During the 1960s, the 1970s, and the 1980s, Korean seafarers who worked for foreign shipowners outnumbered those who worked for Korean shipowners. Japanese and US shipping companies such as Sanko Steamship Co., Ltd attracted many Korean officers. Partly because Korean shipping companies gained momentum to expand their fleets and provided many job openings for Korean officers during the 1990s and 2000s, current Korean seafarers who work for Korean owners outnumber those who work for foreign owners. Korean seafarer market experienced a shortage of junior officers, such as the second officer and second engineer, in the 1990s. To cope with the difficulties of supplying junior officers, the Korean government passed a law named as the Korean International Ship Registration Act (KISRA), allowing foreign seafarers to be employed by the Korean owners who registered vessels in the International Ship Registration.[16]

153. Several big shipping companies, such as the Hyundai Shipping Co., Ltd, the Hanjin Shipping Co., Ltd, and the Pan Ocean Co., Ltd operate independent ship management companies such as Haeyoung Maritime Services Co., Ltd, Hanjin Ship Management Co., Ltd, and Pos Ship Management Co., Ltd respectively. The main purpose of establishing such companies was partly to provide their own fleet with management functions such as crew training and ship repairs and partly to provide third-party shipping companies with ship management services, like Wilhelmsen Ship Management (formerly known as Barber Ship Management). Korean ship management companies have not yet reached the level of Wilhelmsen Ship Management as an independent third-party ship management service provider. However, the Korean government passed a law to expand the ship management business by providing benefits for the Korean ship management companies in 2012.

§2. Employment Contract

154. An owner makes employment contract with masters or crews for operating a vessel at sea. The employment contract is subject to the Korea Seamen's Act. If the agreement puts the seafarer into unfavored position than that in the Act, the agreement is regarded as null and void (Article 28). The owner should provide a

16. It is implied that only Korean nationals are allowed to work on board the Korean-flagged vessel according to Korean Seamen's Act.

seafarer with a paid vacation of six days per month as a reward for working on board the vessel (Article 70(1))). The seafarer is eligible for paid vacation after eight months working on board (Article 69(1)).

155. According to the Korea Ship Officers Act, only officers of Korean nationality should be on board the Korean-flagged vessels. However, in order to fill the gaps of shortage of low-ranking officers, a special agreement between shipowner's association and crew association based on KISRA was made in 2005, which resulted in starting foreign national officers working on board Korean vessels. As a result, hundreds of foreign crew and officers work on board Korean-flagged vessels in conjunction with Korean nationals.

156. The master is appointed by the shipowner or the bareboat charterer unless otherwise agreed (The KCC Article 842). When a vessel is operated by the time charterer, the master is appointed by the shipowner or the bareboat charterer. As a result, the time charterer is not vicariously liable for damages caused by the negligence of the master. Rather, the shipowner or the bareboat charter is vicariously liable for the damages caused by the negligence of the master as far as the ship's maneuvering is concerned, such as ship collision. However, the master is regarded as the servant of the time charterer as far as the ship's business is concerned, and thus, the time charterer is vicariously liable for the cargo damages caused by the master's negligence in relation to ship's business.

157. Apart from an employment contract, a boarding contract may exist in Korea. A certain company does not like to pay salary for the seafarer's waiting period, and thus, as soon as the seafarer disembarked from the vessel, the effect of employment contract ends.

§3. Master's Status and Liability

I. Master as a Servant or Agent of the Owner

158. From the legal point of view, the master is a servant or agent of the owner. When the collision accident occurs due to the negligent navigation of the master and, as a result, the owner of the opposite vessel suffers damages, the master is subject to liability against the victim based on tort law theory under the Korean Civil Code Article 750. In addition, the owner of the vessel is vicariously liable for the damages as the employer of the master according to Korean Civil Code Article 756(1). The victims can choose either the master or the owner as the defendant. When the owner compensates the damages, it is entitled to raise a recourse claim against the master in accordance with Korean Civil Code Article 756(3). In such recourse action, Korean courts usually reduce the indemnification amount to a substantially low level. The master is eligible to invoke the shipowner's limitation of liability (Article 774).

159. In contrast, when cargo on board was damaged by a negligent act of the master, the cargo interest cannot bring an action against the master based on the breach of contract because the master does not have any contractual relationship with the cargo interest. However, it is subject to claims based on the cause of action in tort.

160. The pilot is regarded as a temporary servant of the shipowner or the master. The pilot is engaged for easy approaching and berthing to harbor or leaving the harbor. Most major ports are designated as a compulsory pilotage area. The shipowner and pilot enter into the pilotage contract in which the liability of the pilot is limited to the pilotage for the relevant pilotage service. It is not applicable where the accident occurs due to the intentional act or gross negligence of the pilot. If that is the case, the pilot should compensate for full damages sustained by the shipowner. There is no statutory law to allow the pilot to limit its liability against the third party based on the cause of action in tort, which is different from the U.K. Pilotage Act in which the pilot is allowed to limit its liability. However, the pilot is eligible to invoke the shipowner's limitation of liability.

II. Master's Power of Delegation

161. The most important provision of the master in the KCC is the provision related to the scope of the master's power of delegation as an agent of the shipowner. The master is a designated agent by the shipowner, but the scope of delegation is fixed by the operation of the law in the KCC. The master has a very extensive scope of power of delegation when the vessel stays in the non-registered port, while it has a limited power of delegation when the vessel stays within the registered port (Article 749).

162. When the vessel is away from the port of registry, the master shall have the authority to perform all judicial and non-judicial Acts which are necessary for continuing the voyage (Article 749(1)). If the master enters into a food supply contract with a shipchandler, the contract is enforceable against the shipowner because the parties of the contract are the shipowner and the shipchandler. The master has a delegation to enter into the contract for the carriage on behalf of the shipowner as the status of an agent of the shipowner. If the master receives a legal notice from the court, it is regarded as the receipt of the notice by the shipowner pursuant to Article 749. However, the vessel is in the port of registration, and the scope of the master's power of delegation becomes narrowed down only to the employment and dismissal of crews (Article 749(2)). This is because, when the vessel is staying at the port of registry, the owner is able to carry out business activities directly without relying on the master, and thus, the scope of the master's power of delegation is not required to be expanded broadly. The owner is not allowed to submit the fact as a defense against the innocent third party that certain scopes of the power of delegation prescribed in Article 749 are excluded (Article 751). This provision provides the third party with a certainty that the contract is enforceable when it makes a contract in which the shipowner is one of the parties.

163. The scope of the master's delegation power differs between the port of registry and the non-port of the registry. In the Korean Supreme Court case *1991.12.24. Docket No. 91da30880,* the court rendered that the port of registry should be decided by the place where the headquarters of the real shipowner for the vessel exists. Therefore, while the vessel is registered in Panama but the real operation of the vessel is done in the Pusan port, Pusan port will be regarded as the port of registry for the purpose of master's scope of the delegation under Article 749 of the KCC.

164. The general average arises under the KCC Article 865 only by the master's intentional act to dispose of the vessel or cargo on board in order to avoid the common danger to the vessel and cargo on board as well. When the salvage operation of a vessel is successful, the salvage award is distributed equally between the crews and the owner of the vessel from the remainder after damages and expenses incurred to the vessel were subtracted in advance, according to Article 889(1). The above distribution is made by the master of the vessel (Article 889(2)).

§4. Special Compensation Scheme for the Seamen

165. The master and crew's compensation are regulated by the Korean Seamen's Act. The Seamen's Act aims partly at providing adequate compensation for dead or injured crew members on board seagoing vessels. The Korean Worker's Act is a general law for compensating all kinds of workers, whereas the Seamen's Act is a special law for the crew on board a seagoing vessel. Accordingly, the provisions on compensation in the Seamen's Act prevail over those in the Worker's Act. If there is no provision applicable in the Seamen's Act, the provisions in the Worker's Act will be applicable for the case.

166. Under the Korean Worker's Act, for the bereaved family to recover compensation, the family must prove that the accident was caused while the worker was in the course of his or her employment.[17] However, under the Seamen's Act, the bereaved family of the crew does not necessarily need to prove that the accident occurred during the course of employment. Even if it proves the fact that the crew member involved in the accident was employed on board, it is eligible for receiving compensation (Article 99(2).[18]

An insured crew is entitled to full recovery from the injury, for which the employer should pay all expenses if the crew was injured during the course of its employment (job-related work) pursuant to Article 94(1). Even where the injury is not related to the employment, the injured crew can recover a limited compensation and treatment from the employer in accordance with Article 94(2).

17. The bereaved family can get compensation equal to the average salary for 1,000 days. Otherwise, the family cannot get any compensation (Article 99(2)).
18. If the accident is involved in job-related works, the bereaved family is entitled to payment equal to average salary for 1,300 days (Article 99(1)). If the accident is not involved in job-related work, the bereaved family is entitled to compensation equal to average salary for 1,000 days.

The master and crew under the Seamen's Act are put in a favored position compared with the Worker's Act.

167. There were many disputed cases between the crew and shipowner, whether an accident occurred during crew's being on board and whether it was a job-related accident. The Korean Supreme Court shows a tendency to accept the case positively in favor of the crew. It is partly because Article 94(1) stipulates that being on board the vessel includes periods for crew's going ashore and crew's travel in order to embarkation or disembarkation. Going ashore is usually regarded the same as being on board the vessel. In the Korean Supreme Court case *1999.9.17. Docket No. 99da24836*, the chief cook was presumed to have slipped over from the pier after going ashore and died at sea. Whether he was eligible for compensation based on Seamen's Act or not was at issue. The court decided that he died while on board the vessel, and thus, the owner should pay compensation for the bereaved family of the diseased crew.

In the Korean Supreme Court case *2011.5.26. Docket No. 2011da14282*, a seafarer X took rest at his cabin in a building for crews on shore after voyage. He was heavily hurt while he tried to support the ladder on the container box at the request of a neighbor. He applied for injury compensation and hospital treatment based on Article 94(1) of the Korean Seamen's Act, which stipulates to the effect that the shipowner should compensate for curing injured crew if the injury was sustained while he executed job-related work. The court decided that where a crew member was injured while he was staying at the place on shore or at port, like his residence, it did not fall within the definition of job-related injury under Article 94(1) unless there was any special situation such as he was preparing for imminent sailing when he was injured. In this case, the crew member at issue was not obviously on board the vessel, and thus, he could not rely on the compensation or treatment even based on Article 94(2) because it was obvious that he was on shore, not on board. The only resort for the crew to get compensation or treatment was that based on Article 94(1). The crew should prove that the accident occurred while executing job-related work. The court took into consideration that the crew stayed at a residence which was very similar to the private home and decided that the injury while supporting a ladder in the vicinity of the residence was not job-related work. As a result, the compensation and treatment of the insured crew X as the plaintiff were denied.[19]

168. The definition of crew under the Seamen's Act does not extend to the workers on board the oil rig or other off-shore facilities. Therefore, they are subject to the Korean Worker's Act. As a result, their protection is not good enough, as opposed to the crew on board.

169. The Industrial Accident Compensation Insurance Act (IACIA) was first introduced in 1964 to protect workers from accidents in Korea. It is a compulsory

---

19. Please refer to In Hyeon Kim, *Korean Maritime Law Update: 2008*, for Korean crew's compensation matters, 40-3 JMLC 446.

insurance imposed upon the employer of workers to discharge its obligation of compensating the worker's death or injury during the course of employment. The employer should pay insurance premiums to the Korea Worker's Compensation & Welfare Service.

170. The compensation scheme under the Korean Seamen's Act is similar to that of the Jones Act in the U.S. However, it has several different aspects. First, the seamen are still eligible to exercise claims based on the cause of action in tort admitted in the Civil Code, in addition to that in the Seamen Act, as opposed to that in the Jones Act. Second, the breach of seaworthiness obligation of the owner for seamen's safety does not provide crews with any valid cause of action, which gives seamen the cause of action under the Jones Act.

§5. Voting Right and Right to Strike

171. Korean crews cannot exercise their voting rights during the service on board at sea. In the Korean Constitutional Court case *2007.6.28. Docket No. 2005 Hunma772*, the Civil Servant Election Act was decided by the Korean Constitutional Courts as being against the Korean Constitution because the Act did not provide crews at sea with any methods to cast ballots. There is a discussion in the Korean Parliament on how Korean crews on board cast ballots.

172. The crews' right to strike is allowed in a very limited fashion under the Korean law. Taking into consideration the ship's safety, the Seaman's Act does not allow the crew to strike on board in several cases including: (i) the vessel stays at a foreign port; (ii) a passenger boat is under sailing with a passenger on board; (iii) a vessel for carriage of dangerous goods is under sailing laden with cargo; (iv) when a vessel or person may put in serious danger if a strike goes on (Article 27).

Chapter 5. Owner's Obligation and Liability

§1. General

173. A shipowner is a person or legal entity to have ownership of a vessel. The owner does not necessarily operate its vessel by entering into the contract for carriage with the shipper. It may charter out the vessel to the charterer and thus may not operate the vessel. In the latter case, the owner is satisfied with earning charterage from the charterer rather than earning freight from the shipper.

174. A bareboat charterer is called an ad hoc owner in Korea. Even though the bareboat charterer does not own the vessel, it possesses the vessel and employs the master and crew to operate the vessel. Therefore, it is called as an ad hoc owner. In terms of liability, the bareboat charterer is no different from the shipowner in that it is vicariously liable for damages caused by the negligence of the master of the vessel whom it employs (Article 850). In this respect, according to the Korean Supreme Court, the time charterer is not vicariously liable, at least for the damages during the ship maneuvering, because damages are caused by the master employed by the shipowner or bareboat charterer.

§2. Shipowner's Obligation and Liability

175. In a typical situation of the vessel operation, the owner is the operator. The master and crew are employed by the owner. The owner may be held vicariously liable for the damages caused by the master or crew's negligence. The owner is entitled to invoke limitation of liability (global limitation) according to the KCC.

176. When the bank is registered as the owner of the vessel, it is not regarded as the owner in terms of liability caused by the operation of the vessel, but the bareboat charterer is liable as the owner.

177. The owner's obligation or liability in tort is not stipulated in the KCC except in the collision case. It is a matter of the application for the Civil Code. The owner is vicariously liable for the damages caused by its crew or master pursuant to the Korean Civil Code Article 756.

178. The shipowner is also statutorily liable against the third party. According to Article 809, the shipowner is liable for the cargo damages in addition to the carrier in case the vessel is chartered out to the time charterer or voyage charterer. The registered owner of oil tanker is statutorily liable for oil pollution damages even though the vessel is operated by the charterer pursuant to KOPCA (Article 2(4) & Article 5)-(CLC Articles 1(4) & 3(1)). The registered owner of the oil tanker is obliged to enter into liability insurance in order to compensate for oil pollution damages. The shipowner or bareboat charterer has an obligation to remove wreck according to the Korean law. The shipowner is also statutorily liable for wreck removal. It has an obligation to remove its own wreck according to the Ship Entering and Leaving Act and Maritime Safety Act. It is usual manner in Korea for the shipowner to enter into a contract for liability insurance. Korea P&I club is a kind of liability insurer which undertakes these kinds of shipowner's risks.

179. The shipowner has an insurable interest in the vessel which it owns. The shipowner as the insured enters into the hull insurance contract with the insurance company. The shipowner gets insurance proceeds equal to the amount of the vessel's price when the vessel becomes a total loss.

180. When a vessel is chartered out to the bareboat charterer, the bareboat charterer enters into an employment contract with the master and crew. Therefore, the bareboat charterer rather than the owner is vicariously liable for the damages caused by its master or crews, in accordance with the KCC Article 850.

Ship management company is active in providing crew management and ship's repair on behalf of the shipowner. Crews provided by the ship management company are servants of the shipowner. Therefore, where an accident occurs and victims raise a lawsuit for compensation of damages, the owner rather than the ship management company is vicariously liable.

181. The shipowner has an obligation to provide the seaworthy vessel with the charterer in the bareboat charter contract. However, the shipowner should provide a seaworthy vessel and crew to the charterer at the time of the charter contract.

182. When the owner acts as the carrier, the owner is liable for the cargo damages based on the breach of the contract. It is entitled to invoke package limitation in the same lawsuit as the carrier. It is also entitled to invoke global limitation (Article 797(4)).

§3. Shipping Partnership

183. The KCC has several provisions for ship partnership. In a ship partnership arrangement, multiple people own a particular vessel. This type of ownership of a vessel is very rare in Korea. However, it is still found in a small vessel such as a fishing vessel and pleasure boat.

184. In a ship partnership, all partners are liable for the loss incurred during the operation of the vessel. It is different from the shareholder's liability in a corporation. The shareholder's liability is limited to its share. The ship partners are liable for the cargo damage in accordance with the portion of their share in the partnership (Article 756(1)), as opposed to the evenly divided liability in the partnership of the Civil Code (Article 712).

185. A manager should be designated by the partners (Article 764).

186. Unless the ship management company does not employ the master and crew as its employees, it will not be vicariously liable for the liability caused by the master of the vessel. In this case, the ship management company may act as the agent of the shipowner. If the ship management company is large enough to employ the master and crew, it may be vicariously liable for the damage caused by the master as its employee. Under the current ship management business in Korea, there is no independent management company. Almost all ship management companies are a subsidiary of the shipping company and, thus, it does not have any power to employ its own master or crew. The liability of the management company is limited to ten times the management fee per year for the relevant vessel involved in the accident. Korean government enacted the Act for the Development of Ship Management Company in 2012.

Chapter 6. Liability and Limitation of Liability

§1. General

187. Limitation of liability regime exists in order to protect shipowner's interest under the KCC. There is a necessity to protect the shipowners because they are exposed to heavy loss or injury during the operation of the vessel at sea. There are criticisms in Korea that the global limitation scheme should be eliminated from the KCC. Several scholars defend that it is still required to facilitate liability insurance. Without it, it is very difficult for the insurer to calculate the maximum insurable exposure to the owner as the insured during the operation of the vessel.

188. Korea is a contracting party neither to the 1976 International Convention on Limitation of Liability for Maritime Claims (LLMC) nor the 1996 Protocol to the 1976 LLMC. However, Korea adopted almost all of the provisions in the 1976 LLMC into the KCC. Korea's position is identical to that of China but different from that of Japan. Japan is a contracting party to the 1996 Protocol to the 1976 LLMC.

§2. Person Eligible to Limitation

189. A shipowner is a person who is entitled to invoke or limit his liability under the KCC (Article 769). The limitation scheme initially aims to protect shipowners. With development of the shipping business, bareboat charterer, time charterer and voyage charterer appeared. These persons have characteristics similar to those of the owner in that each person is engaged in the maritime business by means of the vessel and thus faces unexpected heavy liability or loss. Reflecting these developments, charterers were inserted in the KCC as the eligible persons who can enjoy benefits of the limitation (Article 774(1)).

190. A ship management company and a ship operator are also eligible persons who can invoke the limitation of liability according to Article 774(1). The ship management company may employ its own master; thus, it may be vicariously liable for damages in tort. The ship operator is a broad concept. It is obvious that the definition of the ship operator should not include the charterer because it is stipulated as another person to invoke the limitation of liability like the shipowner. Therefore, the F/F (or Non-Vessel Operating Common Carrier (NVOCC) in the U.S.) may be a good example when it acts as the carrier. A shipyard may fall within the definition of the operator when it has a sea trial during the construction of the vessel. If there is a collision with a third party during the sea trial, the shipyard is vicariously liable for the negligence of the dock master employed by it (Korean Supreme Court case *1992.10.27. Docket No. 91da37140*).

191. The servants or agents, such as the master or pilot of the shipowner, are included in the category of the person (Article 774) who is entitled to invoke the limitation.[20]

192. The liability insurer is also entitled to limit its liability according to the Convention. However, the liability insurer is not listed as a beneficiary in the KCC. Under Korean law, the victim, in a liability insurance arrangement, is entitled to bring about direct action against the liability insurer, in addition to the shipowner as the insured (Article 724(2)) (1996 Protocol to 1976 LLMC Article 1(6)). When the victim exercises the direct action, the insurer can invoke the same limitation of liability as the insured can invoke against the victim. The insurer is not listed as the person who is entitled to limit its liability in the KCC Article 774. However, according to Article 724(2), the liability insurer can raise the same defense as the insured can do against the victim. In a recent Korean Supreme Court case *2009.11.26. Docket No. 2009da58470*, the court admitted that the liability insurer is entitled to limit its liability just as the shipowner as the insured can invoke in the limitation of liability proceeding. This judgment is welcomed because it fills the gap between the Convention and KCC on the beneficiary of limitation of liability.

193. Whether a slot charterer is entitled to invoke the limitation of liability is an issue in Korea. There is no court case on the issue, but prevailing view is that it falls within the definition of the "charterer" in Article 774(1), and thus, it is for an eligible person to enjoy the limitation of liability.[21]

194. An F/F often acts as the carrier. Whether an F/F as the carrier is allowed to invoke global limitation of liability in addition to the package limitation is in question in Korea. The views are split. Even when the F/F acts as a carrier, it does not operate a vessel; therefore, it lacks the possible links to the factors justifying the limitation of liability. Accordingly, it seems that it does not fall within the scope of the person eligible for the limitation.[22] New development of the F/F's owning the container box may well be reflected in deciding whether the F/F can be regarded as the shipowner which is entitled to invoke the limitation. For example, Taewoong Logistics in Korea owns lots of containers for liquid cargo. It provides its own container to the shipper. Even though it is a kind of F/F and acts as a contractual carrier, it may invoke global limitation, arguing that it has a physical facility just as an actual carrier.

---

20. The Korean Supreme Court *(1995.3.24. Docket No. 94ma2431)* upheld that the master of the vessel is the person who is entitled to invoke the limitation of liability in accordance with the KCC Art. 774.
21. *In the MSC Napoli case, a slot charterer was allowed to invoke global limitation. [200] 1 Lloyd's Rep 246.*
22. There is an opinion that the F/F as a carrier should have the right to invoke the global limitation. Kyun Sung, Lee, *Maritime Law* 278 (2010).

§3. Claims Subject to or Excepted from the Limitation

I. Claims Subject to the Limitation

195. The claims subject to the shipowner's limitation of liability under the KCC are as follows (Article 769):

(1) Claims regarding loss of life or personal injury, or loss or damage to any property other than the offending ship itself, which have occurred on board, or in direct connection with the operation of, a vessel.
(2) Claims regarding losses resulting from delay in the carriage of cargoes, passengers, and their luggage.
(3) Claims regarding all other losses resulting from infringement of rights other than contractual rights, which occurred in direct connection with the operation of a vessel.
(4) Claims regarding measures taken for the purpose of averting or minimizing loss for which the shipowner may limit its liability and for further loss caused by such measures.
(5) Claims regarding loss occurring in direct connection with salvage operations.

196. Where a collision occurs between vessel A and the opposing vessel B with cargo on board, fishermen suffer damages caused by the leaked bunker oil from vessel B. The owner of the opposing vessel B and cargo may have claims against the owner of the vessel A. These claims fall within the definition of Article 769(1). The victims resulting from bunker oil have a claim against the shipowner of vessel A based on Article 769(3). If the victims took measures to minimize the loss and expenses incurred, the claim of the victims is a good example of claim based on Article 769(4).

197. The KCC does not have a provision to the effect that the claims in Article 769 shall be subject to the limitation of liability even if it is brought by way of recourse or for indemnity under a contract or otherwise, unlike 1976 LLMC Article 2(2). However, the prevailing view supports the application of it to the KCC.[23] When an insurer who stands in the shoes of an insured tries to recover damages in subrogation, its recourse claims are subject to the limitation of liability under Article 769.

II. Claims Excepted from Limitation

198. According to the KCC Article 773, the following claims are not subject to the limitation under the KCC:

23. Lee Sik Chai, *An Introduction to Korean Maritime Law* 84 (1999).

(1) Claims against the shipowner of the master, crew, or other servants whose duties are connected with the ship, including claims of their heirs, dependents, or other persons entitled to make such claims.
(2) Claims for salvage or contribution in general average.
(3) Claims for oil pollution damage within the meaning of the CLC, dated November 29, 1969, or of any amendment or Protocol thereto which is in force.
(4) Claims in respect of the raising, removal, destruction, or rendering harmless of a ship which is sunk, wrecked or abandoned, including anything that is or has been on board such ship.
(5) Claims in respect of nuclear damage.

199. In a Korean Supreme Court case *2014.5.9. Docket No. 2014ma223*, the time charterer as the carrier issued B/L to the shipper after it received the cargo from the shipper. The vessel laden with the cargo on board arrived at Inchon port in Korea and the cargo was discharged and stored in a warehouse. The cargo was wrongfully handed over to the consignee without exchanging the cargo with the B/L by the warehouse keeper. The shipper as the B/L holder brought about the law suit for the loss of the cargo against the carrier. The carrier applied for the limitation of the liability in a separate legal proceeding. In that proceeding, the time charterer as the carrier argued that the cargo claim due to the wrongful delivery of the cargo by the warehouse keeper as the agent of the carrier was claiming subject to limitation according to Article 769(1)(1976 LLMC Article 2(1)(a)). However, the court rejected the argument of the applicant. It rendered that the wrongful delivery claim of the carrier did not fall within the definition of wording "claims in respect of loss of or damage to property, occurring on board or in direct connection with the operation of the ship."

200. The KCC adopted Article 773(4) in order to protect the government in accordance with the reservation provision of the LLMC Article 18(1). Claims resulting from oil pollution are subject to the separate limitation of liability scheme called the CLC and Oil Pollution Compensation Act. Crew claims and claims from salvage and general average should not be subject to the limitation of liability because, if the limitation is allowed, the salvage and general average may be hampered. The claims regarding wreck removal are exceptions from the claims subject to the limitation of liability. It is the outcome that Korea reflected the reservation provision in the 1976 LLMC Article 18 and adopted it in the KCC. This exception is intended to protect the public authorities responsible for keeping the safety of fairways in port from wasting removal costs of wrecks when the shipowner does not discharge its duty to remove the wreck at its own expense.

201. Oil pollution damages can be classified into two types. One is the oil pollution caused by the oil tankers. The other is that caused by bunker from the general cargo vessels. While the former is subject to the separate and independent limitation of liability scheme under the CLC and KOPCA, the latter is subject to the LLMC and the KCC. Therefore, the victims of oil pollution from the general cargo vessel are disadvantageous to those by the oil tankers because the claims are subject to limitation of liability under the KCC, which results in competing with other claimants.

202. Removable expenses against the oil pollution caused by the oil from the oil tanker are subject to the limitation of the liability, according to the KOPCA and CLC. However, removal expenses against the pollution caused by the bunker oil from the general cargo vessel are not subject to the limitation pursuant to the KCC Article 773(4). It is the result of adopting the Bunker Convention in which no limitation scheme is established, and thus, it is left to the national law. The KOPCA Article 45 confirmed that the shipowner is not allowed to invoke the limitation against the removal expenses for pollution caused by the bunker oil from the general cargo vessel.

§4. Exclusion of the Limitation Right

203. The right of the shipowner to limit its liability is not allowed if the accident resulted from its personal act or omission committed with the intent to cause such loss or recklessly with the knowledge that such loss would probably occur (Article 769). Under the Korean civil law, there are only three subjective mind requirements which trigger the liability to the wrongdoer. Intentional acts, gross negligence, and slight negligence are those requirements. The subjective mind of "recklessly with the knowledge that such loss would probably occur (hereinafter "reckless behavior")" is a new concept adopted in the KCC from the viewpoint of civil law. Therefore, confusion was followed regarding the interpretation of the meaning of reckless behavior. One school regards it as a kind of gross negligence, while the other schools understand it as a standard higher than gross negligence. In the Korean Supreme Court case *2012.4.17. Docket No. 2010ma222 (Hebei Spirit Oil Pollution case)*, the court decided that gross negligence did not meet the requirement. It can be interpreted that the Korean Supreme Court accepts that reckless behavior is a subjective standard beyond gross negligence but lower than intentional act. The burden of proof on the presence of reckless behavior or intentional act rests upon the claimant under the KCC Article 769.

204. However, in the above *Hebei Spirit Oil Pollution* case, the Korean Supreme Court rendered that the proof in low standard that there was no reason to break the shipowner's limitation right rested upon the shipowner as the applicant in the limitation proceeding pursuant to Article 10 of the Shipowner's Limitation of Liability Procedural Act. Therefore, the relationship between Article 10 of the Procedural Act and the KCC Article 769 in relation to who has burden of proof to prove that there was reckless behavior to break the right of the applicant's limitation of liability became in dispute. The burden of proof rests upon the applicant where it applied for the limitation in the limitation proceeding but upon the claimant in other cases, such as the case that the claimant makes an appeal against the court's decision allowing the limitation for the benefit of the applicant and that the claimant brings about separate proceeding outside the limitation proceeding.

205. This is an extremely high standard that the claimant is not likely to prove the above requirement. There is no such precedent in the Korean court wherein the shipowner was not allowed to invoke the limitation of liability under the KCC. However, there is one case in which the carrier's right to limit its liability was not accepted by the Korean Supreme Court. It is relevant to the case because the requirement in the carrier's limitation case (package limitation) is identical to that in the shipowner's limitation case (global limitation.). In the Korean Supreme Court case *2006.10.26. Docket No. 2004da27082,* the court regarded the low-level managerial staff member as the shipowner's alter ego. When the legal person, such as a company, is concerned, the directing mind in the legal entities should be addressed to find out the carrier's alter ego. It was an accepted view that only the director level or the above falls within the category of the shipowner itself; when the legal person is concerned, the Seoul High Court rendered that the decision of the low-level managerial staff member to load sensitive cargoes on deck rather than under deck against contract fell within the meaning of "reckless behaviour of the carrier" and the Supreme Court also affirmed it.[24]

206. In Korean Supreme Court case *1995.6.5. Docket No. 95ma325*, the court upheld that the master's reckless behavior does not meet the requirement to exclude the owner's limitation of liability. The master's reckless behavior only bars the master from invoking its own limitation of liability.

207. The limitation of the carrier can be invoked as a defense in the lawsuit dealing with merits of the case. However, the limitation of the shipowner cannot be invoked as the defense in the lawsuit dealing with the merit, but it should be applied in a separate court proceeding (Article 776(2)).

§5. Effect of Limitation

I. Limitation Amounts

208. Limitation amounts under the KCC Article 770(1) are identical to those of the 1976 LLMC except for the passenger claims, which are as follows:

(1) The limit of liability in respect of claims for loss of life or personal injury to passengers of a ship is an amount of 175,000 Special Drawing Rights (SDR) multiplied by the number of passengers which the ship is authorized to carry in accordance with the ship's inspection certificate (Article 770(1)(i)).
(2) The limit of liability in respect of claims for loss of life or personal injury to persons other than passengers shall be calculated as follows:

24. Refer to In Hyeon Kim, *The Carrier's Loss of Right to Limit Liability and Piercing Corporate Veil*, The Asian Business Lawyer 1, p. 101 (Spring 2008).

167,000 SDR for a ship with a tonnage below 300 tons.
333,000 SDR for a ship with a tonnage of 300 tons or more but not exceeding 500 tons.
For a ship with tonnage in excess of 500 tons, the following amount shall be added to 330,000 SDR.
For each ton from 501 to 3,000 tons, 500 SDR.
For each ton from 3,001 to 30,000 tons, 333 SDR.
For each ton from 30,001 to 70,000 tons, 250 SDR.
For each ton in excess of 70,000 tons, 167 SDR (Article 770(1)(ii)).

(3) The limit of liability in respect of any other claims other than (i) and (ii) shall be calculated as follows:

83,000 SDR for a ship with a tonnage below 300 tons.
167,000 SDR for a ship with a tonnage not below 300 tons but not exceeding 500 tons.
For a ship with a tonnage in excess of 500 tons, the following amount shall be added to 167,000 SDR.
For each ton from 501 to 3,000 tons, 167 SDR.
For each ton from 30,001 to 70,000 tons, 125 SDR.
For each ton in excess of 70,000 tons, 83 SDR (Article 770(1)(iii)).

209. The limitation amounts set out above apply to all claims arising from one distinct occasion (Article 770(2)). There are three different and separate categories of limitation funds such as for passenger claims (Article 770(1) (i))(ii)) for loss or injury claims for crew (Article 770(1)(ii)), and for the property damages claims (Article 770(1)(iii)). The claims subject to the limitation of liability under Article 769 compete with each other within the same category of claims under (Article 770(1) and 770(3)). Where the amount calculated in accordance with Article 770(1)(ii) is insufficient to pay the claims mentioned therein in full, the amount calculated in accordance with Article 770(1)(iii) shall be available for payment of the unpaid balance of claims under Article 770(1)(ii) and such unpaid balance shall rank ratably with claims mentioned under Article 770(1)(iii) (Article 770(4)).

A salvor definition for the purpose of limitation of liability was elaborated in the 2007 revision of the KCC. The salvor may be subject to liability where it or its servant commits tort to a third party or the salved vessel. Basically, the salvor's limitation amount is the same as that of the shipowner. However, the salvor who provides assistance for salving not from the salving vessel or on board the salved vessel is allowed to limit its liability to that of 1,500 gross tonnage.

210. Where a tug-barge is involved in an accident, how to calculate the limitation amount has been disputed several times. The Korean courts show a tendency to calculate in such way as to protect claimant as much as possible. If the tug X tows the barge Y, first, calculate the tug X's limitation of the liability amount, and then calculate the barge Y's limitation of the liability amount. Second, add the two figures together. In the Korean Supreme Court case *1998.3.25. Docket No. 97ma2758,* the court adopted the above calculation methods. This calculation method was once again adopted in the famous Hebei Spirit Oil pollution case by the high court for limitation proceeding (Seoul High Court *2010.1.20. Docket No. 2009la1045*).

The author thinks that the limitation amount for the space charterer under the current Korean law is not reasonable because there is no partial limitation of liability calculation method for the space charterer. The space charterer uses only part of the vessel through the contract with the shipowner. Therefore, the space charterer should not be liable for whole tonnage of the vessel which it partially borrows. Limitation amount of servant or agent of the shipowner, such as the master and the pilot, is too high to sustain. There is no reduced limitation amount scheme for them. The author argues that the limitation amount for the servant or agent of the shipowner should be liable in a substantially reduced amount. The pilot's limitation of liability amount is limited to that of the shipowner with 2,000 gross tons when the vessel over 2,000 gross tons is involved in the accident.

II. Single Liability

211. The KCC Article 771 is identical to the LLMC Article 5. Where a person entitled to the limitation of liability has a claim against the claimant arising out of the same occurrence, their respective claims shall be set off against each other, and the provisions of the KCC shall only apply to the balance, if any. It aims at protecting the claimant. Without set-off, the claimant is placed in a disadvantageous position. Where a collision occurred between vessels X and Y, Let's say X's limitation amount is USD 5 million, X's damages USD 20 million, and Y's damages USD 30 million with a 50% fault ratio. X's liability against Y is USD 15 million. If the limitation is allowed without set-off, X is required to pay only USD 5 million owing to the limitation and will receive USD 10 million from Y. If the set-off is adopted, X is required to pay USD 5 million to Y after both claims are set off (USD 15 million minus USD 5 million= USD 5 million). In the latter case, Y does not need to pay 10 M. Consequently, Y is more protected than in the former case without set-off.

III. Relationship with the Package Limitation

212. When a carrier is liable for the cargo damage and a subsequent lawsuit is raised against the carrier, it is entitled to invoke both the global limitation and the package limitation. When a big accident, such as an explosion on board, occurs, the carrier may select the global limitation rather than the package limitation in order to limit its liability. In this case, the owner should apply for the global limitation in a separate proceeding apart from the lawsuit for the merit of cargo damages.

§6. Procedural Rules for Limitation

I. Governing Law

213. The procedural rules for the shipowners' limitation are not regulated by international conventions but by domestic laws. The 1976 LLMC has a provision on this matter. Article 14 says that subject to the provisions of this chapter, the rules relating to the constitution and distribution of a limitation fund, and all rules of procedure in connection therewith, shall be governed by the law of the State Party in which the fund is constituted. Korea has a special law for this purpose called the Shipowner's Limitation of Liability Procedural Act (hereinafter "the KSLLPA").

II. Procedure for Limitation under the KSLLPA

214. An applicant who wants to invoke the limitation of liability should make an application in writing to the effect that the total claim amounts may exceed the limitation amounts (Article 9). The application should be made within one year from the date when the applicant receives claims in writing, which exceeds the limitation amounts (KCC Article 776). It is a practice in Korea that the application is possible even though the applicant applies for the limitation in case the actually received claims do not exceed the limitation amounts but the applicant verifies that the total claims may exceed the limitation amounts.

215. The court may order the applicant to deposit a limitation fund equal to the limitation amount when it decides that the application is appropriate (Article 11). The limitation fund is constituted as per the substantive law of the KCC. If there is only a property claim, the limitation fund only for property claims is established. The applicant may deposit the limitation fund either in a bond or in cash. If the court decides the application is not appropriate, it may reject the application.

216. The court will make a decision on the commencement of a limitation proceeding (Article 19). It should fix the due date when all possible claimants should file claims to the court. It should be a certain date between thirty days and ninety days from the above date of the decision. The court should also fix the due date for the assessment of the claims which were filed with the court. It should be a certain date between seven days and thirty days from the due date of filing of the claims. It also designates an administrator.

217. The court will receive claims from the claimants (Article 42) and then assess whether the filed claims are appropriate for the case (Article 53). The court will decide whether the filed claim is appropriate (Article 56).

218. The court will receive a complaint on the assessment from the claimant, who is not satisfied with the assessment of the court. The court will accept or reject the appeal as a ruling (Article 57). The claimant is allowed to file the appeal in the second instance court (Article 59).

219. The court makes an allocation list among claimants for distribution from the limitation fund (Article 66). The claimants can make a complaint on the allocation list of the limitation fund (Article 68).

III. Legal Effect

220. From the moment the court decides to commence the limitation proceeding, the legal effect of the decision takes place. The rightful claimants are entitled to receive compensation for their claims within the limit of the limitation fund (Article 27).

221. The claimant no longer exercises its right upon any assets of the applicant other than the limitation fund (Article 27). As a result, it is not allowed for the claimant to arrest a vessel that the applicant owns. The arrested vessel should be released upon the commencement of limitation proceeding.

222. The claimant will receive a proportionally reduced amount from the limitation fund (Articles 65, 69) when the limitation amount does not fully cover the admitted claim among filed claims in the proceeding. When the claimant becomes able to receive the allocated amounts from the limitation fund, the applicant is exempted from the liability against the claim concerned (Article 73)

223. In the famous Hebei Spirit Oil Pollution case (2014), the Korean Supreme Court reiterated that the claimant was able to bring about the law suit for its own benefit without relying on the limitation of liability proceeding, on the presumption that the shipowner's right to invoke limitation of liability be rejected in the lawsuit. According to the court, the claimant has an option between participation in the limitation proceeding and bringing about a lawsuit in merit. If the claimant wants to bring about a lawsuit in merit, it should not participate in the limitation proceeding.

§7. Special Case for the Oil Pollution

224. The CLC, as the special convention of the LLMC, is applicable to the legal issues regarding compensation caused by oil pollution from oil tankers. In order to implement the CLC, the Korean government made a special domestic law called the KOPCA. According to the KOPCA, the shipowner is entitled to invoke the limitation of liability against the claimants who suffered from oil pollution. The amount of limitation of a particular vessel under the KOPCA is higher than that in the KCC. The shipowner is strictly liable for oil pollution damages, and the shipowners of tankers should compulsorily make an insurance arrangement with the liability insurer. The victim has a right to bring an action directly against the insurer. The liability insurer is entitled to limit its liability.

225. The other source of oil pollution is bunker oil, which is used as a fuel for vessels. To cope with the compensation for oil pollution damages caused by the bunker oil, the Bunker Convention was made and came into force in 2008. The convention does not have any independent regime of limitation of liability. Rather, it synchronizes the limitation of liability with that in the LLMC (Article 6). Korea ratified the Bunker Convention in 2009, and then it incorporated the Bunker Convention into the KOPCA. Accordingly, the limitation of liability of the shipowner in case of bunker oil pollution is the same as that in the KCC. Therefore, the compensation for the victims caused by bunker oil pollution is not sufficient compared with the victims for oil pollution caused by oil tankers.

§8. Jurisdiction and Governing Law

226. When the limitation of liability is at issue, the owner of a vessel liable for damages may find a proper court for the purpose of applying for the limitation of liability. There is no unified international convention on the jurisdiction of the limitation of liability procedures. Therefore, each country's domestic law is applicable for the case involved in the limitation of liability.

227. The shipowners try to seek for the forum which provides them with the most favorable results. According to the Korean law, a district court of the following places has the exclusive jurisdiction over the limitation of liability procedure: (i) where the vessel involved in the claims locates; (ii) the applicant's residence; (iii) the place that the accident occurred; (iv) the first arrival port after the accident occurred; and (v) the place that the prejudgment attachment or arrest was executed (KSLLPA Article 2).

228. In recent days, two same limitation proceedings have been competing among three East-Asian countries such as Korea, Japan, and China. Because the limitation amount for the shipowner under the Japanese law is higher than that in Korea or China, new tendency was brought about for the claimant to apply for limitation proceedings in Japan rather than Korea or China. Because Korea is not a contracting party to the 1996 Protocol to 1976 LLMC, the effect of limitation proceeding does not bind the Korean limitation proceeding. The shipowner as the defendant is forced to deposit limitation funds twice. Because there is no rule on how the court treats the double limitation proceeding before two different countries, the parties involved in the proceedings are in a confused condition.

229. When a foreign factor is involved, the KIPL is applicable for the case in order to ascertain the governing law. The governing law for the purpose of deciding: (i) whether a certain shipowner, charterer or others are the right persons eligible for invoking the limitation of liability, or (ii) how much the limitation amount is the law of state of flag which the vessel involved in the accident flies in accordance with the KIPL Article 60(4). For example, in a collision case between a Korean-flagged vessel and a Japanese-flagged vessel, the owner of the Korean vessel suffered from damages may file a claim in a Korean court. The Japanese owner may apply to limit its liability in a certain Korean court. The Korean court will decide which law is the governing law regarding the limitation in consultation with the KIPL because a foreign factor is involved in the case. Japanese law will be designated as the governing law because the flag of the vessel is Japan's.

230. There are criticisms in Korea that the KIPL should be revised in order to adopt *lex fori* approach in the same situation. It is not easy for the court or parties to ascertain the law of the flag State in case the vessel is registered in FOC countries such as Saint Vincent, and Panama. China and Japan follow *lex fori* approach in deciding the governing law for limitation by the operation of law (Chinese Maritime Code Article 275) and the case law, respectively. *Lex fori* approach seems to provide more simplicity and predictability to the parties involved in the case.

231. If Korea ratifies the 1976 LLMC, the LLMC may be the governing law for the limitation of liability when a Korean court seizes the case, regardless of the nationality of the vessel involved in the accident (Article 15(1)).

Chapter 7. Charter Parties

§1. General

232. Three different types of charter parties, such as bareboat charter party, time charter party, and voyage charter party, are prevalent in Korea. They have common legal characteristics as a kind of lease of the vessel rather than the contract for carriage of goods. Apart from these three typical charter parties, new types of charter parties, such as slot charter party or Contract of Affreightment (COA), have appeared and are widely used in Korea.

§2. Bareboat Charter Party

I. General

233. The bareboat charter party is the most widely used charter party in Korea. A vessel may be very high-valued movable, and thus, an owner who wants to expand its fleet may not have enough money to purchase a vessel. In this case, the owner may borrow a vessel rather than purchase it for a certain period of time or construct it and thus make use of the vessel for its business. This kind of arrangement is called the bareboat charter party. The lender of the vessel is called the owner and the borrower of the vessel is called the charterer. Historically, Korean shipping companies have used the bareboat charter party as a means to expand their capacity to operate vessels.

234. Under the bareboat charter party, the shipowner charters out the vessel to the bareboat charterer. The latter makes an employment contract with the master or crew. Accordingly, the bareboat charterer is vicariously liable for damages caused by the negligence of the master or crews.

235. There is no dispute in Korea that the bareboat charter party is not a contract of service but as a hire or lease of a movable. It is different from the typical lease in that the charterer has the obligation of maintenance for the vessel. In a typical lease, the owner of the movable has an obligation to repair and maintain.

II. Types of Bareboat Charter Party in Korea

236. Many Korean shipowners operate vessels as bareboat charterers. Several different types of bareboat charter parties exist in Korea. A shipping company (A) may contact another shipping company (B) and borrow a vessel of B for a period of five or ten years while paying a certain amount of fee for reward. B delivers the vessel to A without its crews on board. This kind of charter party is a kind of lease.

237. According to the KCC Article 847, the shipowner promises to provide the vessel for the charterer and, in return, the charterer promises to pay the charter fee to the shipowner in a bareboat charter party (Article 847(1)). Even if the shipowner has an obligation to provide the crew, but the crew operates the vessel under the management and control of the charterer, it is still regarded as the bareboat charter party (Article 847(2)).

238. However, A (lessee) may contact a bank and request to buy (or construct) a certain vessel from a supplier for the benefit of itself. The bank (lessor) may contact the supplier to purchase the vessel. Subsequently, the supplier delivers the vessel to A. A will pay a lease fee to the bank on a regular basis. The bank has ownership of the vessel, whereas A has possession of the vessel and a right to use it. This type of bareboat charter party is a kind of finance lease. This kind of charter party is a combination of lease and borrowing money from the bank.

239. In the finance lease of constructing a new vessel, the Korean shipowners register the newly built vessel in the FOC countries in accordance with the request of the banker as a lender. If the Korean local currency was leaked to a foreign country without government permission against the Korean Foreign Currency Control Act, the bareboat charterer would be punished in accordance with the Act Articles 19 and 31(1).

240. There is a very special kind of bareboat charter party called the Bareboat Charter Party Hire Purchase (BBCHP) in Korea. In this arrangement, when the charter party period expires, the Korean charterer does not return the vessel to the owner. Rather, the Korean charterer obtains ownership of the vessel and registers it in Korea. It was widely used by Korean shipping companies for the purpose of obtaining Korean-flagged vessels during the 1960s and 1970s. Korean government borrowed purchasing money from the Korean shipping companies to facilitate this arrangement.

241. According to the KCC Article 848(2), the above financial lease and BBCHP are also regarded as a kind of bareboat charter party, and thus, the relevant provisions on the BBC will be applicable. As a result, the charterer in the financial lease or BBCHP is vicariously liable for the damages in tort according to Article 850 of the KCC.

242. In contrast, the charterer should return the chartered vessel to the owner when the charter period expires in a simple bareboat charter party as opposed to the BBCHP.

III. Standard Forms of the BBC

243. Legal issues between the owner and the bareboat charterer can be easily solved pursuant to the prearranged agreement called a bareboat charter party.

244. The BARECON is in a wide circulation in Korea. Provisions regarding the bareboat charter party in the KCC applicable between the parties are not mandatory, and thus, a special agreement between parties prevails over the provisions in the KCC based on the principle of party autonomy. Therefore, the crew can be supplied by the owner under the BBC regardless of Article 847(1).

245. A Delivery and Redelivery clause is an important provision to trigger the commencement and the end of the charter party periods. The obligation of repair and maintenance of the chartered vessel falls upon the charterer (BARECON Article 9), which differs from that in the general lease. The duty to maintain insurance coverage for the vessel falls upon the charterer (Article 12).

IV. Who is the Obligor

246. When a vessel is operated under the bareboat charter party, there is ambiguity as to who the obligor is for damages, which the third-party victims suffer from because there are two possible obligors in the bareboat charter party arrangement.
The issue is who is the obligor between the owner and the bareboat charterer against the third party victim.

247. The KCC has a provision to address this issue, to the effect that the bareboat charterer has the same right and obligation as the owner when the vessel is operated under the bareboat charter party arrangement (Article 850). Under Article 809, the bareboat charterer rather than the shipowner is liable by the operation of the law where the vessel is chartered out to the time charterer or voyage charterer (Korean Supreme Court case *2004.10.27. Docket No. 2004da7040*).

248. In the Korean Supreme Court case *1975.3.31 Docket No. 74da847,* the court rendered that only the bareboat charterer was liable for the damages caused by the collision when a vessel was under the bareboat charter party. It is an established law in Korea that the bareboat charterer, instead of the owner, is liable for damages which third-party victims suffer during the bareboat charter party pursuant to the KCC Article 850.[25]

249. There is no dispute that the bareboat charter party falls outside the definition of contract for the carriage. Rather, it is regarded as a kind of lease agreement in Korea. The bareboat charterer may enter into the contract for the carriage with the shipper or charterer, and then it becomes the carrier. The bareboat charterer as the carrier has rights and obligations as the carrier. It is still subject to vicarious liability because it is the employer of the negligent master or crew.

25. In Hyeon Kim, *Study on Leading cases of Korean Maritime Law over past 50 years*, Study of Commercial Law Cases 23-1, p. 224 (2010).

250. When the bareboat charterer operates a vessel as a carrier, it is entitled to invoke both the package limitation and global limitation pursuant to the KCC Article 797(4).

251. When the bareboat charterer operates the chartered vessel and brings about maritime claims such as collision damage or crew wages, the claimants are entitled to exercise maritime lien under the KCC (Article 850(2)).

V. Special Provisions under the KCC

252. Under Korean law, the contractual right of the lessee is very weak in that if the lessor sells a movable, which is the subject of lease to an assignee, the lessee no longer has the right of possession against the assignee.[26] A vessel is a kind of movable, and thus, this rule is applicable to the case of the vessel. If this general rule is applicable to the vessel's lease, the bareboat charterer as the lessee no longer use the vessel, which will result in an impediment to the stable operation of shipping business. The KCC solved this problem by inserting a provision to the effect that the bareboat charterer as the lessee is entitled to request the owner to help with the bareboat registration. The KCC Article 849 provides the bareboat charterer with a mechanism to maintain the possession of the vessel even though the vessel was sold to the assignee. By registering the fact that the vessel is bareboat chartered, the bareboat charterer is entitled to raise a defense that the vessel is still under the bareboat charter party against the new purchaser.

253. In the 2007 revision of the KCC, the Korean government newly inserted a time-bar provision. The time-bar period is two years, according to Article 851. The parties in the bareboat charter party can no longer raise claims after two years since the vessel was redelivered to the owner.

§3. Time Charter Party

I. Definition

254. Under the time charter party, the time charterer borrows a vessel with the master and crew on board who are employed by the shipowner (Article 842).

255. In practice, there are two different kinds of time charter parties in Korea. One type is that an ordinary shipping company borrows a vessel from a shipowner, and it makes use of the vessel for its own business. In this case, the time charterer usually enters into a contract for the carriage with a shipper and it acts as a carrier. The other type is that an industrial carrier borrows a vessel from an owner and it uses the vessel for transportation of its own cargoes. In this case, the time charterer has the status of the shipper. In the former type, there are two contracts: contract for

26. Kwak Yun Jik, Contract (II), Parkyoungsa, 328.

the time charter party and for the carriage of goods by sea, but in the latter type, there is only one contract for the time charter party. The former is the typical time charter party. The time charter in the latter is called as the industrial carrier.

II. Legal Nature

256. The legal nature of the time charter party has long been discussed in Korea. There are two conflicting views regarding the legal nature of the time charter party. The majority view is that it is less like a contract for the carriage of goods and more like the bareboat charter party. However, a minority view is that it is more akin to a contract for the carriage of goods by sea.

257. The most controversial issue regarding the time charter party in Korea is focused on who is the obligor for claims between the shipowner and the time charterer.

258. In the Korean Supreme Court case *1992.2.25. Docket No. 91da14215* (Polsa Dos case),[27] the cargo was on board the vessel under the time charter party. The holder of the B/L claimed against the time charterer. In turn, the time charterer argued that it was not liable for the cargo damages, but the owner was liable for it. The court rendered that the time charter party is very similar, in the legal nature, to the bareboat charter party, and thus, the time charterer is liable for the damages as if the bareboat charterer is liable under the bareboat charter party pursuant to Article 766 (New Article 850). The court relied on the legal nature of the time charter party and decided that the time charter party is a kind of lease (bareboat charter party), as a result of which Article 850 is applicable for the time charterer.

259. However, this judgment was condemned because the obligor, in a case involved in the breach of the contract, should be judged by factors in relation to the contract. In the above case, the claimant was the holder of the B/L. The prevailing view is that the obligor should be decided by factors such as the logo of the shipping company that appeared in the B/L and who the receiver of the freight is.[28]

There was a serious discussion about whether the time charter would be decided as the obligor for the damages caused by the collision or not. If the Korean Supreme Court faithfully follows the previous judgment, the time charterer rather than the shipowner would be decided as the obligor. Several commentators opposed this kind of scenario and argued that the shipowner as the employer of the master should be regarded as the obligor.

---

27. (1992) Korean Case Reports, 1120.
28. In Hyeon Kim, *Maritime Law* (2007), 136. In the *Jasmine* case of Japanese Supreme Court(1998.3.27), the ship owner rather than the time charterer was regarded as the carrier. The Court reached the conclusion after considering several factors such as the logo in front of the B/L, the fact that the master signed on the B/L and the effectiveness of identity carrier clause. It is interpreted that the Japanese Supreme Court did not take consideration of the legal nature of the time.

260. In the Korean Supreme Court case *2003.8.22, Docket No. 2001da65977,*[29] a vessel under the time charter party collided with an opposing vessel, as a result of which the opposing vessel suffered damages. The victims brought a lawsuit against the time charterer. The court rendered that under the time charter party, the shipowner is liable for the maneuvering of the vessel while the time charterer is liable for the business of the vessel. The collision resulted from the negligence of the master of the vessel, who was employed and controlled by the owner, and thus, the owner was liable for the damages caused by the ship's collision. This judgment is different from that in the Polsa Dos case. If the court faithfully followed the Polsa Dos case, it might have decided that the time charterer rather than the owner was liable for the damages. The court upheld the so-called Maneuvering-Business separation theory.[30] It can be found at the time charter party such as NYPE.[31] *Under the Maneuvering-Business separation theory, ship's maneuvering is left to the shipowner, while engagement of the vessel for the purpose of business is shifted to the time charterer.*

261. In the Korean Supreme Court case *2010.4.29. Docket No. 2009 da 99754,* carrier A entered into a contract for the carriage of goods by sea with the shipper. In order to perform the contract, A borrowed a barge from B and a tug from C. The owner C of the tug hired master D. While D was towing the barge to perform the carriage in accordance with the instruction of A, master D could not control the tug-barge due to the strong current and the collision occurred between the tug and the barge. The owner B of the barge brought about claims for damages against owner C of the tug rather than A as the charterer. C argued that he lent his tug to A and A was operating the tug when the collision occurred, and thus, he was not liable for the damages.

The court expounded the difference of legal nature between the time charter party and the bareboat charter party as follows: in the time charter party, the owner or bareboat charter of the vessel lends its vessel to the time charterer with the master and crew on board and, in return, the charterer promises that it will pay hires to the owner or the bareboat charterer. The main purpose of the contract is to receive service from the owner of the vessel through the master and crew supplied by the owner or the bareboat charterer. However, the main purpose of the bareboat charter party is to make use of the vessel itself, and thus, the charterer hires the master and crew to operate the vessel as if it is its own vessel.

The court regarded the contract for the case as a time charter party rather than a bareboat charter party because C as the owner of the tug supplied the tug with the master and crew on board to carrier A (charterer) for the carriage of goods and, in addition, the master employed by C commanded the tug and the barge. The court ruled that because the person who hired and supervised the master is C as the owner

29. (2003) Korean Case Reports, 1912.

30. *This theory is adopted in the French law (The 1966 Charter Party and Contract for Carriage by Sea Act No. 66-420, Arts. 8 & 9 and Decree Arts. 20 & 21). Under the French law, it is understood that the shipowner has the right and obligations respecting the ship's navigation while the time charterer has the same concerning the ship's commercial operation.*

31. NYPE 93 Arts. 6 & 7.

of the tug, C was vicariously liable for the damages from which the owner of the barge suffered based on the Korean Supreme Court case *2003.8.22. Docket No. 2001da65977.*

262. When the time charterer operates a vessel as a carrier, it is entitled to invoke both package limitation and global limitation. The obligation as the carrier, such as to carry out seaworthiness and to take care of cargo during shipment, is imposed upon the time charterer.

III. Standard Forms of the Time Charter

263. Provisions in the KCC are not obligatory, and thus, if parties in the contract make an agreement different from the provision in the KCC, the agreement is valid.

264. NYPE 81 and NYPE 93 are the most widely circulated form of charter parties in Korea.

265. Charter hire is calculated by the duration of the time charter party, and thus, delivery time and redelivery time are very important. If the time charterers were not able to use the chartered vessel, the hire should not be paid. It is materialized in the name of an off-hire clause in the standard forms of time charter party such as NYPE Article 3.

266. The duty to maintain and repair the vessel rests upon the owner. The time charterer has a duty to designate the safe port. However, the shipowner should provide vessel with seaworthiness to the time charterer when the vessel is delivered. There are clauses neither on the demurrage nor on the dispatch money, unlike the voyage charter party. However, there are clauses on delivery and redelivery of the chartered vessel.

IV. Special Matters in the KCC

267. The KCC has several provisions to strike a balance of interests between the owner and the charterer. These provisions are default rules, and thus, the parties are allowed to make different arrangements from the provisions in the KCC. The provisions regarding the time charter party in the KCC stand on the premise that the parties under the time charter party have equal bargaining power.

268. According to the KCC Article 843(1), the time charterer has a right to order and direct the master for the employment of the chartered vessel. If the time charterer sustained damages because the crew, master or other servants did not follow the time charterer's instruction, the owner of the vessel should indemnify the damages to the charterer according to Article 843(2). This provision is very similar to NYPE Article 8.[32]

269. There is no express provision to apply the famous KCC Article 850 to the time charter party situation. However, the Korean Supreme Court still maintains that the legal nature of the time charter party is a kind of lease, and thus, there is a possibility that the time charterer will be held liable for the third-party victims pursuant to Article 850. However, in the Korean Supreme Court case *2003.8.22. Docket No. 2002da65977,* in which a time-chartered vessel was involved in a collision, the Korean Supreme Court rendered that the time charterer was not liable for the damages which the opposing vessel sustained because the collision falls within the scope of the owner's control and responsibility. The court explained that the accident was caused by the negligent maneuvering of the vessel by the master of the time-chartered vessel, and under the time charter party, the maneuvering of the vessel is allocated as the portion of the shipowner under the time charter party. It appears that the court imposes vicarious liability upon the shipowner because the master of the vessel was employed and controlled by the shipowner in accordance with the time charter party.

270. Whether the bunker supplier or pilot who enters into a contract with the time charterer has a maritime lien on the claims resulting from bunker supply and pilot service or not is at issue. The KCC stipulates that the claimants are eligible for maritime lien based on the claims incurred by the bareboat charterer. If the court follows the position of the Korean Supreme Court that the time charter party is very similar to that of the bareboat charter party, then Article 850(2) is applicable to the time charter party *mutatis mutandis*. The author thinks that the claimants have a maritime lien against the time charterer.

271. In the Korean Supreme Court case *2019.7.24. Docket no.2017ma1442* decision, the Court admitted that the claims incurred by the time charterer brought about the maritime lien. Owners of the tugs brought about an auction sale based on the maritime lien against a vessel for which they provided tug service. The ship owner argued that the plaintiff did not have such right because the maritime lien in the matter was not listed in the KCC Article 777. The Court reflected the legal nature of the time charter party when it made such decision. It regarded the time charter party as one very similar to the bareboat charter party so that it can borrow Article 850(2) as the legal basis for the claimant to be entitled to exercising the maritime lien against the vessel involved in the service.

---

32. In *the House of Lords of the U.K.* case (2000.12.7.) called *Hill Harmony*, the Court decided that the selecting routing for sailing falls within the category of the business which is left to the time charterer, and thus, the master of the vessel, even though employed by the ship owner, should follow the order of the time charterer.

272. The scope of the charter party subject to Article 809 was expanded in the 2007 revision of the KCC. There was ambiguity on whether the owner of the chartered vessel was jointly and severally liable for cargo damages even when the time charterer acted as the carrier under Article 806. Article 806 required that the carrier was in the status of having a double contract for the carriage. When the vessel is chartered out to the time charterer, and then the time charterer enters into the contract for the carriage, the former contract is not the contract for the carriage but the lease. Therefore, the time charterer did not fall within the scope of Article 809. However, when the vessel is chartered out to the voyage charterer, and then the voyage charterer enters into a contract for the carriage, the former contract is regarded as a contract for the carriage. Therefore, the voyage charterer is in the status of having a double contract for the carriage, as a result of which the voyage charterer falls within the scope of Article 809. In order to protect the cargo interest more thoroughly, the KCC inserted an express provision to the effect that even if the time charterer acts as a carrier, the owner is liable for the cargo damages.

273. The KCC inserted a time-bar provision in the 2007 revision. The parties in the time charter party can no longer raise claims two years after the vessel was redelivered to the owner, according to Article 846.

274. When the time charterer does not pay hire duly to the owner, the master has a right to retain the cargo on board the vessel in accordance with Article 844. The master has a right to hand over the cargo in exchange for the payment of the hire. However, the master cannot exercise the above right against the bona fide third-party holder of the B/L issued by the time charterer.

275. If the time charterer did not pay hire by due date, the owner is entitled to terminate the time charter party (Article 845(1)). When the time charterer entered into a contract for the carriage of goods with the third party, the vessel was at sea after sailing laden with cargo, and the owner terminated the time charter party, the same obligation as the time charterer has against the cargo interests is imposed upon the owner (Article 845(2)). If the owner notifies the termination of the time charter party to the cargo interests with its intention to continuously perform the transportation of cargo on board, the owner has a right of pledge on the claims which the time charterer has against the cargo interests, in order to guarantee the owner's claims against the time charterer including hires (Article 845(3)). Article 845 aims to protect the owner in case of the time charterer's breach of the time charter party and simultaneously protect the cargo interests by imposing the same obligation as the time charterer as the original carrier.

276. The necessity of inserting default rules in the time charter party is increasing. When parties do not enter into a time charter contract in writing, they may have difficulties in seeking a solution. If several provisions are inserted in the KCC, the parties may rely on the default rule to solve their dispute. Chinese Maritime Law and Japanese Commercial Code show good examples. Pilot charges and bunker expenses are borne by the time charterer. KCC does not have such a default rule.

§4. Voyage Charter Party

I. Definition

277. There is no dispute on the legal nature of the voyage charter party in Korea; it is a kind of contract for work rather than a lease of the vessel, and therefore, it is regarded as a type of contract for the carriage of goods by sea in Korea.[33] The contract for the carriage of goods is a kind of contract for work specified in the Korean Civil Code Article 664, in which a party promises to complete a work, and the other party promises to pay remuneration for the result of the work. The remuneration is paid at the same time when the work was completed (Article 665). Unless otherwise agreed, the carrier cannot claim charterage (freight) from the shipper when it did not complete the carriage of goods to the promised destination, according to the Korean Civil Code.

II. Legal Nature

278. In the normal voyage charter party, the charterer is at the capacity of the cargo owner while the owner acts as a carrier. In this situation, the voyage charterer is equivalent to the shipper in the common carriage.

279. However, the voyage charterer occasionally acts as a carrier. When it finds any space large enough to lend to the other charterer, it enters into another contract for the voyage charter party with a cargo owner, by which it becomes a carrier. Under this arrangement, the cargo owner will make claims against the voyage charterer as the carrier. However, the voyage charterer does not possess the vessel carrying out the contract and furthermore, it may not own any other assets. Accordingly, the realization of the cargo interests' claims against the voyage charter party is not easy. The KCC Article 809 functions to provide a mechanism to cope with the above problem.[34]

III. Voyage Charterer as the Carrier

280. In order to solve this issue, the Korean government inserted a provision to the effect that the owner of the vessel is additionally liable for the cargo damages with the voyage charterer or the time charterer as a carrier when the master acted in breach of the duty of seaworthiness and duty of taking care of the cargo (Article 809).

33. In Hyeon Kim, *supra*, 139; Lee Sik Chai, *supra*, 119.
34. Article 809 is the successor of Art. 806 in the old KCC. There was dispute on whether the provision is applicable, and thus, the owner is liable when the time charterer acts as a carrier.

281. When many shipping brokers act as voyage charterers for the purpose of earning differences between hires, the provision is a very useful tool to protect innocent cargo interests. When the voyage charterer as the carrier goes bankrupt or cannot be found in Korea, the cargo claimants are able to raise a lawsuit against the owner of the vessel pursuant to Article 809. In addition, the cargo claimant is allowed to apply for the prejudgment attachment against the vessel, which incurred damages because the shipowner was forced to become the obligor.

282. However, the provision has been under heavy criticism by several academics and practitioners.[35] When the vessel is under the bareboat charter party, the shipowner under Article 809 should be substituted by the bareboat charterer according to Article 850, and thus, the bareboat charterer stands in the shoes of the shipowner. The bareboat charterer as the obligor does not own the vessel; therefore, the cargo claimant is not entitled to arrest the vessel pursuant to Article 809. Accordingly, the rationale to protect the cargo interest cannot be achieved by Article 809.

283. The other strong criticism is that when the F/F acts as the carrier, Article 809 is not applicable. In terms of financial stability, the F/F as the carrier is as bad as the voyage charterer. Therefore, when the cargo interests enter into the contract for carriage with the F/F, they should be protected in the same way as in Article 809. However, there is no such provision in case the F/F acts as the carrier. Further doubt is raised when we read Article 809 more carefully because it is placed on the common carriage, but there is no provision to apply the same for the voyage charter party case. It is a mistake during the enactment. It should be interpreted that Article 809 is applicable for the common carriage as well as voyage charter party case, the same as the 1991 KCC Article 806.

284. When the voyage charterer operates a vessel as a carrier, it is entitled to invoke both the package limitation and global limitation. The voyage charterer has rights and obligations as the carrier pursuant to the KCC.

IV. Special Provision under the KCC in Case of the Voyage Charterer as the Shipper

285. Under the voyage charter party's agreement, the owner of the vessel acts as a carrier. The KCC has several provisions for the voyage charter party. Both the voyage charter party and common carriage have the same characteristic in that the counter party of the carrier is the shipper. In other words, both contracts are regarded as the contract for the carriage. However, there is a difference in that the freedom of contract prevails in the voyage charter party while it does not in the common carriage. The owner as the carrier on the one hand and the charterer as the shipper on the other hand are regarded as having the same bargaining power under

35. In Hyeon Kim, *supra*, 148.

the voyage charter party. Therefore, the KCC shows the policy that it does not interfere with the relationship between the owner and the charterer except in case of seaworthiness.

286. When the B/L is issued and the third party holds it, the KCC tries to protect the innocent third party. When a third party holds the B/L, any agreement in the B/L against Article 799 is null and void according to Article 855(4). The amount of liability less than that of Article 797 in the B/L is null and void pursuant to Articles 799 and 855(4) in a case that the bona fide third party holds the B/L issued by the voyage charterer as the carrier.[36]

287. It is well settled in Korea that even though the B/L is issued by the carrier under the voyage charter party, the legal relation between the carrier and the charterer or the shipper will be governed by the voyage charter party.

288. The owner as a carrier under the voyage charter party has a duty of exercising seaworthiness and due care for cargo (Article 841). The KCC Article 841, which says that Articles 794 and 795 are applicable *mutatis mutandis* to the voyage charter party, means that the legal nature of the voyage charter party is a contract for the carriage like common carriage, not the lease of the vessel.

289. The seaworthiness duty has a characteristic of a compulsory nature between the owner and the charterer. When the B/L is issued, these obligations and liabilities are transformed as being mandatory between the owner as the carrier and bona fide holder of the B/L (Article 839).

290. The owner of the vessel has a duty to notify the readiness of loading to the charterer. The time of the above notification plays an important role in deciding the commencement of lay times (Article 829(1)). Lay times start from 1300 hours on the same day if the above notification was given before noon or 0600 hours on the following day if the above notification was given after noon (Article 829(2)). The time can be changed by party's agreement because Article 829(2) is a kind of default provision. The day when the work cannot be done due to force majeure and according to the custom at the particular port of loading is not calculated as lay times (Article 829(2)).

291. The right and obligation of the shipowner against the charterer or consignee are extinguished, regardless of a cause of action, unless the lawsuit is brought within two years after the cargo was delivered or should have been delivered (Article 840(1)). Even though the claim is raised based on the cause of action in tort, the two years time-bar provision is applicable to the case. The period can be extended by the party's agreement (Article 840(1)). However, an agreement to

---

36. Article 799 prohibits the carrier from derogating its obligation and liability prescribed in the KCC. It is an equivalent to the Hague-Visby Rules Art. 3(8). Article 855(4) is an equivalent to Art. 799. It is applicable when the innocent third party obtains the B/L issued under the voyage charter party.

shorten the period in Article 840(1) between the owner and the charterer is null and void, unless it is expressly stated in the voyage charter party (Article 840(2)).

V. Standard Forms of Voyage Charter Party

292. Gencon is the most widely circulated form of standard voyage charter party form. Lay time is important for calculating hire between parties. Therefore, there are several clauses on the calculation of lay times in the charter party.

The starting point of the lay time depends on the agreement. Where the allowable lay times expire the charterer should pay demurrage to the shipowner. However, where the vessel did not use the period of the allowable lay times, the shipowner gives the dispatch money to the charterer. The liquidated amount was fixed when the agreement was made. The demurrage and dispatch money accrues only if the fact that the vessel leaves the port later than agreed or earlier occurs, regardless of the presence of negligence from the charterer or the shipowner.

293. Because the voyage charter party is a kind of contract for carriage of goods by sea, there are several clauses regarding for carriage of goods, such as the seaworthiness obligation and taking care of the cargo obligation for the carrier. Error of navigation exemption clause is also found. If the Hague-Visby Rules is adopted as the governing law by party's agreement, any agreement against the mandatory provision in the rules becomes null and void. Almost all of voyage charter party has an arbitration clause to the effect the legal disputes shall be solved before the London Maritime Arbitration with the English governing law.

§5. Slot (Space) Charter Party

I. Definition

294. A slot charter party or space charter party is widely used between liner shipping companies in Korea. A slot charterer or space charterer is an operator of a vessel in a sense that it borrows a part of a vessel's space and makes use of this space for the benefit of its own business. Accordingly, the particular vessel involved in the slot charter has several operators, as a result of which several different B/Ls are to be issued by the different carriers, including the slot charterer.

II. Legal Nature and Liability

295. If damages occur in a container under the slot charter operation, the carrier which issued the B/L will be liable for the cargo damages and other carriers will not be liable. Under the slot charter operation, the slot charterer is liable only for the portion that it undertakes to carry as the carrier. In other words, the slot charterer is not liable for the damage of the cargo interest which enters into a contract with the carrier. The holder of the B/L issued by the slot charterer is not allowed to invoke the cargo claims against the carrier. The shipowner or the bareboat charterer, as the carrier, not the slot charterer, is vicariously liable for the damage caused by the master's negligence.

The slot charter party is regarded, in legal nature, as a hybrid between the voyage charter party and the time charter party.[37] The slot charterer is not allowed to invoke the global limitation against damages to the chartered vessel itself because Article 769 clearly states that claims subject to the global limitation should be incurred from damages other than those of the vessel itself.[38]

III. Issues to be Solved

296. The KCC does not have any express provision addressing the slot charter party, and thus: (i) whether the slot charterer is entitled to limit its liability, and (ii) how much it can limit its liability is at issue in Korea. Under the current law, the slot charterer can be regarded as one of the charterers, and thus, the general provision on the charterer will be applicable to the case. Accordingly, even though the slot charterer operates only part of the vessel's tonnage or space, it is entitled to limit its liability based on total tonnage or space of the vessel itself rather than the actually engaged space of the space-chartered vessel. Taking into consideration that the space charterer uses only part of the tonnage or space of the vessel, it appears that the above application is unrealistic.[39]

§6. COA

I. Definition

297. A COA is also one of widely engaged ways of vessel operation in Korea. For example, Pohang Steel Co., Ltd, as a steel company, is required to import iron ores from foreign countries such as Australia and Brazil. A shipping company such as the Korea Line Co., Ltd enters into a COA contract with Pohang Steel Co., Ltd for the carriage of iron ores covering ten years. In return, the shipping company as the carrier earns a great amount of money as freight. Immediately after entering into the COA contract, the owner of the vessel seeks to borrow money from the banks by depositing the COA agreement as a security. The COA agreement over the years functions as the security for the shipowner to construct new vessels at the shipyard.

II. Legal Nature

298. It is a kind of voyage charter party. However, it is different from a typical voyage charter party in that the owner undertakes to perform a series of voyages to

37. John Richardson, *Combined Transport Documents*, LLP 145 (2000).
38. Jong Hyeon Choi, *Maritime Law* 137 (2009).
39. Jong Hyeon Choi, *ibid.*, 133.

transport a large volume of cargo covering five or ten years. The owner of the vessel acts as a carrier, and the charterer acts as a shipper.

§7. Feeder Operation

I. Definition

299. Feeder operation is well engaged in liner shipping. When the container cargo is shipped by the liner company, the cargo is discharged temporarily in the hub port and it is shifted to the last port by the relatively small vessel. The small container vessel is called a feeder vessel.

II. Legal Nature

300. Where the feeder operation is involved, only one B/L is issued by the liner as the ocean carrier. The feeder company does not issue another B/L. The B/L issued by ocean carrier is the only B/L and it regulates all scope of the transportation. The feeder company is an independent contractor for the benefit of the ocean carrier. Where cargo is damaged during the feeder operation, the ocean carrier is liable for the cargo damages in breach of contract as the obligor. The feeder company may be subject to tort liability.

Chapter 8. Transport under B/L

§1. General

I. Definition of Common Carriage

301. There are two kinds of contracts for the carriage of goods by sea under the Korean law. One is a voyage charter party, and the other is a contract for the carriage of individual goods (hereinafter "the common carriage"). The latter is a pure contract for the carriage of goods. It is very similar to a common carriage under U.S. law. The carrier undertakes to carry goods from one place to the other place, and the shipper undertakes to pay the freight as a reward in return for the carriage to the carrier. It is one type of typical contract for work.

302. Under the common carriage, the written document for a contract for the carriage is not issued except for some domestic carriage, but instead, the B/L is usually issued by the carrier to the shipper. The B/L functions as an evidence of the contract.

II. Source of Law

303. The Hague-Visby Rules and Hamburg Rules are two international conventions which regulate legal issues regarding the common carriage. Korea is a contracting party neither to the Hague-Visby Rules nor to the Hamburg Rules. Unlike the U.S., Japan, the U.K., and Canada, Korea *does* not have a special and distinctive law known as the COGSA. The COGSA addresses legal relationship between the carrier and shipper in the common carriage. The KCC addresses legal issues involved not only in the voyage charter party but also in the common carriage and includes other maritime issues such as limitation of liability and collision liability.

304. Provisions in the voyage charter party have a characteristic as default rules, but those in the common carriage as a kind of compulsory rules. Regulating legal relationships in case of the voyage charter party is left to the party's autonomy with the exception of seaworthiness matter. The shipowner and the charterer under the voyage charter party are regarded as having equal bargaining power, and thus, there is no urgent need for the government to intervene.

305. However, in the common carriage, the bargaining power of the carrier prevails over that of the shipper. Accordingly, there is an urgent need that the government should intervene in order to protect the shipper. The Hague-Visby Rules do not allow the carrier to derogate from its duty and obligation stipulated in the rules (Article 3(8)). The KCC adopted these rules and if the carrier and the shipper made an agreement to allow the carrier to derogate from its obligation and liability imposed by the KCC, the agreement became null and void (Article 799).

306. The Hague-Visby Rules is adopted as the governing law by the parties' agreement. The KPIL admits the party autonomy in relation to governing law where there is a foreign factor in the contract for the carriage (Article 25(1)).

307. It is a new development in Korean maritime transport activities that the shipper with large cargoes gains bargaining power over the carrier, and thus, it requests the carrier to give up immunity or exceptions of liability against the cargo damages and, furthermore, to pay all damages regardless of the presence of the negligence of the carrier. Therefore, the compulsory provision of Article 799 is no longer reasonable. According to the Rotterdam Rules, the shipper as well as the carrier are subject to the compulsory provision similar to the KCC Article 799. The shipper is also not allowed to lower its obligation less than stipulated in the Rotterdam Rules Article 79(2).

§2. Parties in the Common Carriage

I. The Carrier, Shipper, Consignor, and Consignee

308. The parties to the contract for a common carriage are the carrier and the shipper. The consignor and consignee are not the parties in the contract for the common carriage. The consignor is the person who sends the cargo at the loading port, while the consignee is the person to receive the cargo at the discharging port. When the B/L is issued, the holder of the B/L becomes the consignee. In the Cost Insurance & Freight (CIF) terms, the consignor as the shipper has the obligation to enter into a contract of carriage with the carrier, and thus, it becomes the counter party against the carrier. In the Free on Board (FOB) terms, the consignee as the shipper has the obligation to arrange transportation, and thus, it becomes the counter party against the carrier.

309. In the Korean Supreme Court case *2000.8.18. Docket No. 99da4844*, the court rendered that the importer, under the FOB terms, was the shipper even though the exporter physically made a contract with the carrier, the exporter acted as the agent of the importer and that the party in the contract of the carriage was the importer. Therefore, the carrier is not allowed to get freight from the exporter. However, the exporter in the FOB terms is equivalent to the documentary shipper under the 2008 Rotterdam Rules (Article 1(9)).[40] The rules impose the same obligation as the shipper upon the documentary shipper, under which it may pay freight to the carrier (Article 33).

---

40. Documentary shipper means a person, other than the shipper, that accepts to be named as "shipper" in the transport document or electronic transport record.

II. Contracting Carrier and Actual Carrier

310. The development of door-to-door transportation led to the appearance of the NVOCC. The F/F in Korea is equivalent to the NVOCC in the U.S. The F/F carries out three different kinds of functions in Korea. One of the functions is that of the carrier.

311. The F/F undertakes the carriage of goods from the shipper. However, the F/F does not possess any means of transportation, and thus, it enters into another contract for the carriage with the ocean carrier. In this mechanism, the F/F is called the contracting carrier, while the ocean carrier as the actual carrier. The cargo claimant can invoke claims against the F/F as the contracting carrier based on the cause of action for the breach of contract. However, it can bring about a lawsuit against the ocean carrier for the cargo damages based on the cause of action in tort but cannot raise a lawsuit based on the cause of action in breach of contract because there is no contractual relation between the shipper and the actual carrier. The contracting carrier issues the House B/L, and the actual carrier issues the Master B/L. The former is used as the document for the purpose of negotiation with the issuing bank of the Letter of Credit (L/C).

312. The actual carrier enjoys a special protection under the KCC. According to Article 798(4), the actual carrier is entitled to invoke the package limitation when the cargo claimant raises a lawsuit against it based on the tort. Other independent contractors, such as the warehouse keeper and stevedores, are not allowed to invoke the package limitation under Article 798(2).

313. Unlike the Hamburg Rules (Article 10), the Rotterdam Rules (Article 19) and Chinese maritime law (Article 61), there is no provision in the KCC to the effect that the actual carrier is jointly and severally liable for the cargo damages in conjunction with the contractual carrier. However, the actual carrier is entitled to invoke the same right and defense as the contracting carrier, according to Article 798(4), when it becomes a defendant by the shipper's raising a lawsuit for cargo damages on the cause of action based in the tort (the Korean Civil Code Article 750).

314. There are several carriers in a vessel operated in the name of alliance. In the Alliance arrangement, several shipping companies take part in using the same vessel together. Each carrier has an obligation to take care of its own cargo as the carrier. The ocean carrier of the vessel on board which the cargo is shipped is not the carrier of all other cargo except its own cargo. Therefore, if the owner of the cargo suffered damages, it could raise a lawsuit against its own carrier based on the breach of the contract and against the ocean carrier based on the tort. Only one B/L is issued by each individual carrier.

§3. CARRIER'S OBLIGATION AND LIABILITY

I. Obligation

315. Under the KCC, the carrier has two obligations: (i) to exercise due diligence to make a vessel seaworthy (Article 794), and (ii) to carry the cargo as promised (Article 795). The carrier is not allowed to derogate from these obligations by agreement with the shipper (Article 799).

II. Duration of the Obligation

316. The KCC does not specify the duration for which the carrier takes responsibility. It states that the carrier's obligation includes from the receipt of cargo to the delivery of cargo (Article 795(1)). From this provision, it is implied that the period of carrier's responsibility starts from the receipt of cargo and ends with the delivery of cargo. In the 1991 revision of the KCC, the Korean government expanded the carrier's scope of the obligation from loading to receipt and from discharging to delivery.

317. It can be said that the KCC is based on the port-to-port concept. In this respect, the duration of the carrier's obligation in the KCC is the same as the Hamburg Rules but different from that in the Hague-Visby Rules. In this regard, several disputes are still on-going. When a B/L stating the carrier's liability start from the loading of the cargo and cargo damages happened within a Korean port area, the carrier argues that it is not liable for cargo damages during shifting at terminal. However, the carrier's obligation starts from the receipt of the cargo and ends at the delivery of the cargo, according to Article 795. This obligation is subject to the compulsory provision of Article 799. Therefore, if the Korean law governs the case, the agreement is null and void, and the carrier has a duty to receipt the cargo with due care. As a result, the carrier is liable for the cargo damages.

318. The carrier's liability starts from the receipt of the cargo under the KCC Article 795(1). The scope of the receipt can be extended to the shore. If the carrier receives the cargo at the warehouse far from the port area, the carrier's obligation and liability provisions are applicable to the case. Therefore, the carrier is entitled to invoke the package limitation. 1

III. Basis of Liability

319. Under the KCC, the carrier's liability is based on the presumed fault liability rather than the strict liability (Article 795(1)). Because the carrier's fault is presumed, the carrier will be liable for the cargo damages unless it proves that it or its servant or agent exercised due diligence for receiving, loading, carrying, keeping, stowing, discharging, and delivery.

320. If the cargo was damaged because the officer in charge was negligent in maintaining temperature according to the instruction of the shipper, the carrier may be liable for the cargo damage because it breached the duty to exercise due diligence to discharge the duty of "keeping the cargo" under Article 795(1). If the cargo was damaged during the discharging at berth due to the negligence of its crew, the carrier is also liable for the cargo damages unless it proves that it exercises due diligence to discharge the duty of "discharging cargo."

321. In general contractual claims, the obligor has the burden of proof that it exercised due diligence for discharging its obligation under the Korean Civil Code Article 390. Therefore, some scholars view that the KCC Article 795(1) is the natural result of the KCC's faithful adoption of the relevant provision in the Korean Civil Code. However, Article 795(1) gives the carrier benefit from the view of common law in which the common carrier is strictly liable for cargo damages.

322. Due to the obligatory nature of the carrier's duty of care for the cargo, the carrier cannot derogate from its obligation, such as loading or discharging by agreement (Article 799). If the carrier enters into the contract for the carriage with the shipper to the effect that it does not have the duty to deliver the cargo, it is against Article 799 because it makes the shipper disadvantageous, and thus, the agreement becomes null and void. In the Korean Supreme Court case *2010.4.15. Docket No. 2007da50649*, the court rendered that the carrier has the duty to exercise only when it makes an agreement with the shipper to assume each stipulated separate duty. It means that the carrier does not have the duty to load the cargo unless it does not assume. Consequently, the carrier is allowed to derogate the duty of loading the cargo by agreement. However, the author thinks that the duty of receipt and delivery of cargo is not allowed to be derogated because this duty is the fundamental one for the carrier to exercise.

323. Seaworthiness obligation should be exercised before or on leaving the port by the carrier (Article 794). The carrier is liable for the cargo damages resulting from a certain event caused by the carrier's breach of the seaworthiness. Even though the carrier breached the duty of maintaining seaworthiness, if that is not related to the cause of the damages, the carrier is not liable for the damages (Article 794).

324. It is well settled in Korea that the carrier is not entitled to enjoy the error of navigation defense if it breached the duty of seaworthiness, which resulted in cargo damages.[41]

41. Korean Supreme Court case *1998.12.10. Docket No. 96da45054;* In Hyeon Kim, *supra*, 164; Lee Sik, Chai, *supra, 143.*

IV. FIO Clause

325. There were several court cases between the holder of the B/L and the carrier on the meaning of the Free In and Out (FIO) agreement in Korea. When the charterer has specialty on the loading or discharging in a voyage charter party situation, it makes an arrangement with the owner to the effect that it will load or discharge cargo instead of the owner[42] The FIO agreement is a matter of voyage charter party, and thus it regulates legal relation between the shipowner and the charterer. However, the shipowner issues the B/L into which the charter party is incorporated, and then the holder of the B/L is affected by the FIO clause in the voyage charter party. Recently, the separate wording of FIO in the liner trade, which has nothing to do with the voyage charter party, appears. In this context, the FIO agreement is related to the common carriage.

326. There is no dispute that the FIO agreement shifts the burden of paying expense of loading or discharging from the owner to the charterer. Whether the FIO agreement shifts the obligation of loading or discharging from the owner (carrier) to the charterer or not has been internationally disputed.[43] Without sufficient incorporation of the FIO agreement in the B/L, the shipowner is not allowed to make avail of the agreement against the B/L holder.

327. In the Korean Supreme Court case *2010.4.15. Docket No. 2007da50649*, the court rendered that the obligation of the carrier was shifted to the shipper, and thus, if the accident occurred during discharging under the FIO agreement, the liability for cargo damages should be imposed upon the shipper.

328. In the above case, the shipowner and the charterer entered into a voyage charter party and then the shipowner as the carrier issued the B/L. There was a wording of the FIO BASIS on the front page of the B/L. During discharging by the charterer, the cargo was damaged due to bad stowage done by the charterer's stevedores. Cargo interests as a holder of the B/L brought a lawsuit against the carrier for the cargo damages. The carrier argued that: (i) the wording of the FIO in the B/L meant that both expenses and liability were shifted to the charterer, and thus, the carrier was not liable for the damages. The court decided that in the FIO agreement, the charterer assumed not only expenses but also liability. As a result, the carrier was not responsible for the damages. In addition, the charterer argued that if the FIO agreement was regarded as shifting the carrier's obligation and liability on to the charterer, this kind of agreement was against Articles 795(1)[44] and

42. On the other hand, the carrier in the liner trade carries out the loading and discharging without exception.
43. 1994 GENCON Article 5(a) stipulates that the cargo shall be brought into the holds, loaded, stowed and/or trimmed, tallied, lashed and/or secured and taken from the holds and discharged by the charters, free of any risk, liability and expense whatsoever to the owners.
44. Act 795(1)) (The old KCC Art. 788(1)): If the carrier fails to prove that he or crew or other employees of the vessel did not neglect to pay attention to the receiving, loading, stowing, carrying, keeping and caring, discharging, and delivering goods, he shall be liable for damages resulting from loss, destruction, or delay in delivery.

799(1)(3)[45,46] as a result of which it was null and void. The KCC Article 795(1) is similar to the Hague-Visby Rule Articles 2 and 3(2). The KCC Article 799(1) is similar to the Hague-Visby Rule Article 3(8). The court rendered that KCC Article 795(1) does not mean that this provision should be applicable for all the cases but only when the carrier agrees to assume to receive, load, delivery and discharge, respectively. Therefore, under the FIO agreement, the carrier did not make any agreement to discharge the cargo in this particular case, and thus, the carrier did not have an obligation to discharge under Article 795(1). The court finally reached a conclusion that the agreement was not against Article 799(1)(3).

V. Delivery Issue

329. The shipper is the person who is entitled to demand the cargo from the carrier. The right to demand the cargo stems from the contract for the carriage. The right to demand the cargo transfers from the shipper to the consignee by the operation of the KCC Article 140. When the cargo arrives at the discharging port, the consignee obtains the same right as the shipper (Article 140(1)). Furthermore, when the consignee demands the delivery of the cargo after the cargo arrives at discharging port, the right of the carrier prevails over that of the shipper (Article 140(2)). The carrier has an obligation to deliver the cargo to the consignee (Articles 795, 815, 140). When the B/L is issued, the holder of the B/L becomes the consignee.

330. According to the KCC Article 140, where the cargo becomes a total loss just before it arrives at the destination, the consignee does not obtain any legal right for the cargo. The shipper is the only person to request the delivery of the cargo from the carrier. Therefore, there is a need for revision of the KCC Article 140 to the effect that the consignee has a right to obtain the delivery of the cargo from the carrier.

331. The carrier has an additional obligation to deliver the cargo in exchange for the B/L under the KCC (Articles 129 and 861) in addition to the duty of delivering the cargo with due diligence under Article 795(1). If the carrier hands over the cargo without exchange of the B/L, the carrier should be held liable for the loss of cargo to the holder of the B/L. The holder of the B/L is entitled to claim based on the cause of action for a breach of contract and in tort. According to the Korean courts, the carrier cannot invoke the package limitation if it hands over the cargo intentionally or recklessly with the knowledge that damages would probably occur (Article 797).[47]

45. Act 799(1)) (The old KCC Art. 790(1)): No special contract between parties that reduce or exempt any obligation or liability of the carrier contrary to the contents of from Art. 794 (The old Act Art. 787) to Art. 798 (The old Act 789ter) shall be effective.
46. The KCC Art. 799(3): The relationship between the carrier and the holder of the B/L in the voyage charter party is also subject to Art. 799(1).
47. Korean Supreme Court case *2001.4.27. Docket No. 99da71528*. However, the court decided that the warehouse keeper's intentional act or reckless behavior in the case did not prohibit the carrier from invoking the package limitation.

332. The KCC does not have any provision on the definition of delivery. According to the Korean Supreme Court, a delivery is completed at the time when the consignee starts to have actual control over the cargo. Accordingly, when the cargo was stored in a business warehouse, the court decided that the delivery is completed at the time when the cargo leaves from the warehouse because the carrier had control over the cargo through the warehouse keeper as his servant or agent.[48] In the meantime, in the case that the cargo is stored in a consignee's warehouse, the court found that the delivery is completed at the time when the cargo enters the warehouse.[49] In this case, the carrier no longer controls the cargo during the period that the cargo is stored at the warehouse.

333. In conclusion, the carrier should hand over the cargo in exchange for the B/L at the time when the cargo leaves the warehouse in case of a business warehouse and when the cargo enters the warehouse in case of a consignee's warehouse.

334. The KCC has a provision (Article 803) to address the cases that the consignee does not appear or reject to receive it. The carrier is allowed to deposit the cargo to the deposit office or deliver it to the place designated by the government. The carrier should notify the charterer or shipper of the deposit or delivery. When the carrier deposits the cargo at the deposit office or delivers the cargo to the designated place, the carrier's obligation to deliver the cargo in exchange for the B/L ends.

335. The Letter of Indemnity (L/I) is widely used in the discharging process in Korea. Regardless of the wide circulations of the L/I, the Korean Supreme Court showed firm views on the legal nature of the L/I that it was valid among the consignee, the guarantor, and the carrier but invalid between the carrier and the holder of the B/L.[50]

336. In the L/I transaction, the carrier hands over the cargo to the consignee who does not possess the B/L, relying on the promise in the L/I that the carrier can make recourse claims against the guarantor when the holder of the B/L makes claims against it for the loss of cargo as a result of its handing over the cargo to the person designated in the L/I. According to the Korean Supreme Court, the act of handing over the cargo to the designated person other than the holder of the B/L constitutes a tort against the holder of the B/L. Therefore, the carrier is liable for the loss of cargo against the holder of the B/L. Relying on the promise in the L/I, the carrier, however, who handed over the cargo to the consignee, is entitled to make claims against the guarantor.

337. In the L/I transaction, the carrier is not allowed to invoke the package limitation for the loss of the cargo because the carrier must have known the fact that the

---

48. Korean Supreme Court cases *1992.2.14. Docket No. 91da4249; 2000.11.14. Docket No. 2000da30950.*
49. Korean Supreme Court case *1990.2.13. Docket No. 88daka23735.*
50. Korean Supreme Court case *1992.2.25. Docket No. 91da30026.*

holder of B/L would appear at a later stage due to its loss of cargo (Article 797). The carrier's liability involved in the wrongful delivery of the cargo based on L/I is not compensated by the carrier's P&I insurance.

338. The D/O (delivery order) is not terms in the KCC. However, it has been circulated for a long time and became important in the issue of delivery of the cargo. The carrier issues the D/O to the warehouse keeper or to the master of the vessel, stating that the cargo may be handed over to the holder of the D/O. Whether the warehouse keeper has the obligation to exchange the cargo with the D/O or not has been at issue in Korea. A court admitted that such practice is well settled in a Korean port, and thus, the warehouse keeper was in breach of the contract because it handed over the cargo to the shipper without exchanging the cargo with the D/O.

§4. Shipper's Obligation and Liability

I. General

339. It is not easy to find provisions regarding the shipper's obligation and liability in the KCC. It is partly because the shipper is regarded as a weaker party than the carrier in the contract for the carriage of goods by sea. The KCC Article 799 is not applicable against the shipper. Therefore, the shipper is allowed to derogate from its obligation and liability. For example, the shipper is allowed to make an agreement to the effect that it does not guarantee the accuracy of the information about the cargo (Article 853(3)). The agreement is valid, and thus, the shipper will be liable for the carrier's damage due to inaccuracy of the figures only if the damage was caused by the shipper's negligence.

340. However, there is a criticism that the KCC should impose stricter obligations upon the shipper than the current KCC, reflecting the modern trend in container transportation. The carrier's interest argues that: (i) the shippers with volume cargoes prevail over the carriers in respect of the bargaining power in modern trade; (ii) under container transportation, the Korean carriers experienced several total loss cases caused by the explosion of the cargo packed in the container; (iii) under the carriage of containers, the carrier cannot inspect contents inside the container and thus the shipper's notification to the carrier of the content in the container becomes very crucial for the safe transportation.

341. There is a strong voice that the strict obligation to notify the dangerous condition of the cargo to the carrier should be inserted in the new KCC. Without such notice, there is no way for the carrier to become aware of the presence of the dangerous cargo on board within a container box. Recently, lots of explosion accidents have occurred in the container vessel. New Japanese Commercial Code adopted a provision to impose an obligation for the shipper to notify the carrier of the cargo condition.

II. Special Obligation of the Shipper in the KCC

342. The conditions of cargo are furnished by the shipper. The shipper guarantees the accuracy of contents such as weight and quantity of cargo which it submitted to the carrier as stated in the B/L. If the figures or characteristics of the cargo submitted to the carrier are different from the actual condition, the shipper is liable for the damages even though it did not act negligently (Article 853(3)).[51] The provision is interpreted that the shipper will be strictly liable for the damages caused by inaccuracy of the condition of cargo on board.

343. The KCC has a provision on dangerous cargo (Article 801). However, the provision does not mention the issue of liability of the shipper. There are split views in Korea on whether the shipper is strictly liable for the damages caused by the dangerous goods when it was loaded without the shipper's knowledge of dangerous characteristics. The KCC does not have a liability provision regarding dangerous goods, different from that in the Hague-Visby Rules.[52] Because Korean law is based on the presumed fault liability principles, there is a view that the Korean courts cannot easily impose strict liability upon the shipper without such express provision of the Hague-Visby Rules, which impose strict liability upon the shipper.[53]

§5. Transport Document- B/L

I. Definition and Functions

344. The KCC does not have a provision on the definition of the B/L.[54] Upon the request of the shipper, the carrier should issue the B/Ls to the shipper after the receipt of the cargo (Article 852(1)) or after loading on board the vessel (Article 852(2)). The main purpose of the contract for carriage is to transport cargoes from the seller at the loading port to the buyer at the discharging port.

345. Several legal hurdles arise in connection with the transportation of cargoes. First, when the vessel arrives at the discharging port, the master should hand over the cargo to the eligible consignee. However, it is not easy for the master to ascertain the consignee. Second, the buyer may want to pay the purchasing price after it receives cargoes. However, the carrier may want to obtain the price as soon as it

51. It is very similar to Hague-Visby Art. 3(5).
52. According to the Hague-Visby Rules Art. 4(6), the shipper of such goods shall be liable for all damages and expenses directly or indirectly arising out of or resulting from such shipment.
53. Lee Sik, Chai, *supra*, 171.
54. Under the Rotterdam Rules, transport document means a document issued under a contract of carriage by the carrier that: (a) evidences the carrier's or a performing party's receipt of goods under a contract of carriage; and (b) evidences or contain a contract of carriage. Under the Hamburg Rules, B/L means a document which evidences a contract of carriage by sea and the taking over or loading of the goods by the carrier, and by which the carrier undertakes to deliver the goods against surrender of the document. A provision in the document that the goods are to be delivered to the order of a named person, or to order, or to bearer, constitutes such an undertaking.

loads cargoes on board the vessel. Third, the seller may request the buyer to provide a guarantee to it for the purpose of securing the purchasing price. The buyer sends the L/C issued by a bank to the seller to the effect that the bank will pay the purchasing price instead of the shipper. Instead, the bank requests a guarantee for securing its risk from the shipper. In order to solve these problems involved in international trade and transportation, the merchants invented a document called the B/L.

346. The B/L has three different functions under the Korean law. The B/L acts as a good evidence for proving the presence of a contract for the carriage of goods by sea, especially in the common carriage. In the common carriage, the document evidencing the contract for the carriage is generally not issued. Instead, the B/L plays the role of document evidencing the contract.

347. The B/L functions as an evidence of the receipt of cargo. In the front of the B/L, there is a column for the quantity of the cargo to be transported. The KCC also requires the carrier to enter the characteristics of cargo, such as numbers and weights of cargo, onto the B/L (Article 853(1)).

348. The B/L also functions as the document of title. By operation of the law in the KCC, the holder of the B/L has title to the cargo when it is under transport, even at sea. In order for the buyer to have the title to a movable, it is one of the requirements that the possession of the movable should be transferred to the buyer from the seller (Korean Civil Code Article 188). The B/L represents the cargo under the transportation at sea, and thus the fact that the purchaser obtains the B/L means that it obtains the possession of the cargo at its hand (Articles 861, 133). As a result, the buyer obtains the title to the cargo. Under the Korean law, the holder has the right to demand the cargo from the carrier. In this sense, the B/L is a document of title in which such right is embodied.

349. Both a negotiable B/L and a non-negotiable B/L can be issued by the carrier at the request of the shipper. When the negotiable B/L is issued, the carrier should hand over the cargo to the holder of the B/L in exchange for the B/L at the discharging port. When the non-negotiable B/L is issued, whether or not the carrier is required to hand over cargoes in exchange for the B/L is in dispute in Korea.

350. There are three different kinds of B/L in Korea in terms of negotiability: Order B/L, Bearer B/L, and Straight B/L. When the order B/L is issued, the B/L can be assigned to the assignee by the designation of the holder. Even though the B/L that the consignee's name is designated is issued, the B/L can be assigned by endorsement, and thus, it is regarded as one of the negotiable B/L according to the KCC Article 130 (It is called the Straight B/L in Korea). When the designated B/L with remarks of non-negotiable is issued, it cannot be assigned (Article 130). In this sense, it is equivalent to the straight B/L in the U.S. Sea waybill is a kind of non-negotiable document.[55]

55. In the Korean Supreme Court case *2003.1.10. Docket No. 2000da70064*, the Court decided, *inter alia*, that a straight B/L not marked non-negotiable can be transferred by endorsement; however,

II. Evidential Effect of the B/L

351. Under the common carriage, the B/L is usually issued. The B/L has an evidentiary effect. If the claimant is the shipper and holder of the B/L as well, the statement on the B/L has a prima facie effect (Article 854(1)). Accordingly, the carrier is allowed to rebut the evidentiary effect in the statement on the B/L. For example, if there is a remark that ten pieces of goods were on board, the carrier can rebut it with different evidence. However, if the claimant is a bona fide third-party holder of the B/L, the statement on the B/L has a conclusive effect in evidence, and thus, the carrier no longer can rebut it (Article 854(2)) (The old Article 814*bis*). It is an equivalent to Article 3(4) of the Hague-Visby Rules. These provisions aim at fortifying the effect of the B/L. Without such provisions, the export or importer should verify the condition of the cargo at loading port. Without proving the evidence, the export and importer will lose the law suit.

352. In the Korean Supreme Court case *2002.2.9. Docket No. 98da49074*, the court explained the legal meaning of the evidentiary effect of the B/L as follows: according to the KCC Article 854, the carrier is presumed to receive goods as stated in the B/L, and thus, if the clean B/L was issued with a remark that the cargo was received in an apparently good order, the carrier is presumed to have received the goods in an apparently good order at the loading port. Accordingly, the holder of the B/L is required to prove only the damaged condition of the goods when it received the goods at the discharging port.

353. According to the Korean Supreme Court, the condition of the goods at the loading port should be proved by the carrier when a clean B/L was issued. In a lawsuit for cargo claims without the B/L, the plaintiff should prove the presence of damages. In order to prove the damages, the plaintiff should prove the alleged condition of the cargo at the loading port when it was handed over to the carrier and the damaged condition of the cargo at the discharging port when it was received from the carrier. Owing to the evidentiary effect of the B/L, the holder of the B/L as the plaintiff is not required to prove the condition of the cargo at the loading port; that is, the burden of proof is shifted to the carrier as the defendant. Evidentiary effect on the B/L gives benefit to the holder of the B/L.

354. In the above case, the Korean Supreme Court admitted the effect of the so-called Unknown Clause. In order to evade an unfavorable evidentiary effect of the B/L on the carrier whenever the carrier believes that it is necessary, the carrier inserts a wording of "said to contain (STC)" in the B/L. In the above case, the court rendered to the effect that when there is an unknown clause in the B/L, the evidentiary effect of the B/L in the KCC Article 854 does not apply, and thus, the holder

---

even though the straight B/L was not endorsed and the transferee, therefore, cannot prove his entitlement as the due holder by reference to the succession of the endorsement, the transferee can exercise his right under the B/L by proving that it obtained the B/L legitimately, In this case, all rights, including right to sue based on both breach of contract and tort, were transferred to the due holder when the B/L was transferred.

of the B/L should verify the condition of the cargo at the loading port. The finding is based on the provision in the KCC Article 853(2),[56] which says that the carrier is allowed to omit stating the weight, volume, number, or marks submitted by the shipper when it has reasonable ground for suspecting that there is a considerable reason that they are different from those it actually received or it has had no reasonable means of checking.

355. The unknown clause or Said to Contain remarks plays a role in giving benefit for the carrier not to be subject to the evidentiary provision of Article 854. In order for the carrier to enforce the unknown clause, it should verify that there was a reasonable ground not to believe the accuracy of the remarks in the B/L. Therefore, even though the carrier could weigh the weight of the container box at loading, it did not weigh the box, and then the court may not admit the effect of the clause.

III. Identity of the Carrier Clause

356. Almost all B/Ls issued by Korean Shipping companies include the so-called Identity of the Carrier's clause.

357. It is a clause in the rear side of the B/L to the effect that the owner is still liable as the carrier even though the vessel is operated under the time charter party. Where the time charterer enters into the contract for carriage with the shipper, and it is subject to cargo claims from the shipper, the time charterer argues that it is not liable for the cargo damage because the owner is the carrier by the agreement evidenced in the B/L pursuant to the identity of the carrier clause. The clause is also known as the Demise clause.

358. Identity of the carrier clause affects who is the obligor in the cargo claims. If it is valid, the courts may decide that the shipowner rather than the time charterer is liable for the cargo damages as the carrier. If the court finds that it is null and void because it is against the Hague-Visby Rule 3(8), the time charterer is liable for the cargo damages. In the *Jasmine* case, the Japanese Supreme Court supported the former and the shipowner was decided as the carrier. Neither the Hague-Visby Rules nor the Hamburg Rules does have any provision on the identity of the carrier. However, the Rotterdam Rules has a provision for it. It is generally invalid under the Rotterdam Rules (Article 37(1)).[57]

359. The Korean courts addressed several times the validity of the Identity of Carrier clause or Demise clause in the B/L. In the *Polsa Dos* case, the Seoul High Court rendered that the demise clause was an agreement between the carrier and the

56. It is an equivalent to Article 3(3) proviso.
57. Article 37 (identity of the carrier) 1. If a carrier is identified by name in the contract particulars, any other information in the transport document or electronic transport record relating to the identity of the carrier shall have no effect to the extent that it is inconsistent with that identification.

shipper, and thus, it did not affect the third-party holder of the B/L. The court regarded the clause as being null and void and upheld that the time charterer was liable as the carrier against the holder of the B/L.[58]

A. *Exclusive Jurisdiction Clause*

360. The B/L issued by Korean shipping companies necessarily includes an Exclusive Jurisdiction Clause except for a liner company.[59] It states to the effect that a Korean court has an exclusive jurisdiction over legal disputes regarding the contract for the carriage. Because Korea is the place where the carrier as the defendant resides, there is no difficulty in the Korean court; it exercises jurisdiction based on the exclusive jurisdiction clause in the B/L.

361. However, when the lawsuit is raised in a Korean court based on the B/L with a foreign jurisdiction clause, the Korean Supreme Court showed the tendency that only when the case meets four requirements, the Korean court stays the action to send the case to the foreign court designated in the B/L; otherwise, the Korean court exercises jurisdiction on the case. One of the requirements is the substantial relationship between the case and the foreign country of the court designated as having the jurisdiction. It means that if a Japanese court is designated as the court having jurisdiction in the B/L, Japan should have a certain connection with the case in order for the Japanese court to exercise jurisdiction, excluding the Korean court.

362. It is noteworthy that Korea is not a party to the Hamburg Rules in which the exclusive jurisdiction clause has only a limited power, and thus, the claimant is allowed to select a forum among several forums other than the forum designated in the exclusive jurisdiction clause.

363. In the Korean Supreme Court case *2004.3.25. Docket No. 2001da53349,* the B/L designated a Japanese court as having exclusive jurisdiction. The carrier was a Japanese company, the accident occurred during the voyage and the governing law was the Japanese COGSA. The Korean cargo claimant as the holder of the B/L raised a lawsuit based on the cause of action in tort. The Korean court examined whether the case met the requirements. The carrier as the defendant argued that the case should be sent to the Japanese court based on the Exclusive Jurisdiction clause. It relied on the Japanese governing law clause in the B/L as a substantial connector between Japan and the case. The court rendered that the case did not have a substantial connection with Japan, considering that the cause of action was based on tort, and in such case, the governing law was the Korean law based on KIPL. Accordingly, the carrier's argument was rejected, and the case was dealt with in the Korean court.

---

58. Seoul High Court case *1991.4.2. Docket No. 90na43614.*
59. One Liner company has an arbitration clause instead of jurisdiction clause in the B/L.

B. Both-to-Blame Clause

364. When the collision occurs, the cargo owner may suffer damages. The carrier may be held liable for the cargo damages. However, the collision may be the result of the master's error of navigation, and then the carrier (A) is easily allowed to invoke the error of navigation defense based on the KCC Article 795(2). Consequently, the cargo interest is not allowed to claim damages against the carrier (A) on board the cargo. However, the cargo interest may seek to collect damages against the opposite vessel (B) involved in the collision. According to the KCC Article 879, in the both-to-blame collision case, the third party, such as the cargo interest, can claim against the tortfeasors only the portion of damages which each tortfeasor is responsible for. Therefore, the cargo interest in the above scenario is entitled to collect only part of its claims from the opposite vessel (B), which is not the full amount of damages.

365. However, the cargo interest is allowed to claim full amount of damages to each carrier involved in the collision, according to U.S. law or Japanese law. Under these jurisdictions, the *carrier* pays the full amount of damages due to the presence of the joint and several liabilities as if there is no error of navigation defense. To solve this anomaly, the carrier and the shipper insert a clause called "Both-to-Blame" clause in the B/L to the effect that the cargo interest should return the half-collected money from the opposite carrier to the carrier in the both-to-blame collision case.

366. When Korean law is applied, the both-to-blame clause has no meaning because a carrier is liable for only its share of liability in a both-to-blame case in accordance with the KCC Article 879(1).

§6. Other Transport Documents

I. Sea Waybill and Surrendered B/L

367. The sea waybill is also widely used instead of the B/L in Korea. It is a non-negotiable document and is not regarded as a document of title. Therefore, the carrier is not required to hand over the cargo in exchange for it. The carrier is obliged to hand over the cargo to the eligible consignee regardless of presenting the sea waybill. The holder of the sea waybill is presumed as the consignee. The consignee rather than the holder of the sea waybill has a right to demand the cargo against the carrier. Under the contract for the carriage, the shipper is the right person to demand the delivery of the cargo. The consignee's power to demand the delivery of the cargo is given by the operation of the law. The consignee has the same right as the shipper when the cargo arrives at discharging port, and furthermore, it prevails over the shipper when it demands the delivery of the cargo to the carrier (the KCC Articles 140, 841).

368. In the 2007 revision of the KCC, the Korean government inserted a provision on the sea waybill. According to the KCC Article 863, the information contained in a sea waybill is deemed prima facie evidence not only between the carrier and the shipper but also between the carrier and a bona fide third-party holder thereof. It means that the holder of the sea waybill is not required to prove the fact that the number of the cargo stated therein was actually loaded at the loading port. The fact is presumed to be true. The carrier is allowed to rebut the fact by other evidence. Even though the new KCC referred to the Comité Maritime International (CMI) model rule on the sea waybills, it does not go far enough to adopt the conclusive effect of the sea waybill as opposed to the CMI model rules.

369. The carrier is not liable for the cargo damages if there is a reasonable ground for it to believe that the receiver is such a consignee or its agent stated in the bill even though the receiver is not in fact the consignee according to Article 864.

370. Surrendered B/L is widely engaged in Korea and other Asian countries, including China and Japan. It is very similar to the sea waybill in that it is not the document of title, and the carrier is not required to hand over the cargo to the holder of the surrendered B/L in exchange for the B/L. The surrendered B/L is issued as soon as the shipper returns the original B/L to the carrier for the purpose of erasing the function of the document of title and presentation rule from the original B/L. In trading within very close neighbor countries such as Korea, China, and Japan, the shipper or consignee does not want to delay the receipt of the cargo due to later arrival of the B/L than the vessel laden with the cargo at discharging port. The shipper approaches the carrier and requests to issue the surrendered B/L, which does not have the function of a document of title. The carrier issues a surrendered B/L with a remark of "Surrendered" on the front page of the B/L. At the discharging port, the consignee submits the front page of the surrendered B/L. Only after the carrier confirms that the holder of the surrendered B/L is the consignee does it hand over the cargo to the holder of the surrendered B/L. There is no duty for the carrier to deliver the cargo only to the holder of the surrendered B/L in the KCC.

371. Whether the agreement in the rear side of the original B/L is binding the shipper and the holder of the surrendered B/L or not is at issue. In the Korean Supreme Court case *2006.10.26. Docket No. 2004da27082*, the court decided that no original B/L was issued in the case, and thus, the carrier's argument that the lower limitation amount in the rear side of the original B/L should be applied to the case was denied.

372. However, the author thinks that the agreement in the rear side of the original B/L may be applicable to the case if the party prove that there was such agreement between parties. In a certain case, a special stamp containing "all terms, conditions and exceptions as per original bill of lading. SURRENDERED" appears in the surrendered B/L, in which the shipper may be bound by the terms and conditions in the original B/L. In the Korean Supreme Court case *2016.9.28. Docket No. 2016da213237*, the original B/L had been issued to the shipper at first but it returned to the carrier at the request of the shipper. The carrier argued that he was entitled to invoke the package limitation stated in the original B/L. The Court accepted it and allowed the carrier to invoke the package limitation. In the Korean Supreme Court case *2019.4.11. Docket No. 2016da 276719, the importer requested the issuing bank to issue a set of Letter of Credit for the benefit of the export. The carrier issued a set of Bill of Lading to the shipper and it was handed to the issuing bank. However, the importer and exporter changed the method of payment from the L/C to direct payment. The shipper requested the carrier to reissue the surrendered B/L. The surrendered B/L was handed over to the local agent of the carrier in the discharging port. The agent issued the delivery order to the importer. Relying on the name of the consignee, the warehouse keeper handed over the cargo to the consignee. In the meantime, the issuing bank, which lost its security for the payment, raised claims against the local agent, arguing that it breached its duty to issue a delivery order only after it received the B/L from the consignee. The Court decided that where the B/L was issued in the form of the surrendered B/L, there is no duty for the local agent to rely on the B/L. By following the order of the carrier, it discharged its obligation.*

II. Electronic B/L

373. In the 2007 revision of the KCC, the Korean government inserted a provision on the electronic B/L.

Article 862 (Electronic B/L):

(1) Instead of issuing B/L pursuant to Article 852 or 855, the carrier may issue electronic B/Ls by way of registering it in the Title Registry designated by the Ministry of Justice upon the assent of the shipper or charterer. The electronic B/L issued thereon has the same effect as the B/L issued pursuant to Article 852 or 855.
(2) The electronic B/L should include information stated in Article 853 (1). Only after the carrier makes an electronic signature and sends it to the shipper or the charterer and when they receive it, the electronic B/L becomes effective.
(3) The holder of electronic B/L can assign the right to the assignee by the way that it makes electronic documents with information of endorsement and sends it with the electronic B/L to the assignee through the designated registry.
(4) When the assignee receives the above electronic document with the information of the endorsement according to paragraph 3, the electronic B/L has the same effect as the assignor makes an endorsement and hands it over to the assignee pursuant to Articles 852 and 855. The assignee of the electronic B/L acquires the same effect as the assignee who obtains the B/L pursuant to Articles 852 and 855.
(5) The details regarding the requirement for the designation of the registry for the electronic B/L, how to issue and endorse electronically and procedure for receiving cargo will be provided in the presidential decree.

374. According to new Article 862(5), the Presidential Decree was prepared[60] and took effect as of August 4, 2008.

375. Under the KCC, the Title Registry plays a pivoting role in the issuance and assignment of electronic B/L (hereinafter "e-B/L"). In relation to the Title Registry in Article 862(1), Article 3 of the Presidential Decree regulates the Title Registry as follows: the persons who want to be designated as the Title Registry should: (i) be a legal person; (ii) possess more than twelve expert technicians such as holders of licenses for electronic information technology; (iii) have net assets of KRW 20 billion (about USD 20 million) and enough liability insurance to compensate the victims caused by the fault of the Registry in relation to its operation; and (iv) furnish equipments: (a) in relation to registering, endorsing, assigning, presenting the e-B/L, (b) regarding confirming the date of transmitting and receiving the e-B/L and recording, preserving the records, and (c) regarding security of the equipments.[61]

376. In relation to issuing e-B/L, Articles 862(2) and 6 of the Presidential Decree say that: (i) the carrier should transmit electronic documents, including some required information, plus the carrier's certified electronic signature and document showing that the consignor agreed on the issuance of the e-B/L, to the Title Registry; (ii) the carrier should transmit the terms of general clauses in the B/L to the Registry; and (iii) the Registry should record the issuance register including the above information and general clauses in the Title Registry and immediately transmit the fact that the e-B/L is issued to the consignor.

377. Regarding the assignment of the e-B/L stated in Article 862(3), Article 8 of the Presidential Decree provides that: (i) the titleholder of the e-B/L should make an electronic document showing his intention of endorsement and apply for transmission of the attached e-B/L to the assignee; (ii) the electronic document for assignment should include the information about authenticity of the e-B/L, assignee, and certified electronic signature of the assignor; (iii) the Title Registry should enter the statement on the assignment including information and immediately transmit the fact to the assignee in the electronic document; and (iv) the Title Registry should notify the assignor of the fact that it has transmitted the fact in (iii).

378. There is no mechanism to guarantee international convertibility, even in the Presidential Decree. If the e-B/L is involved in international trade, a foreigner should record it as a party in the Korean Title Registry. The author believes that the KCC should provide the mechanism for the Registry designated by the Korean government to be used not only domestically but also internationally. Partly because the

60. Refer to Wan Yong Chung, *Study on the newly adopted Electronic Bill of Lading Provision*, Journal of KMLA 30-1 (2008): 86.
61. The KT Net and KL-NET in Korea are andTitle Registries designated by the Korean government as of this date.

registry is operated by a Korean company with the permission of the Korean government, foreign banks as a frequent holder of the B/L do not participate in the collective use of the electronic B/L. Without international convertibility, the scheme will be frustrated.

III. Letter of Indemnity

379. The L/I is frequently used as a substitute for the B/L when the cargo importer tries to receive the cargo from the carrier at the discharging port without exchange of the B/L. Instead of presenting the B/L, the consignee as the importer submits the L/I to the carrier and the carrier hands over the cargo to the importer. Taking the risk of indemnifying loss of cargo to the holder of the B/L, the carrier hands over the cargo to the importer. If the importer pays purchase price of the goods to the bank in order to obtain the B/L and it becomes the due holder of the B/L, the above risk of the carrier is not materialized. However, if the importer does not try to collect the B/L, then the bank as the holder of the B/L exercises its right as the consignee because it is the holder of the B/L. However, the carrier has an obligation to hand over the cargo to the holder of the B/L, and thus, it should be held liable for the loss of cargo to the bank as the holder of the B/L. In turn, the carrier seeks recourse claims against the guarantor in the L/I who promised the indemnification.

380. There is a split view on the validity of the L/I in Korea. There are views that the delivery of the cargo to the importer in exchange for the L/I is an established practice in Korea, and thus, the carrier is no longer liable for the loss of the cargo against the bona fide holder of the B/L. However, the Korean Supreme Court has a firm position on the legal effect of the L/I; the court says that the L/I is effective between the issuer and the carrier; however, it is null and void between the holder of the B/L and the carrier.

381. In the Korean Supreme Court case *2009.10.15. Docket No. 2008da33818,* the court upheld once again that the carrier is not allowed to argue that the carrier's obligation to hand over the cargo in exchange for the B/L ends when it hands over the cargo in exchange for the L/I based on the fact that the Korean shipping business has a practice of using the L/I instead of the B/L. The carrier is liable for the loss of cargo to the holder of the B/L. In this case, the holder has the causes of action based on the breach of the contract and in tort as well. The carrier is not allowed to invoke the package limitation. The Korean Supreme Court rendered that the carrier handed over the cargo recklessly with the knowledge that damages might occur.[62]

382. The author agrees with the Korean Supreme Court judgment that the carrier's obligation to hand over the cargo to the holder of the B/L is not discharged even though the L/I is issued.

---

62. The Korean Supreme Court cases *1992.2.14. Docket No. 91da4249; 1992.2.25. Docket No. 91da30026.*

383. Major P&I clubs make it a rule that they will not indemnify the carrier's liability caused by their delivery of cargo in exchange for the L/I.

384. The L/I is not a negotiable instrument. It is a kind of a guarantee letter. Because it is not a kind of liability insurance, the holder of the B/L as the victim is not allowed to make direct action against the guarantor. The carrier may enter into a liability insurance contract with the liability insurer. Where the guarantor does not collect the B/L by paying the price of the goods, the carrier will be subject to the recourse claim from the issuing bank. The liability insurer should pay insurance money to the carrier. In this context, the carrier is allowed to exercise direct action against the liability insurer according to Article 724(2).

IV. Delivery Order

385. The Delivery Order (D/O) is also frequently used in Korea. The holder of the B/L as the consignee should submit the B/L to the carrier in order to obtain the cargo. The master also has an obligation to hand over the cargo in exchange for the B/L. When the consignee submits the B/L to the carrier at office, the carrier issues the D/O to the consignee and then the consignee goes to the master or the warehouse keeper at the port. It is an order from the carrier to the ship's master or a warehouse keeper to hand over the cargo to the holder of the D/O. The D/O implies that the B/L was duly collected by the carrier, and thus, there is no risk of handing over the cargo to the wrong person.

386. There is a dispute on whether the D/O is a negotiable instrument.[63] When the carrier receives the B/L and, in return, issues the D/O and hands it over to the holder of the B/L, the carrier intends that the B/L's function as the document of title ends. There is no need to admit an extended substitute for the B/L called the D/O. Even though the D/O is not a document of title, the holder of the D/O is still fully protected by the operation of the law under the KCC. The holder of the D/O is presumed as the rightful consignee. The consignee has the right to obtain the cargo from the carrier pursuant to Article 140 of the KCC.

387. The D/O is not a terminology stipulated in the KCC. It has been widely circulated in practice. There is an issue on whether the warehouse keeper should hand over the cargo to the consignee in exchange for the D/O. Even though there is a provision that the carrier should deliver the cargo to the holder of the B/L in exchange for the B/L, there is no provision which imposes the master or the warehouse keeper to hand over the cargo to the holder of the D/O with exchange of it. Such obligation may be imposed upon the warehouse keeper by party's agreement. There are several cases that the court imposed liability based on tort upon the warehouse keeper where the holder of the B/L made claims against the warehouse keeper. In the

63. Dong Yoon Chung, *Commercial Law(II)*, Bummoon Publishing Co., Ltd, 2008, cp. 857. Prof. Chung regards the D/O as a negotiable instrument

Korean Supreme Court case *2009.10.15. Docket No. 2009da39820*, the court imposed the duty to hand over the cargo in exchange for the D/O upon the warehouse keeper.

388. In the Korean practice, both Master D/O and House D/O are issued and circulated. The House D/O is issued by the contracting carrier to the consignee as the importer, whereas the Master D/O is issued by the actual carrier to the contracting carrier or its agent. Recently, the Korean Supreme Court addressed their legal implications.

389. In the Korean Supreme Court case *2009.10.15. Docket No. 2009da39820*, the contracting carrier (A) entered into the first contract for the carriage with the exporter in China and then the second contract for the ocean carriage with the actual carrier (B). A issued the House B/L and handed it to the exporter. However, B issued the Master B/L and handed it to A. While the cargo was kept in a warehouse, the importer presented the Master D/O to the warehouse keeper (C) and requested the delivery of the cargo and subsequently C handed it over to the importer. In the meantime, the exporter as the holder of the B/L who did not receive the sales proceeds from the importer made claims for loss of cargo against C with the cause of action based on tort. C argued that it was not responsible for the damages because it delivered the cargo in exchange for the Master D/O. The Pusan High court *(2009.4.22. Docket No. 2008na10754)* upheld C's argument.

390. On October 15, 2009, the Korean Supreme Court rendered as follows: the House D/O is issued by the carrier to the importer after the importer pays sales amounts, and thus, it functions as the supporting document for the importer to receive the cargo from the warehouse keeper. However, the Master D/O is issued by the actual carrier only for the purpose of receiving the cargo from the warehouse, and thus, it cannot be the D/O for the benefit of the importer. In this case, the warehouse keeper handed over the cargo to the importer after receiving the Master D/O instead of the House D/O, as a result of which the plaintiff who possessed House B/L lost the cargo. Consequently, the warehouse keeper committed a tort against the plaintiff as the holder of the House B/L.[64]

391. When the F/F acts as the carrier, two different contracts exist. First, the F/F enters into the first contract for the carriage with the cargo owner. Because the F/F does not possess any transportation facilities for the ocean carriage, it enters into a second contract for the carriage of goods with the ocean carrier. In the first contract, the F/F as the contracting carrier issues the House B/L to the shipper or the consignor. Under the House B/L, the issuing bank of L/C obtains the status of the consignee for the cargo. The importer obtains the House B/L from the issuing bank of L/C after paying purchase price for the goods and thus obtains the consignee status for the cargo. It goes to the carrier to collect its goods in exchange for the House B/L. In the meantime, under the second contract, the ocean carrier issues the Master B/L to the contracting carrier as the consignor. In the Master B/L, the local agent of

64. (2009) Korean Case Reports, 1837.

the contracting carrier is designated as the consignee. In turn, the local agent of the contracting carrier, in advance, requests the actual carrier to hand over the cargo to it in exchange for the Master B/L. In the end, when the holder of the House B/L requests the contracting carrier to hand over the cargo to it, the contracting carrier delivers the cargo which had been ready for delivering through the above mechanism.

392. The carrier should hand over the cargo to the holder of the B/L when the B/L is presented by the holder. However, the cargo is not at the hand of the carrier but on the vessel or in the warehouse. Therefore, the carrier orders the ship's master or the warehouse keeper to deliver the cargo to the holder (with the D/O). In this situation, the warehouse keeper should exchange the cargo with the D/O. The D/O for this purpose is not the Master D/O but the House D/O, according to the Korean Supreme Court. The Master D/O is the order that the actual carrier gives to the ship's master to hand over the cargo to the contracting carrier. The House D/O is the order that the contracting carrier gives to the ship's master to hand over the cargo to the importer as the holder of the House B/L.

393. In the above case, the warehouse keeper mistakenly handed over the cargo to the importer in exchange for the Master D/O, not the House D/O. By doing this, it committed a tort against the holder of the House B/L as the titleholder of the cargo. The author agrees with the Korean Supreme Court's interpretation to this effect.

394. In a recent Korean Supreme Court case *2015.4.23. Docket No. 2012da115847*, the court rendered that there was a practice in the PyungTaek port for the business warehouse keeper port to exchange the cargo with the D/O. The court concluded that if the warehouse keeper handed over the cargo without exchange of the D/O to the consignee, it was liable for the cargo damages against the holder of the B/L based on the tort.

V. Mate's Receipt

395. The Mate's Receipt (M/R) is a document that the Chief Officer (C/O) issues to the consignor as evidence of the receipt of the cargo. It is not a negotiable instrument because it is issued by the C/O without right to issue any document with negotiability. When the B/L is issued by the master or the carrier, it plays a role as an important reference for the items loaded or received on board. When there is any dispute on the contents of the cargo, the M/R becomes good evidence to verify the actual condition of the cargo when it was loaded or received by the carrier. There is no provision on the M/R in the KCC.

§7. PROTECTION OF THE CARRIER

I. Package Limitation

396. The carrier has a right to limit its liability against the cargo damages. This limitation is called the package limitation. The limitation amount is the higher one between 666.67 SDR per package and 2 SDR per Kg (Article 797(1)). The package is calculated by the number of the package or container enumerated in the B/L or similar transport document, where a container, pallet or similar one is used to consolidate goods (Article 797(2)(i)). The amount was increased through the 2007 revision of the KCC. Under the 1991 KCC, the limitation amount was 500 SDR per package. There was no kg limitation (Article 789*bis*(1)). Even though the 1991 revision of the KCC adopts almost all of provisions in the Hague-Visby Rules, the limitation amount was not so. It was heavily criticized by the cargo interests, and furthermore, the Kg limitation regime was not adopted. To alleviate the anomaly detrimental to the cargo interest, the court also showed a tendency to render judgment in favor of the cargo interest.[65]

397. In the Korean Supreme Court case *2004.7.2. Docket No. 2002da44267*, carrier H entered into the contract for carriage of goods with S computer manufacturing company. S packed a personal computer unit into a carton and then put 24 of these units on a pallet. Twenty-six pallets were then stowed in a container. Therefore, 624 computers were in a container. A total 2,496 PC were stowed in four containers by S. After the cargo was loaded on board, in the Kind of Package: Description of Goods column, “Shipper Load Stowage & Count, Said to be 104 plts (2,496 units) of micro PC station” and in the Number of Containers or Packages column, 40' x 4 (104 plts) was recorded in the B/L issued by H (which means 4 of 40 feet container with total 104 plts. Therefore, 26 plts in a container). One container among four containers was totally lost.

Carrier H argued that its liability is limited to 26 pallets x 500 SDR, based on the figure written in the Number of Containers column, whereas the cargo interest insisted that the limitation amount should be calculated by multiplying 624 units times 500 SDT, based on the figure in the Kind of Package column. The court ruled that the number in the Kind of Package column rather than in the Number of Containers column reflected more closely the parties’ intention. The court explained that, for the carrier limitation of the liability, the meaning given to package should be based on the parties’ intention, and when large package units (26 pallets) and small package units(624 units) were recorded, large package units should be regarded as the packages as the standard for calculating the limitation amounts unless otherwise agreed by the parties. In conclusion, the court supported the cargo interest’s argument, and thus, the carrier’s limitation of liability was limited to 624 x 500 SDR rather than 26 x 500 SDR.[66] It seems that the court tried to protect the cargo interest, taking risk of departure from the explicit stipulation in the KCC Article 797(2)(i).

---

65. Korean Supreme Court case *2004.7.2. Docket No. 2002da44267.*
66. For details, In Hyeon Kim, *Korean Maritime Law Update: 2004*, 36-3 JMLC (July 2005) 366.

398. The carrier is entitled to enjoy the package limitation without prejudice to its right of the global limitation pursuant to Article 797(4). In a big accident, the carrier is allowed to invoke the global limitation at the special proceeding called shipowner's limitation of liability proceeding in addition to invoking the package limitation in the lawsuit for merit.

399. This limitation can be raised as a defense even if the claimant brings about the action based on tort (Article 798(1)). Korea is a country where the cause of action can be raised based on either the breach of contract or tort.[67] Under the 1962 KCC, the Korean Supreme Court did not allow the carrier to limit its liability in case the action was raised based on the cause of action in tort.[68] There were heavy criticisms against the judgment because both parties in the contract for carriage had a mutual understanding that the carrier's liability had to be limited regardless of the type of cause of action, and thus, court should have interpreted the provision in the KCC as such, reflecting party's intention in the agreement. In the 1991 revision of the KCC, the Korean government solved this issue by adopting the provision in the Hague-Visby Rules Article 4*bis*(1). This provision exists in the 2007 revised KCC.

400. The carrier's right to limit its liability is not allowed if the carrier acted with intent to cause damages or "recklessly and with knowledge that the damages would probably result" (Article 797). The subjective requirement in this provision is a very high standard. The case that the carrier's limitation of liability was denied is very rare. There are split views on the meaning of the "recklessly and with knowledge that the damages would probably occur" (hereinafter "*reckless behavior*"). Minority regards it as gross negligence, while majority regards it as one of subjective mind of higher than gross negligence but lower than the intent.

401. In the recent Korean Supreme Court case *2006.10.26. Docket No. 2004da27082*,[69] the court denied the carrier's right of limitation of liability. The shipowner (S) time-chartered M/V Empress out to D which entered into, in turn, a contract of carriage of goods by sea with a shipper. Two low-level managerial staff who were in charge of carriage department in the company decided to load a part of cargoes on deck against the contract. The on-deck cargo was damaged during the voyage from Korea to Taiwan. The plaintiff brought an action against the carrier. The carrier tried to limit its liability for the cargo damages pursuant to KCC Article 789*bis*(1).[70]

67. Korean Supreme Court cases *1962.6.21. Docket No. 62da102; 1983.3.22. Docket No. daka 1533; 1989.4.11. Docket No. 89dakal1428; 1999.7.13 Docket No. 99da8711.*
68. Korean Supreme Court case *1989.1.24, Docket No. 88da16294.*
69. (2006) Korean Case Reports 1027.
70. The Old KCC Art. 789*bis*(1) A carrier can protect its interest by limiting its liability to 500 SDR per package or shipping unit of the cargo, but the carrier loses the benefit of the package limitation when the injury to the cargo resulted from the carrier's personal act or omission, committed with the intent to cause such loss, or committed recklessly and with knowledge that such loss would probably result. This wording came from the Art. 4(5)(e) of Hague-Visby Rules. The U.S. COGSA does not have these provisions because it does not adopt Visby amendment.

Two separate issues were dealt with in depth in the Seoul High Court and Supreme Court: (1) piercing corporate veil,[71] and (2) proving the carrier's personal act committed recklessly and with knowledge that such loss would probably result.

402. In Seoul High Court case *2004.5.4. Docket No. 2003na48176*, the court rendered that two low-level managerial staff acted recklessly and with knowledge that such loss would probably result when they decided to load a part of cargo on deck against the contract rather than under deck, taking into consideration that a wooden-boxed cargo which was loaded and carried on deck for six days was exposed to the seawater involving dangers of cargo damage, which could have otherwise been avoided by way of under-deck loading. The court further regarded them as the carrier's person or the alter ego on the ground that they had an exclusive power to decide the carriage of cargo based on the company's job distribution chart.[72]

403. On October 26, 2006, the Supreme Court affirmed the Seoul High Court's judgment on the issue of the scope of the carrier's alter ego as follows:

> If the court limits the meaning of the carrier's person only to the representative organization of the company, the current provision of the KCC Art. 789bis(1) will be meaningless in the case of the company, considering the company usually delegates its power of decision-making to the low-level managerial staff. Therefore, when the power of the company for decision-making is delegated to the low-level managerial staff, the staff should be regarded as the carrier's person or alter ego.[73]

404. It is the first case in the Korean court to admit the presence of *reckless behavior* of the carrier involved in the transportation cases.[74] Although the Korean Supreme Court has not explained the meaning *of reckless behavior*, several scholars and practitioners regarded it as conscious gross negligence rather than mere gross negligence.[75] If it is equal to conscious gross negligence, the carrier should

---

71. The cargo interest argued that D as the carrier was the same entity with S, and thus, the corporate veil of D should be pierced in order to hold the ship owner liable for the cargo damages.
72. In addition, the court rendered that Dainty shipping was only a paper company which S/M established for the purpose of evading its liability. The Court accepted several facts as proofs of S/M's complete control over Dainty Shipping such as using the same address of the office and same e-mail address between two companies and the fact that the freight was paid to S/M. As a result, the court pierced the corporate veil of Dainty Shipping and imposed the liability of Dainty Shipping as the carrier on S/M.
73. It seems to the author that the court might take into consideration that there was no other high ranking officer except the president of the company between the two low-level managerial staffs and the president.
74. The Korean Supreme Court has applied the conscious recklessness test in several air carriage cases governed by the Warsaw Convention in which the plaintiffs failed to prove the presence of the conscious recklessness of the carrier or his servant. Korean Supreme Court cases *2004.7.22. Docket No. 2001da58269; 2005.9.29. Docket No. 2005da26598; 200610.13. Docket No. 2005da3724.*
75. Dong Hoon, Kim, *Loss of carrier's right to limit liability*, Journal of KMLA 15-1 (1993): 103; Chang June, Kim, *Carrier's loss of limitation right*, Proceedings at the Spring Seminar of 2007, Korea Maritime Law Association (2007.5.4.): 38. However, two more different views exist in Korea; one

know that the accident probably occurred with a 50% chance of the possibility; nevertheless, it did not take action to avoid the danger.

405. It is a general view in Korea that the alter ego in a legal entity means a person who has legal status as a director or the above (equal to the representative of the organization in the above case). However, there is a view that the scope of an alter ego in the legal entity, such as a company in maritime law, can be expanded to the middle of the managerial staff if the exclusive right of decision-making on the specific matter is delegated to them.[76] The court case resulted in the expansion of the scope of the alter ego from the director level to the low-level of managerial staff. However, the author thinks that the ruling of the court should be interpreted in a limited fashion as the court stated very cautiously in its ruling, that is, only when the exclusive right of decision-making is delegated down to the low-level managerial staff.

II. Himalaya Protection

406. A carrier usually entrusts the performance of parts of its obligations to others, such as a servant or agent or an independent contractor. An independent contractor, such as the warehouse keeper or stevedores, is distinguished from a servant of the carrier in that the carrier does not exercise control over the performance of the independent contractor even though the two are related by the contract.[77] When the cargo interests raise a cargo claim against a servant, agent or independent contractor with the cause of action in tort, the question arises as to whether it can invoke the package limitation the same as the carrier. The carrier makes an agreement with the shipper to the effect that they are entitled to invoke the rights that the carrier can. This arrangement in the B/L is called the Himalaya clause.

407. The Hague-Visby Rules Article 4*bis* also adopts a very similar provision to the Himalaya clause in the B/L, except that the independent contractor is explicitly not allowed to invoke the rights. The KCC followed the example of the Hague-Visby Rules in adopting the Himalaya protection.

408. There are two differences in the Himalaya protection between the KCC and the Hague-Visby Rules. First, the actual carrier is an additional beneficiary for the Himalaya protection according to Article 798(4), unlike in the Hague-Visby Rules. Second, the independent contractor is not expressly excluded from beneficiaries in the KCC, unlike in the Hague-Visby Rules. Due to the absence of the express stipulation, the Korean Supreme Court had to address the issues several times on whether independent contractors such as warehouse keepers or stevedores are entitled to

view regards the *reckless behavior (*recklessly and knowingly that such loss would probably result) as gross negligence and the other, as contingent intent.

76. B.T. Bae, *Annotated Maritime Law* 209 (1981).
77. Warehouse keeper (Korean Supreme Court case *2004.2.13. Docket No. 2001da75318*) and terminal operator (Korean Supreme Court case *2007.4.27. Docket No. 2007da4943*) were regarded as independent contractors by the Korean Supreme Court.

enjoy the benefit under Article 798(4). The court takes a firm position that the independent contractor is not one of beneficiaries under Article 798(4).

409. In the Korean Supreme Court case *2004.2.13. Docket No. 2001da75318*, a warehouse keeper for the carrier delivered the cargo without exchange of the original B/L. The holder of the B/L claimed damages for the loss from the warehouse keeper, which responded that the claim was time-barred by the KCC Article 811 because the suit was filed after the expiration of the one-year time-bar period and it fell within the servant or agent who can enjoy the protection of provisions for the benefit of the carrier under Article 789*ter* (2)(Article 798(2) under the current KCC). However, the cargo claimant argued that the defendant acted instead as an independent contractor and that the KCC excluded the independent contractor from the class of persons who could enjoy the benefit of the carrier, such as time-bar protection. On February 13, 2004, the court affirmed that:

> the warehouse keeper does not follow the order or instruction of the carrier like the master but acts at its own discretion; for this reason, it is entitled to the status of an independent contractor. As a result, the warehouse keeper is not within the scope of the definitions of servant or agent under Article 789ter (2) and thus is not entitled to invoke the carrier's defence of time bar under Article 811.[78]

410. In the Korean Supreme Court case *2007.4.27. Docket No. 4943,* the validity of the Himalaya clause in the B/L was addressed in detail. The plaintiff argued that the Himalaya clause was null and void because it was against the KCC Article 790(1), which prohibited the carrier from derogation of liability and obligation, contrary to the provisions of Articles 787–789.[79]

411. When a terminal operator in Korea was sued by the cargo interests due to its negligence, it invoked the limitation of liability based on the Himalaya clause in the House B/L. The House B/L contained a typical Himalaya clause and the Korean governing law clause. The terminal operator invoked the limitation of liability based on the Himalaya clause in the House B/L. The plaintiff argued that the clause was null and void because the clause allowed the carrier to derogate its liability against the KCC Article 790(1) (Article 799(1) under the current KCC). The Korean Supreme Court explained that even though the KCC did not include the independent contractor, such as the terminal operator, as among the persons who were entitled to enjoy the benefit of the carrier's right to limit its liability, the carrier and the consignor were free to make an agreement freely to include any third party as a beneficiary in the Himalaya clause. On that basis, the court decided that the terminal operator was an eligible third party in the Himalaya clause. The court further explained that Article 790(1) in the KCC was applicable only for the carrier for the

78. In Hyeon Kim, *Korean Maritime Law Update: 2005*, JMLC 36, No. 3, p. 367 (July 2005).
79. It is similar to Art. 3(8) of Hague-Visby Rules.

purpose of protecting the cargo interest, and thus, the terminal operator was not subject to Article 790(1). In conclusion, the court upheld that the terminal operator was entitled to limit its liability pursuant to the Himalaya clause in the House B/L.[80]

412. As the Korean Supreme Court ruled in the above case *2007.4.27 Docket No. 4943*, the independent contractor can be fully protected by the party's agreement only if the carrier and the shipper agree to allow the independent contractor to be protected like other servants or agents and make clear entry it into the B/L. As we *see* above, if there is no such wording in the B/L, the independent contractor except the actual carrier is not protected by the operation of the law under the Korean law. However, the independent contractor can be protected by the operation of the law under the Rotterdam Rules. The Rotterdam Rules allow the independent contractor called maritime performing party to invoke the same right as the carrier against the shipper (Article 19(1)).

413. In the Korean Supreme Court case *2002.2.8 Docket No. 2001da58641,* the court held that a stevedore could not invoke the package limitation because its contract was with the consignee rather than the carrier. In this case, the stevedore did not fall into the scope of the independent contractor because it was not employed by the carrier. The Himalaya protection was allowed only to the servant or agent who had a contractual relationship to carry out part of the carrier's obligation against the cargo interest.

III. Exemption

414. The carrier enjoys the error of navigation and fire exemption from liability in accordance with the KCC Article 795(2). The KCC Article 795(2) says, *inter alia*, that the carrier shall be relieved of the liability to compensate for any damages caused by navigation or act concerning management of ship by the master, seaman, pilot, or other employee of a ship, or by fire except in case that any of fire is caused by the privity or fault of the carrier. If the damages are caused by the navigational fault of crew on board during the navigation, the carrier is exempted from liability. Damages caused by collision, grounding and bad decisions of the master under heavy weather are good examples of error in navigation defense in Korea.

415. In the Seoul District Court case *1998.4.9. Docket No. 96gahap80830*, the cargo insurer who paid the insurance proceeded to the cargo owner as the insured brought about a recourse claim against the carrier. The damage was caused by the collision resulting from the master's negligent navigation. The court ruled that the carrier is exempted from collision liability caused by the master's negligence in the operation of the law (Article 795(2)). "Act concerning management of ship" is

80. In Hyeon Kim, *Korean Maritime Law Update: 2007*, JMLC, 39, No. 3 p. 446 (July 2008).

included in the concept of "the error of the navigation." Act concerning management of ship is not related to the maneuvering of the vessel. A crew's act of mistakenly leaving the valve open, followed by the water ingress into the cargo hold resulting in cargo wet damage, is a good example of an act concerning management of ship.

416. The Korean courts have been very lenient in allowing carriers to invoke the exemption based on the error of navigation. The collision resulting from the error by the crew while maneuvering the vessel is the most widely accepted example.[81] Even though there is no explicit provision, it is a well-settled issue that the exemption under Article 795(2) is on the premises that the carrier should, in advance, fulfill the seaworthiness requirement under Article 795(1).[82]

417. The carrier is also exempted from liability when the fire causes damages unless the fire was caused by the carrier's personal fault or privity. The Korean courts have been very reluctant to allow carriers to invoke the fire exemption. Only when the carrier proves that the fire caused cargo damage and that the carrier had taken reasonable care to make the vessel seaworthy the carrier is entitled to invoke the exemption; furthermore, the carrier cannot avoid the liability if the fire caused was the carrier's personal fault or privity. The courts and academics do agree that "the fault or privity of the carrier" in Article 796(2) is only that of an alter ego of the carrier and not that of servants or agents such as the crew. There are split views on who should bear the burden of proof in relation to the presence of the fault and privity of the carrier. The author supports that the burden should be imposed upon the cargo interests because the cargo interests will benefit if the presence of the fault of the carrier is proven.

418. In the Korean Supreme Court case *2002.12.10. Docket No. 2002da39364*, the court held that a fire moved from a vessel alongside the defendant vessel could be an exempted fire under the KCC Article 796(2). The fire is not necessarily required to start on board the vessel.

419. Apart from the above two direct exemptions, the KCC has a provision that the carrier's burden of proof on the absence of its breach of due care for the cargo is shifted to the cargo interests (Article 796).

IV. Shifting Burden of Proof from the Carrier to the Shipper

420. According to the KCC Article 796, the carrier shall be relieved of the liability to compensate for damages, if it has proved that any fact of the following subparagraphs existed and that any damage of the goods might usually be caused by such fact. However, the above shall not apply if it was proved that the carrier failed

81. Seoul District Court case *1998.4.9. Docket No. 96gahap80830.*
82. Lee Sik, Chai, *supra*, 143.

to exercise due care mentioned in Articles 794 (seaworthiness) and 795(1) even if the carrier could otherwise have avoided such damages:

(1) *Perils* and accidents at sea or other navigable waters.
(2) Act of God.
(3) War, riot or internal insurrection.
(4) Piracy and other similar acts.
(5) Judicial seizure, quarantine restriction, and other restrictions by public authorities.
(6) Act of shipper or the owner of the goods or his employees.
(7) Strike and other acts of labor dispute or lockout of a ship.
(8) Act of salvage of human life or property at sea, or the deviation from the route thereby, and any other deviation from the route by reasonable cause.
(9) Insufficiency of the packaging of the goods or incompleteness of *the writing* on the package.
(10) *Particular* nature or latent defect of the goods.
(11) *Latent* defect of the ship.[83]

421. Perils at sea, reasonable deviation, shipper's act and insufficient package are examples that the burden of proof on the presence of the carrier's fault is imposed upon cargo interests under the KCC. If the carrier proves the presence of the above fact, the carrier is exempted from liability unless the claimant proves that the damage was caused by the carrier's lack of exercising due diligence on the seaworthiness and care for cargo. Taking into consideration that the carrier is liable for the cargo damages unless it proves that it exercised due diligence on the seaworthiness and on the care for cargo, the above shifting burden of proof to the cargo interest is beneficial to the carrier.

422. The heavy weather is one of the examples of perils at sea. Korean court is very reluctant to allow the carrier to invoke the heavy weather defense. Even though the cargo was damaged under the heavy weather of Beaufort scale 10, the exemption of the liability under Article 796 was not allowed. Piracy is one good example for the carrier to invoke the exemption from liability under Article 796. Where the cargo was lost because the vessel was kidnapped by piracy, the carrier can be exempted from the liability for the loss of cargo if it proves that there was piracy and that the loss can usually occur due to the fact (e.g., piracy). Where an embargoed cargo was on board the vessel and a certain government confiscated it, the carrier may invoke the defense under Article 796.

423. In the Korean Supreme Court case *2006.5.12, Docket No. 2005da21593*,[84] the carrier was exempted from liability based on the presence of the "latent defect of the cargo" under KCC Article 796.

83. Unlike Hague-Visby Rules, the burden of proof on the carrier's negligence on the unseaworthiness is shifted to the plaintiff. This may be one of reasons that the unseaworthiness issue is rarely argued in the Korean courts. Lee Sik, Chai, *supra*, 139.
84. (2006) Korean Case Reports, 1027.

424. The importer tried to import Phenol from the U.S. to Pusan, Korea. The maximum allowance of Phenol's color was twenty points. The importer entered into the contract of carriage by sea with the carrier. The carrier issued a clean B/L without remarks.[85] After the vessel arrived at Pusan, the color of Phenol reached twenty-six points against the maximum allowance in the contract. The importer was forced to sell Phenol at a reduced price. The cargo insurer (the plaintiff) paid insurance proceeds to the importer and, in turn, made a recourse claim to the carrier based on both the breach of the contract and in tort. It argued that the remaining residues of previous cargo of Sulphur affected the color of Phenol. However, the carrier argued that the damage of Phenol was caused by the latent defect of Phenol itself, and thus, it was entitled to exoneration from the liability pursuant to KCC Article 796.

425. The Seoul High Court ruled against the plaintiff's allegation on the ground that the cleanliness certificate of ship tanks had been issued by the surveyor after discharging the previous cargo.[86] Rather, the court rendered that the change of color was caused either by the latent defect of the cargo itself or by the existing residue during manufacturing Phenol based on the fact that the number of Phenol's color in the sample, which was gathered after loading, also increased gradually. Accordingly, the court allowed the carrier to be relieved from the liability. On May 12, 2006, the Korean Supreme Court ruled that the change of color of Phenol was caused by the latent defect of the cargo itself or by the remaining residues during the manufacturing procedure, and such change of color would normally occur, and thus, the carrier was entitled to be exonerated from the liability pursuant to KCC Article 796.

V. Time Bar

426. The carrier's right and liability against the shipper or the consignee's time-barred one year from the date when the cargo was delivered or to be delivered (Article 814) unless the carrier brings about the lawsuit in the court.[87,88,89]

---

85. It stated as "Shipped in apparent good order and condition."
86. Seoul High Court case *2005.3.16. Docket No. 2003na72322.*
87. Article 814(1) Any right and obligation of a carrier to a charterer, shipper, or consignee shall, regardless of cause of action for claims, be extinguished if no application for an action is made within one year after the carrier delivers or is to deliver goods to the consignee: Provided, that the period may be extended by an agreement between parties.
88. There are two different types of time bar in the world. In the prescription period, the right of the person is distinghished after the time-bar period passes. In the limitation period, the right of the person is still alive even after the time-bar period passes. Only the right to exercise his right is barred. The time bar stated in the Hague-Visby and Korean Commercial Code are a kind of the prescription period. However, the time bar in the Rotterdam Rules is regarded as a kind of the limitation period. Please refer to In Hyeon Kim, *The Rotterdam Rules 2008, Wolters Kluwer, 2010, p. 274.*
89. There are two kinds of time bar in Korea. First, the right of the plaintiff is distinguished by the lapse of the time-bar period under Article 184(1) of the Korean Civil Code. It is called as "somyulsihyo,"

427. One year time bar triggers from the date when the cargo was delivered or to be delivered. The delivery of cargo is not defined in the KCC. However, the consignee should have possession or control of the cargo to meet the definition of the carrier. In the Korean Supreme Court case2019.6.13. Docket No. 2019da205947, the lower court regarded the arrival date of the vessel as the delivered date for the purpose of deciding time bar extinction. After the vessel arrived at a port, the cargo should have been delivered to the land. The cargo was not moved to the land because the customs office confiscated the cargo. The Court decided that the date when the customs office did not allow to custom clear was the date that the cargo was not able to be delivered. The Court decided that the lower court decision was wrong.

428. In the Korean Supreme Court case 2022.12.1. Docket No. 2020da280685, the lower court accepted the consignee's argument that the claim was time-barred because it was raised after a one-year time-bar period had lapsed. In the case, the carrier brought about a lawsuit to collect claims such as detention charges for several containers. However, the Korean Supreme Court said that the lower court was wrong because there were claims which did not pass a year since it was incurred. The court decided that the time-bar period started from the date which the claim was brought about. The decision is highly respected because it reflects the practice very well. The detention charge is incurred every day after the designated free time ends.

429. The time-bar period in Article 814(1) is much shorter than the five-year time bar for claims related to general commercial transactions (Article 64). While the time bar in the Hague-Visby Rules applies only for claims of the shipper against the carrier, the KCC Article 814 applies not only for the shipper's claims against the carrier but also for the carrier's claims against the shipper. The ground for stopping the clock or deferring the time bar in Article 168 of the Civil Code does not apply to the case.

430. It can be extended only by the agreement of both parties. However, according to the Korean Supreme Court case *1997.11.28. Docket No. 97da28490*, the agreement to reduce the period of one year to nine months in the B/L was null and void because it was against Article 814, having a mandatory characteristic for protecting the shipper or the holder of the B/L and the time-bar period was extended to one year automatically. Article 814 is also applicable for the action based on the cause of action in tort. In the Korean Supreme Court case *1997.4.11. Docket No. 96da4246*, the court rendered that Article 814 was applicable for the case even if the carrier acted intentionally or recklessly.

---

a statute of limitation, a kind of prescription period. The other type of time bar is called as "jechukglgan" or peremptory period is also a kind of prescription period under Article 814 of the Korean Commercial Code. The right of the plaintiff is distinguished after the given period of time passes. The lapse of the period of time bar can not be stopped in the peremptory period due to any event while it can be stopped in the statute of limitation.

431. In the Korean Supreme Court case 2022.7.9. Docket No. 2017da24748, the validity of the extension for the time bar under Article 814(1) was addressed. Daewoo Shipbuilding &Marine Engineering Co., Ltd. ("Daewoo") entered into a contract of carriage with the defendant carrier for the cargo. As the consignee, Daewoo received the cargo on December 4, 2012. At the time of delivery, the cargo had already been damaged. On December 15, 2014, Daewoo requested an extension of the limitation period for insurance processing, and the defendant agreed on December 18, 2014, to extend the period until 2015. The plaintiff, as the insurer, paid insurance proceeds to the insured Daewoo. The plaintiff, claiming that it had subrogated Daewoo's right to claim damages against the defendant, filed this lawsuit on December 28, 2015, after one year had passed since the delivery of the cargo. The lower court held that "the period prescribed in Article 814(1) of the Commercial Code is a peremptory period, and once that period has passed, the carrier's obligations are definitively extinguished. Even if the parties agree to extend the period after it has passed, the extinguished right cannot be revived. The rights that have expired due to the peremptory period are automatically extinguished, regardless of whether the parties invoke this expiration." The lower court ruled that this lawsuit was filed after the period for filing the lawsuit had expired, and even though the defendant agreed to extend the period on December 18, 2014, after one year had passed since the delivery of the cargo, this did not alter the outcome.

The Korean Supreme Court rendered as followings: Article 814(1) of the Korean Commercial Code concerns a peremptory period (Supreme Court 2019.6.13. Docket No. 2019Da2594). If, after the expiration of the peremptory period prescribed in Article 814(1) of the Commercial Act, the party entitled to benefit from the lapse of the period clearly expresses an intention not to receive the legal benefits resulting from the lapse while being aware of the expiration, it can be recognized that the party has waived the benefit of the right's extinguishment due to the lapse of the peremptory period by analogously applying Article 184(1) of the Civil Act regarding the waiver of the benefit of prescription after its completion.

The peremptory period prescribed in Article 814(1) of the Commercial Code concerns the right of claim, and if the right is not exercised within a certain period, the right is extinguished or loses its effect, which is similar to the statute of limitations. A debtor who benefits from the completion of the statute of limitations can waive the legal benefits resulting from the completion by expressing their intention not to receive those benefits (Korean Civil Code, Article 184(1)). (Omitted) Article 814(1) of the Commercial Code not only sets a one-year period for filing a lawsuit regarding claims arising from legal relationships related to maritime transport but also allows for the extension of this period by agreement between the parties. Although there is a need to promptly resolve legal relationships related to maritime transport between carriers and shippers or consignees, some disputes related to maritime transport are difficult to resolve in a short time, and it may take a long time to clarify liability. This provision allows the parties to extend the period for filing a lawsuit by agreement, considering these circumstances, so they are not bound by the period and can seek an appropriate resolution of the dispute. (Omitted) When reviewing the lower court's decision in light of these legal principles, it is clear that the plaintiff requested an extension of the period after the expiration of the peremptory period prescribed in Article 814(1), and the defendant agreed to this extension.

Therefore, the lower court should have examined whether the defendant, while aware of the expiration of the peremptory period, agreed to the extension with the intention of not receiving the benefits from the expiration and then determined the validity of this lawsuit accordingly. However, the lower court erroneously determined that the benefit of the expiration of the peremptory period prescribed in Article 814(1) could not be waived and failed to properly consider these circumstances, thereby incorrectly judging the lawsuit as inadmissible. The appeal grounds pointing out this error are well-founded.

It is noteworthy that the time-bar agreement with a nine-month period is valid in case the land transport rules are applicable. Articles 121 and 147 of the KCC applicable to land transport state that the time-bar period is just one year. However, the shortening of the period is allowed in the land transport case. In the Korean Supreme Court case *2009.8.20. Docket No.2008da58978*, it became clear that the accident occurred in the land leg, and thus, the land transport rule was applicable. The Court decided that the time-bar period of one year is allowed to lessen to nine months because time-bar period can be reduced according to Article 184(2) of the Korean Civil Code.

432. According to the Korean Supreme Court case *2001.10.30. Docket No. 2000da62490*, old Article 811 (New Article 814(1)) was not applicable for the time bar in case of recourse claims. The period for the time bar in case of recourse has been disputed since the above judgment.

433. There is a new addition in Article 814 regarding the recourse claim. In case the carrier (contracting carrier) enters into the subsequent contract for the carriage with the third party, the time bar will be extended for three months from the date when the carrier settled a claim with the shipper or when the carrier brought an action against the shipper according to Article 814(2). It aims at protecting the contracting carrier. When the cargo is damaged, the cargo interest will seek for compensation from the contracting carrier based on the breach of the contract. The contracting carrier, in turn, may seek for indemnification from the actual carrier. When the contracting carrier receives cargo claims eleven months after the date when the cargo was delivered, the remaining time-bar period which the contractual carrier has against the actual carrier is just one month. Because the contracting carrier is in the status of the shipper in relation to the actual carrier, the one-year time-bar provision under Article 814(1) is applicable. Accordingly, the time-bar period of only a month is left, which puts the contractual carrier in a detrimental position. In order to solve the imbalance, the new Code includes a new provision of Article 814(2), reflecting the Hamburg Rules Article 20(5).

434. The newly adopted Article 814(2) does not solve the time-bar period involved in the recourse claim. However, the time-bar period in case of recourse claim from the contracting carrier against the actual carrier is solved as being three months from the date when the carrier settled a claim with the shipper or when the carrier brought about the action against the shipper (Article 814(2)).

435. The new Article 814(3) includes another mechanism to protect the contractual carrier. Where the contractual carrier becomes a defendant in the lawsuit, the time-bar period of three months does not run until the date when the judgment is finalized and conclusive if the carrier gave prior notice of such lawsuit to the third party. Without bringing about the lawsuit for recourse claim to the third party, such as the actual carrier, the contractual carrier has a full three-month benefit of time bar against the third party upon giving prior notice of the lawsuit to it.

436. The new Code extended the time bar from one year to two years for every charter party, including the voyage charter party (Article 840). In the voyage charter party, the cargo interest's claims against the owner will be time-barred after two years from the date when the cargo was delivered or should have been delivered. The time-bar period is extended from one year to two years in the voyage charter party case.

VI. Dangerous Goods

437. The KCC has a provision on the carriage of dangerous goods. Article 801(1) says, *inter alia*, that if any inflammable, explosive or other dangerous goods might inflict any danger or injury on other goods, even though the carrier has effected the shipment knowing such nature, the master may, at any time, unload or destroy them, or take harmless measures. Furthermore, Article 801(2) states that the carrier shall be exempted from the liability for compensation for any loss caused by goods resulting from the master's disposal of the cargo in accordance with Article 801(1), excluding the liability of general average contribution.

438. The Article 801 is modeled on the Hague-Visby Rule 4(6). However, Article 801(2) does not have the provision in the Hague-Visby Rules to the effect that the shipper of such goods shall be liable for all damages and expenses directly or indirectly arising out of or resulting from such shipment. Rule 4(b) is interpreted as imposing strict liability upon the shipper for damages caused by loading the dangerous cargo.

439. There are two split views on whether the shipper is strictly liable for the damage or not under the KCC Article 801(2). One view is that the shipper is liable only when it is negligent in handing over the cargo to the carrier because there is no explicit provision to impose strict liability upon the shipper.[90] It argues that fault-based liability rather than strict liability is the basic norm under Korean law, and thus, without the presence of a fault, the defendant does not hold liability. The other view suggests that the shipper should be strictly liable for the damage regardless of the presence of the negligence because the provision in the Hague-Visby Rules should be referred to the interpretation of the KCC.[91]

---

90. Jong Hyun Choi, *supra,* 346.
91. In Hyeon Kim, *supra,* 185.

VII. Notice of Loss or Damage

440. The KCC Article 804 imposes an obligation upon the consignee to give a notice to the carrier, in writing, of loss or damage to the cargo. The consignee must do so without delay when it discovers the loss or damage and within three days of receipt when the discovery of the loss or damage is not done immediately. If the consignee does not give notice to the carrier in time, the consignee is not deprived of its right to claim the loss or damages. Rather, the cargo is presumed to have been delivered in good condition, and the burden shifts to the consignee to prove otherwise. However, the burden does not shift if the consignee can establish that the carrier or its employee otherwise had knowledge of the loss or damage.

441. The penalty imposed upon the consignee when it does not exercise the duty stipulated in Article 804 is questionable. The consignee is required to prove that the cargo was damaged at the loading port if it breached the obligation under Article 804. However, the consignee has an obligation to prove the condition of the cargo at the loading port, even in general cargo-claim cases. Therefore, the penalty under Article 804 should be changed.

§8. Protection of the Shipper

I. Shipowner's Statutory Liability under Article 809

442. The KCC has several provisions for protecting the cargo interest in order to strike a balance between the carrier and the shipper while protecting the carrier. The most important provision is imposing joint and several liabilities upon the owner of the vessel with the carrier. According to Article 809, the owner is liable for cargo damages, in addition to the carrier, when the vessel was operated under the voyage charter party or time charter party. In the case that the carrier itself does not possess any assets to pay the claims, the cargo interests make claims against the owner of the vessel by the operation of the law. Where the vessel is under BBC, the BBC charterer puts the shoes of the ship owner. It became liable for the cargo damages instead of the ship owner. Article 809 functions to protect the cargo interests. They are allowed to bring about prejudgment attachment against the owner of the vessel.

443. In the meantime, the KCC has not yet adopted a provision to impose joint and several liability upon the actual carrier and the contracting carrier, unlike the Hamburg Rules Article 10. In this respect, the protection of the cargo interest is not perfect.

II. Mandatory Provision

444. Article 799(1) does not allow the carrier to derogate from its obligation and liability imposed in the KCC upon the carrier by agreement like the Hague-Visby

Rules Article 3(8), which is a powerful tool for protecting cargo interests. If the agreement says that the carrier is not liable for any cargo damages, it is destined to be null and void because it puts the shipper in a disadvantageous position. However, Article 799(1) does not affect the validity of the agreement between the carrier and the shipper in case the carrier's obligation and liability is increased. Package Limitation is allowed under the KCC.

445. The direct action allowed to the victims under Article 724(2) functions as another tool to protect the cargo interests. It is the usual manner in Korea that the carrier enters into the liability insurance with the liability insurer such as a P&I club. When the cargo owner suffers damages due to carrier's breach of the contract, it is allowed to bring about a direct claim against the liability insurer in addition to the carrier as the tortfeasor.

III. Evidentiary Effect of the B/L

446. The KCC provides the holder of the B/L with a certain evidentiary effect in the written statement *thereon*. When the shipper holds the B/L, the statement therein has prima facie evidence. In the meantime, when the innocent third party holds the B/L, the statement on it has conclusive evidence (Article 854). In a general lawsuit, the claimant should prove that it suffered from damages. In order to prove the presence of the damages, the claimant should submit that it handed over the clean cargo or the alleged number of cargo to the carrier. However, the claimant who holds the B/L with statement on weight or number of the cargo does not need to prove the actual condition of the cargo when it is handed over to the carrier at the loading port. If there is a shortage of cargo when the consignee receives the cargo at the discharging port, the claimant may submit the B/L as evidence and then the burden of proof is shifted to the carrier. If the holder of the B/L is a bona fide third party, rebutting the fact in the statement by the carrier is not allowed. As a result, the shipper is protected where the B/L is issued.

IV. Action In Rem

447. Action in rem allows the claimant to arrest the vessel involved in the accident and to apply for the public sale of the vessel and get paid for the damages prior to other creditors against the owner. The Korean government inserted provisions regarding *action* in rem when it enacted the KCC in 1961. It included the cargo claims as one of the claims which trigger *action* in rem. The provision of *action* in rem under Article 777 had played an important role in protecting cargo interests. However, it was deleted when the KCC was revised in 1991. Many countries, such as Panama and Japan, still regard the cargo claims as one of the claims to bring about *action* in rem. There is criticism that the Korean government was too hasty in deleting the provision, and thus, it should be reinstated as soon as possible.[92]

448. Instead of having the right of the maritime lien, the cargo claimant has another resort known as Article 809 solution. The shipowner is subject to prejudgment attachment. When a charterer enters into the contract for carriage with the shipper, the owner of the vessel becomes liable for cargo damages if certain conditions are met. Because the shipowner becomes the defendant, the property of the defendant is allowed to the prejudgment attachment.

92. In Hyeon Kim, *supra,* 315.

Chapter 9. Piloting

§1. General

I. Definition

449. Korea has a special law regulating pilotage. According to the Pilot Act, Korean ports are divided into two different types in terms of the type of pilot. In a case that a vessel is entering or leaving major ports, such as Pusan, Incheon, Pohang, and Mokpo, a pilot should compulsorily be on board pursuant to the Act.[93]However, in a case that a vessel is entering or leaving small ports, the employment of a pilot is at the discretion of the ship's master.

450. To become a pilot, a captain with sea experience of over three years on board the seagoing vessel over 5,000 GRT should pass the pilot apprentice examination, which is held once a year. About ten applicants pass the examination every year. They get an internship period of six months for training. The pilot is one of the highly paid occupations in Korea and is a very popular job among navigators and captains on board the vessel. The retiring age is 65 years old but it can be extended for three years.

II. Piloting in Korea

451. A total of 270 pilots work in eleven Korean ports as of July 2024. Each pilot is necessarily a member of one of the twelve local pilot associations, including Pusan, Incheon, Yeosu, Ulsan, PyungTaek, Daesan, Masan, Pohang, Gunsan, Mokpo, Tonghae, and Juju. In addition, each pilot is a member of the Korea Maritime Pilots' Association (<www.kmpilot.or.kr>). Even though a pilot is a member of the local pilot association, he is not employed by the association. In its legal nature, it is not employed by any other entity. Rather, it is an independent specialist in that it obtains a license from the government and operates its own office and pays tax for running its own business. In practice, pilots are regarded as temporary servants of the vessel's owner for which they work on board. Therefore, the vessel's owner is vicariously liable for damages caused by the fault of the pilot.

§2. Obligation and Liability

I. Contractual Relationship

452. Pilot and shipowner enter into the contract for piloting. Korean pilots make use of a standardized contractual clause (general clause) when they are engaged in piloting. According to the general terms of the piloting contract, the liability of a

93. Jeju port became to join as one of the compulsory pilotage ports as of Jul. 1, 2016.

pilot is limited to the amount of pilotage which the pilot who caused the damages earns in return for the piloting.[94] However, the above limitation of liability is not permitted if the accident occurred due to the intentional act or gross negligence of the pilot. The standard contractual clauses for piloting are authorized by the Korean government according to the Pilot Act, Article 36. Thus, where the pilot made the vessel bottom touched and suffered damages, the liability of the pilot is limited to the pilot charges for the voyage of the vessel.

453. The above legal arrangement is effective between the shipowner and the pilot. If a third-party victim brings a lawsuit against the pilot who caused the damage based on the cause of action in tort, the pilot will be liable for the damages which the victim sustained, based on the tort law. The victim does not have the privity of contract with the pilot, and thus, the limitation in the general clause does not govern the legal relation between the pilot and the victim.

454. In a recent Pusan Eastern District Court case *2009.4.2. Docket No. 2007gahap1479*, the pilot disembarked before it reached the disembarkation position, followed by the vessel's contact with the oil pipeline at sea in the Ulsan port. The damaged owner of the oil pipeline made claims against the owner of the vessel, and it paid damages. In return, the shipowner made an indemnification lawsuit against the pilot. The court rendered that the act of the pilot to get off the vessel even before it reached the disembarkation position was gross negligence, and accordingly, the contractual terms for limitation of liability were not applicable to the case. The court further decided that there was no contractual relationship between the shipowner and the pilot when the pilotage was compulsorily executed in accordance with the Pilot Act, which led to the contractual terms being null and void. The court ordered the pilot to pay 40% of the recourse claim of the shipowner.

455. Even though the pilot is required to take on board the vessel according to the pilot Act, contract for the piloting is also carried out in Korean practices. The time when the piloting contract starts is important when an accident happens while boarding the pilot. When the pilot comes on board is the time for the contract to start, even though the signature of the master was done after the pilot arrives at the bridge, which is a later stage.

II. Tort Liability

456. When a third party suffers from damages caused by a pilot's negligence, the third party is entitled to invoke a claim for damages against the pilot based on the cause of action in tort (Article 750 of the Korean Civil Code). In addition, the third party is able to bring a lawsuit against the master of the vessel or the owner of the

94. However, there is an argument that it is not valid when pilotage is done in a compulsory pilot because there is no contract for the piloting.

vessel. The cause of action for the claim against the shipowner is a vicarious liability under the Korean Civil Code Article 756. This is because the pilot is regarded as a temporary servant of the shipowner. The shipowner and the pilot are jointly and severally liable.

457. Korean law does not have any provision to allow the pilot to limit its liability except the KCC. Under the KCC, the pilot can limit its liability when it is liable for the damages (Article 774(1)). The limitation amount in this case is the same amount as the owner, which is so high that the pilot cannot afford to pay it.

458. It can be said that the pilots are exposed to full compensation when the claims are raised by the claimant based on the cause of action in tort, under the current Korean law except KOPCA. Unlike the U.K. pilot Act,[95] the Korean Pilot Act does not have any provision to allow the pilot to limit its liability. Under the KOPCA, the pilot is not subject to the claim from the victims who suffer oil pollution damages by the oil tankers. The pilot also protects from the shipowner's recourse claims unless the damages were caused by the intentional act or with the knowledge that the damages would probably occur. The author thinks that the pilot should be protected by a limitation provision in the Korean Pilot Act.

459. In relation to the recourse action from the shipowner to the pilot, there had been no precedent in the Korean courts until the above 2009 Ulsan case. However, when a major incident occurred due to the fault of the pilot, the liability insurer of the shipowner considered making a recourse claim against the pilot but, in practice, refrained from exercising the right, considering the pilot's poor economic status and public function.

460. Apart from civil liability, administrative and penal liability are also imposed upon the pilot. The MOMAF as the issuer of the license for the pilot is an eligible administration to admonish the pilot if the pilot acts negligently during the piloting. The actual administrative punishment is done by the KMST. Even though it is the agency to find out the cause of the casualties at sea, it also has the power to punish the holder of navigating licenses, such as the master and pilot. The cancelation of the license for the pilot by the administration is very rarely executed. The order for halting the exercise of the license for one or two months is a usual administrative punishment by the KMST. The pilot has two more chances to argue against the decision of a Local MST. The pilot is entitled to appeal to the Central MST to review the decision by the local MST. The Pilot can make an appeal to the Daejon High Court to cancel the order of the Central MST to halt its exercise of the pilot license.

95. According to Art. 16 of the 1987 U.K. Pilot Act, pilots or port authorities as employers of pilots are entitled to limit its liability.

§3. THE PROTECTION OF THE PILOT

I. Pilot Charges

461. Under the time charter party, the time charterer is the person to arrange the pilot. Therefore, the piloting contract is done between the pilot and the time charterer. The service of the pilot was given for the benefit of the time charterer. As a result, the time charterer is the party to pay the pilot charges. However, there is a clear wording that the shipowner should pay the pilot charges. There the split views on the interpretation of the wording. Recently, in a lawsuit, the shipowner was to pay the remainder of pilot charge incurred by the time charterer.

462. When Hanjin Shipping applied for rehabilitation proceedings in Korea, the pilot who had the remainder of the unpaid pilot charges could not collect its claims. After three years of the proceeding, the pilot at Pusan found the provision and applied a prejudgment attachment against the vessel of the owner. The lawyer who was in charge of the case admitted the liability of the shipowner.

II. Maritime Lien

463. The claimant with pilot charge has the maritime lien against the vessel for which the lien is incurred. Article 777 applies in case the owner incurs the claims, while Article 850(2) applies in case the BBC charterer incurs the claims. Whether the claims incurred by the time charterer bring about the maritime claims or not has long been discussed in Korea. There is no provision for the time charterer.

464. In the Korean Supreme Court case *2019.7.24. Docket. No. 2017ma 1442*, the court admitted that the claimant is allowed to invoke the auction sale against the vessel based on the maritime incurred by Article 850(2) even though the claims were made by the time charterer. The claims rendered by the claimant were related to the tug service. The above case will be applied *mutatis mutandis* in case of the pilot service.

III. Physical Damages

465. The pilot is needed to embark on board the vessel by using a rope ladder. During embarking or disembarking period, the pilot is exposed to the danger of physical damage. He is forced to fall into the sea, leading to death. No rules for protecting the pilot exist in Korea. Neither the KCC nor the Pilot Act does not have any provision to protect the pilot. Where the pilot falls into the sea during its attempt to embark, the pilot should raise claims based on the tort. It should verify the presence of the negligence of the vessel. However, it is a very difficult burden for the pilot because all the evidence is in the hands of the vessel. Therefore, it is recommended that the vessel should prove that there was no negligence to the vessel, which will result in the protection of the pilot.

Chapter 10. Towing and Pushing Contract

§1. General

466. Owing to the geographic characteristics of Korea, a lot of towing operations are engaged in the Korean territorial seas. Towing consists of a tug and a barge or a general vessel. In a towing for a carriage of goods, a tug carries a barge which contains goods in its holds. In this towing, the tug connects the barge with rope or wire. In towing for pushing a vessel, a tug is engaged in helping the vessel's maneuvering. The former type of towing is called the towing as a type of carriage of goods. The latter type of towing is called the towing as a type of employment. The KCC does not have any provision addressing legal issues on towing.

467. However, the Chinese Maritime Code (Maritime Code of the People's Republic of China) has a chapter on towing as a type of carriage of goods (Chapter VII Articles 155–164). Under the Chinese Maritime Code, a contract of sea towage is a contract whereby the tug owner undertakes to tow an object by sea with a tug from one place to another, and the tow party pays the towage. The provisions of Chapter VII shall not be applicable to the towage service rendered to ships within the port areas (Article 155). Where the tow party fails to pay the towage price or other reasonable expenses as agreed, the tug owner shall have a lien on the object towed (Article 161).

§2. Type of Carriage of Goods

468. The towing as a type of carriage of goods is a contract for carrying the barge as the cargo. It is a kind of contract for the carriage of goods by sea. The difference from the general carriage of goods is that the cargo is contained in the barge in the case of the towing. The owner of the barge with the cargo is equivalent to the shipper. Because the cargo contained in the barge is delivered by the shipper to the carrier, the obligation of the carrier may be narrower than that in the general carriage by sea. There is no express provision regulating the towing contract in the KCC. The provisions on the contract for carriage of goods in the KCC may not apply to the contract for carrying the barge. In the Seoul High Court case *2000.1.19. Docket No. 98na31792,* several equipments were carried on board a floating barge which was towed by a tug. The contract for the towing stated that the shipper should keep the cargo to be towed in a safe condition and secured firmly not to be shifted during the voyage. The equipments were damaged during the heavy weather. The shipper as the plaintiff raised claims for damages against the carrier. The court rendered to the effect that the contract for towing was different from the general contract for the carriage by sea in terms of the way of transportation, the shipper's obligation to maintain seaworthiness of the cargo and the fact that a person in charge of safety of the cargo was on board the barge, and thus, that the provision in the KCC would not necessarily be applicable for the towing contract, but the agreement in the towing contract by the parties should be, in advance, applied.

469. This type of towing is variously engaged in Korea. Along the Korean coast line, several sand-catching companies try to transport a barge full of sand to the port. Several shipbuilding yards which make blocks far from the yards try to bring them to the yards. The scene of a tug towing a barge laden with blocks on board is easily noticed on the southern coast of the Korean Peninsula. Big shipbuilding companies such as Hyundai Shipbuilding Co., Ltd make a plant or oil rig bound for the Middle East and try to transport it.

I. Obligation and Liability

470. The standard Towcon form is a widely used standard form for towing contracts worldwide. The towing contract in Korea usually includes a core provision such as a Knock-for-Knock clause. It is influenced by the Protection and Indemnity (P&I) insurance. According to the Korea P&I Club, it may indemnify damage to the owner of an entered ship only when the towing contract is entered into with certain conditions, namely, the contract should be based on Towcon and Towhire or a knock-for-knock clause (Rule 27(2)).

471. In a typical towing contract, the tug owner has the duty to maintain the tug in a seaworthy condition, to tow the barge with due care during the voyage and to follow the towing surveyor's reasonable instruction. However, the shipper should maintain the barge in a seaworthy condition and designate a towing surveyor to inspect the barge's seaworthy condition and provide appropriate instructions for towing to the tug owner as the carrier.

472. In a typical knock-for-knock clause, the owner of tug on one part and the owner of barge or the cargo on the other part shall be responsible for any loss or damage to its own ship, cargo, or property and for loss of life or personal injury on his own ship, without any recourse whatsoever against the other.

473. The owner of tug or barge is vicariously liable for its servant or agent's wrongdoing against the third party based on tort-law theory. It is usual that there is no crew on board the barge, in which case the owner of the tug was only vicariously liable for the damage to the third-party victims. However, where crew was on board and negligent for the safe navigation and thus contributed to the collision with the opposite vessel. The owner of the barge in addition to that of the tug is responsible for the damages of the opposite vessel. In the Korean Supreme Court case *2010.1.28. Docket No. 2008da65686*, there was a crew on board the barge which was towed by the tug. In a restricted visibility, the collision occurred between the above tug-barge and the opposite vessel. The court decided that the failure of the crew on the barge to sound fog signal contributed to the collision, and thus, the owner of the barge was held vicariously liable for the damages to the opposite vessel.

474. When the towing fleet was involved in the collision and incurred damages to the third party, the Korean court found that the owner of the tug was held liable for damages. In the meantime, the owner applied for the limitation of liability in the proceeding. How to calculate the limitation amount became an issue. In the Korean Supreme Court case *1998.3.2. Docket No., 1998.3.25. Docket No. 97ma2758*, the court decided that the limitation amount was a sum of calculating each unit's own limitation respectively. In other words, the limitation amount of the tug and the amount of the barge should be calculated separately and then aggregated together, which became the limitation amount of the owner who operated tug and barge together.

475. The tug owner is not allowed to apply for auction sale based on the maritime lien because the contract of the tug to tow the barge as the cargo does not fall within the definition of the towing in Article 777. Instead, the carrier may exercise the lien on the barge when it has unpaid freight for the carriage.

§3. Employment Type

476. The other type of towing contract is an employment type found within the port area. In this contract, the tug owner enters into a contract to assist in the maneuvering of the vessel with the owner of the vessel to be pushed. The tug is under the full control of the vessel pushed or towed. The tug follows the order of the vessel pushed or towed. This type of towing is not the contract for the carriage, and thus, provisions regarding the contract for carriage under the KCC do not apply to the case. However, the tug owner can limit its liability in case it causes damages to the third party. This type of towing or pushing can be found in ports when a pilot is engaged in making a large vessel alongside the berth at port.

477. An employment type of towing falls within the definition of the towing triggering the maritime lien under Article 777. Therefore, the owner of the tug is allowed to apply for auction sale against the vessel for which it was employed.

Chapter 11. Salvage and Assistance

§1. General

478. The KCC has several provisions on salvage (Articles 882–895). When a vessel renders a voluntary assistance to a vessel in distress at sea with a successful result, the KCC allows the owner of the vessel which rendered the assistance to claim a salvage award (Article 882). The voluntary salvage is legally very similar to services rendered without mandate pursuant to the Korean Civil Code Articles 734–740, under which the service provider is not allowed to demand an award. However, the expenses which were incurred during the service by the provider can be reimbursed (Article 739(1))

479. Voluntary salvage rarely occurs, but contractual salvage occurs frequently in Korea. There are several Korean private salvage companies engaged in salvage, including Korea Salvage Co., Ltd (<www.korsal.com>). A license is not required to be a salvor in Korea. International salvage companies such as SMIT Salvage BV (The Netherlands), SVITZER Salvage BV (The Netherlands) and Nippon Salvage Co., Ltd are also active in Korea.

§2. Source of Law

I. KCC

480. The provisions on salvage in the KCC are applicable to voluntary salvage (Article 882). However, the scope of application was partly expanded to be applicable for the contractual salvage in the 2007 Revision of the KCC. Newly inserted Article 887(1) says to the effect that the provisions in the salvage chapter are applicable to the contractual salvage in case there are no provisions to be applicable under the contract unless they are against the contract.

481. The Korean Seaman Act imposes the obligation to rescue crew from the vessel at distress upon the master of the vessel in the vicinity of the vessel at distress (Article 13). The master of a vessel does his best to assist the opposing vessel's crew and the vessel itself when it collides with the opposing vessel (Article 12).

II. Salvage Convention

482. Korea is not a state party to the 1986 Salvage Convention. The convention addresses contractual salvage. Article 10(1) imposes upon the master of a vessel to render assistance to any person in danger of being lost at sea.

§3. VOLUNTARY SALVAGE

I. Definition

483. The provisions on the salvage in the KCC are applicable basically to voluntary salvage in which the salvor does not have any obligation to render assistance to the vessel in distress.[96] The vessel (A) may receive a distress signal at sea, and then the master of the vessel (A) proceeds to the distressed vessel (B) as quickly as possible to render assistance. The subject of the salvage is the vessel and cargo on board in distress. The salvage of the human being only does not fall within the concept of the salvage under the KCC.

II. Legal Nature

484. The most important provision in the salvage section is that the salvor is entitled to the right of salvage remuneration (or award) from the owner of the salvaged vessel under the KCC. The vessel (A) might spend expenditure on rendering assistance. If the vessel (A) does not receive any recovery from the salvaged vessel (B), the vessel (A) or other vessels will not try to take risks. Because the salvor renders its work voluntarily, the owner of the salvaged vessel is not required to pay remuneration according to the provision of services rendered without mandate in the Civil Code Article 734. A person who manages another person's matters without mandate generally acquires the right to claim payment for costs and expenses according to the Civil Code Article 739(1), but the person is not allowed to receive more than the cost and expenses. However, the salvage at sea should be encouraged in order to facilitate the rescue of property and human life at sea, and thus, the KCC allows the salvor to acquire the remuneration, including cost, expenses and benefits in addition.

485. Remuneration is allowed to the salvor only when it succeeds in the rescue. It is called the no-cure, no-payment rule. In order to solve practical difficulties in the oil pollution case, the no-cure no-payment rule was amended in the 2007 revision of the KCC. The salvor is entitled to receive special compensation regardless of the success of salvage (Article 885(1)).

486. The shipowner of the vessel and other property rescued has the obligation to pay the remuneration and the special compensation in return for the salvage assistance in proportion to their share of the rescued price (Article 886). The owner of the vessel, the master and crew who rendered the rescue to the vessel in distress have the right to request remuneration from the rescued vessel and the cargo's owner. The remuneration obtained from the rescued vessel and cargo should be paid for the expenses incurred for salvage operation. The remainder should be distributed to the shipowner and seafarer, including the master and crew, at the rate of

96. Lee Sik Chai, *supra*, 247.

50:50 (Article 889(1)). The remuneration should not exceed the price of the vessel and other property rescued unless otherwise agreed (Article 884(1)).

487. Under voluntary salvage, there is no time to make an agreement on salvage remuneration because of an emergency situation. According to the KCC Article 883, the court decides the amount of remuneration in the voluntary salvage. When the court decides the remuneration, it should take into consideration the price of the rescued vessel, the extent of the danger, the endeavor and expenses poured by the salvor, the extent of the risk against which the salvor and its equipments faced, the effect of the salvage, and the effort of the salvor for protecting environmental damages. The salvor has a maritime lien upon the salved cargo (Article 893) and the vessel rescued as well (Article 777). However, the salvor is not allowed to exercise the maritime lien on the rescued cargo if the cargo was assigned to a third party (Article 893 Proviso). The salvor has priority on the reimbursement for its remuneration over the mortgagee (Articles 893(2), 777). A claim for salvage reward is subject to two years' time bar from the date when the salvage was completed (Article 895).

488. The master of the rescued vessel has the power to execute all acts related to the legal proceedings and non-legal proceedings regarding the payment on behalf of the obligor who should pay remuneration (Article 894(1). The master can be a party in the legal proceeding on the remuneration; the effect of the concluded judgment against the master is valid for the obligor of the remuneration.

§4. Contractual Salvage

I. Definition

489. The other type of salvage is contractual salvage. When a vessel is in distress, the owner of the vessel will make a salvage agreement with the salvor. The Lloyd's Open Form is one of standard forms for contractual salvage.

II. Legal Nature

490. Provisions in the salvage section in the KCC were not applicable to contractual salvage. However, the Korean government took into consideration the fact that contractual salvage is more widely used, in practice, than voluntary salvage and decided to insert a provision in the 2007 Revision of the KCC in order to apply the salvage provisions to the contractual salvage. Article 887(1) says that even if parties make a prearranged agreement for rendering salvage assistance and no provision is found in that agreement, the provisions in the voluntary salvage in the KCC will be applicable to the case. Therefore, provisions in the salvage subsection are applicable for the contractual salvage as a default rule.

III. Salvage Contracts Engaged in Korea

491. The Lloyd's Open Form is usually engaged in contractual salvage in Korea, in which the salvage remuneration shall be fixed by arbitrators in an arbitration proceeding in London after salvage. However, the Korean style-salvage form is also engaged between Korean salvage companies and Korean shipowners, in which the salvage remuneration is fixed with a certain amount in accordance with the Korean law and by the KCAB.

Chapter 12. General Average

§1. General

492. The KCC has several provisions on general average. When the master of a vessel voluntarily takes an action to cargo on board or the vessel for the purpose of avoiding impending perils which may impact the vessel and the cargo together. The loss of the cargo owner or vessel's owner by the master's intentional act is called the general average loss (Article 865). At the sacrifice of the lost cargo or the vessel, the saved cargo or vessel avoided the impending perils. In other words, the owner of the remained cargo or vessel gains benefit at the sacrifice of the lost cargo or vessel. Under the general principle of law, when an accident occurs, the subsequent loss from the accident falls upon the person who owns the property, such as the vessel or cargo. However, under the general average regime, the loss arising out of the general average sacrifice should be shared by all persons who had interests in the properties which were in common danger but successfully saved.

493. General average occurs frequently in Korean shipping practice. When a vessel's engine breaks down, the owner of the vessel employs a tugboat to tow the vessel. The owner's expenditure due to the employment of the tugboat falls within the definition of the general average.

494. It is a well-settled practice in Korea that the time charterer can be added as a general average contributor. The bunker for the engine may be salvaged with the vessel and cargo. Because the bunker is owned by the time charterer, the time charterer is invited as one of contributors.

§2. Source of Law

I. KCC

495. To qualify as a general average act, the sacrifice or expenditure must be made or incurred by the master's act for the purpose of saving the ship and cargo that are in common danger. The sacrifice or expenditure must be intentionally made.[97]

496. The KCC imposes an obligation to indemnify the loss of the cargo and vessel's owner upon the owners of the saved cargo or vessel (Article 866).

497. The losses in the general average include both sacrifice and expenditures (Article 865). The loss of logs on board by the master's jettison is a good example of the sacrifice in the general average. When the engine of a vessel is in trouble, and the owner arranges the tug for towing the vessel, the expense for engaging the

97. Lee Sik Chai, *supra*, 214.

tugboat is an example of expenditure in the general average. The owner of the lost cargo or the vessel is entitled to claim to the owner of the remained cargo or the vessel the appropriate contribution of the general average (Article 866).

498. The loss caused by the general average sacrifice is borne by the interested parties in proportion to the values of their respective interest in the property involved plus half the amount of freight payable on delivery (Article 866). In practice, the amount of loss, after deducting the amount to be borne by the person who suffers the loss, is apportioned among the shipowner and cargo owners in proportion to the values of their property saved by the general average act.[98]

499. Where the common danger against the cargo and the vessel together was brought about due to the cargo or the vessel, the party who pays general average contribution is entitled to exercise the recourse claims against the party who negligently contributed to the general average expenditures or sacrifices (Article 870).

500. The contribution of the general average of the saved cargo is covered by the cargo insurer (Article 694). When the owner of cargo is subject to pay contribution of the general average to the claimant who lost its property by the intentional act of the master, the insurer of the owner of the saved cargo has an obligation to pay contribution in accordance with the KCC Article 866. Likewise, the contribution of the general average of the saved vessel is covered by the hull insurer (Article 694). However, the provision is regarded as a default rule, and thus, the insurer may make a different agreement with the insured from the provision.

501. General average contribution is exempted from the claims subject to the limitation of liability (Article 773). The rationale behind the provision is to protect the owner of the lost cargo or the vessel in the general average. If the owner of the lost cargo or the vessel does not fully recover the loss due to the application of the limitation of liability, the owner will be put in a very disadvantageous position as opposed to the owner of the saved cargo or vessel's advantageous position, which result in the unjust result. The liability of the owner of saved cargo and vessel is limited to the price of the cargo or the vessel when the cargo was delivered or the vessel arrived (Article 868).

502. The claim for general average contribution or recourse claim against the party who negligently contributed to the general average expenditure or expenses is time-barred unless the claimant does apply it before the court within a year after the calculation ended (Article 875).

II. Party's Agreement and YAR

503. The provisions in the KCC on the general average have characteristics as default rules, and thus, parties are free to make different agreements from the

98. *Ibid.*, 220.

provisions in the KCC. Parties usually include general average stipulations in the contracts of carriage. As in many other countries, the York-Antwerp Rules (YAR) are usually incorporated into almost all of the Korean contracts of carriage such as the B/L, Gencon and NYPE. The distribution of the general average contribution is carried out in the agreement in the YAR. YAR is regularly amended by the CMI.

504. YAR is well-known among Korean practitioners. Whether or not YAR can be a source of law to be applicable to the given case even if there is no agreement that YAR is applicable to the contract between parties is at issue. According to the KCC, if there is no rule in the KCC, the commercial customary law can be a source of law. In order for a certain fact to be a commercial customary law, a commercial customary practice must exist and then the practice must be widely accepted by the person involved in the business. According to a survey in Korea, YAR reached the level of commercial customary law.[99]

§3. Particular Average

505. Particular average is a responding concept against general average. The particular average refers to the loss of a particular cargo or that of a particular vessel which is separate from other cargo or vessel. The KCC does not address the particular average. The particular average is borne by the owner of that particular cargo or vessel, and it is a pure insurance matter under the Korean law.

99. In Hyeon Kim, "A study on the customary commercial law in the area of maritime transaction," Justice Vol. 199 (2023.11.), p.11.

Chapter 13. Collisions

§1. General

506. According to the Korean Civil Code Article 750, damages caused by collision can be compensated based on the cause of action in tort. A both-to-blame case in the collision falls within the definition of mutually committed tort. In a mutually committed tort case, both persons who contributed to the damages are jointly and severally liable for damages caused by the co-tortfeasors under the Korean Civil Code (Article 760). However, in the ship's collision, tort law is modified under the collision provisions in the KCC.

507. Collision cases which do not fall within the scope of definition in the KCC Article 876 may not be subject to the KCC but to the Korean Civil Code. The owner of a vessel involved in a collision enjoys benefit of limitation of liability if the case is subject to the KCC as opposed to the Civil Code. A collision between two seagoing vessels is a good example of a collision in the KCC. A collision between a seagoing vessel and an inland-navigating vessel also falls within the definition of a collision in the KCC. However, a collision between inland-navigating vessels is not regarded as a collision in the KCC Article 876.

508. There are two different kinds of collision. One is the direct contact of two vessels, and the other is the indirect contact of two vessels. A good example of the latter is that the passing vessel makes a high wave and subsequently, a small vessel in the vicinity is capsized by the high wave. If it is within the definition of a collision, the owner of the vessel makes use of the legal regime in the KCC to protect its interest. Otherwise, the owner will be in a detrimental position because the general commercial law or the civil law applies to the case. The Korean government decided to include indirect contact as one of the examples of collision in the 2007 revision of the KCC (Article 876(2)).

509. Many collision accidents occur in Korea within the Korean territorial seas. According to the KMST's statistics, 235 collisions occurred within the Korean territorial seas during the year 2015.

§2. Source of Law

510. Collision is a kind of tort. The legal regime on the ship's collision in Korea is governed by the statutory law named as the Maritime Law Section in the KCC and the Civil Code in addition. Korea is not a party to the 1910 Collision Convention. However, the KCC adopted several provisions from the 1910 Collision Convention. However, Korea is a state party to the International Regulations for Preventing Collisions at Sea, 1972 (1972 COLREG), which stipulates rules for navigators to avoid collisions at sea.

§3. Who Is the Obligor

511. When the owner of a vessel operates the vessel, the owner is liable for the result of a collision based on the vicarious liability under the Civil Code Article 756 or the KCC Article 879. It is because the owner is the employer of the master or crew who committed tort.

512. However, if a vessel is operated by the bareboat charterer, the bareboat charter rather than the owner is vicariously liable for damages caused by the collision because it is the employer of the master or crew who committed tort. According to the same theory, when a vessel is operated under the time charter party, the bareboat charterer or the owner of the vessel who employs the master or crew is liable for the damages.

513. A time charterer or voyage charterer is not liable for the damages caused by the collision. In this regard, Korean law's position is different from that of Japan. Under Japanese case law, the time charterer is liable for the claim caused by the collision. In the Korean Supreme Court case 2003, the court rendered that the navigation matter is subject to the shipowner while business matter is to the time charterer. The collision is a matter of navigation, and thus, the shipowner is a liable party for the collision damages.

§4. Obligation and Collision Avoiding Rules

I. COLREG

514. Korea is a party to the 1972 COLREG. In addition to ratifying the COLREG in 1977, the Korean government enacted a national law called the Korean Maritime Traffic Safety Act (KMTSA) in 1986, which was reinforced with a new name called as Maritime Safety Act (MSA) in 2012. Therefore, the 1972 COLREG and the KMSA are two major governing laws in Korea for the navigator to observe in order to avoid a collision at sea.

II. Basic Collision Rules

515. The collision rules are divided in accordance with visibility. In good visibility, crossing, head-on and overtaking rules apply. When the vessels meet in a crossing situation, the vessel which has the approaching vessel on her starboard side is a give-way vessel and the other vessel is a stand-on vessel (COLREG Rule 15). In a head-on situation, both vessels should avoid the opposing vessel by turning to starboard side (COLREG Rule 14). In an overtaking situation, the overtaking vessel should avoid the overtaken vessel (COLREG Rule 13). When the collision occurs, the give-way vessel holds more responsibility for the collision than the stand-on vessel. In order for the navigation rule to be applied in sight of one another: (i) vessels are under way with the sight of one another, (ii) they are approaching involved in risk of the collision, and (iii) they are set on course. If one of the requirements is not met, the navigation rule in sight of one another is not applicable. The ordinary seamanship provision will be triggered.

If visibility becomes restricted due to fog or heavy rain, the collision rules applicable for good visibility are no longer valid and special rules are applicable. In this case, both vessels should avoid the other vessel with reduced speed (COLREG Rule 27) and should not turn to port. When the vessel is in a narrow channel, it should keep as near to the outer limit of the channel, which lies on her starboard side. A vessel using a traffic separation scheme shall proceed in the appropriate traffic lane in the general direction of traffic flow for that lane. These rules for narrow channel and traffic separation schemes are applicable in any condition of visibility.

516. All navigating vessels have the duty to abide by the following rules regardless of the visibility under the COLREG and KMSA: (i) they should keep a lookout. All available means, such as binoculars and radars, should be employed; (ii) they should maintain a safe speed in a given circumstance; (iii) they should take action to avoid collision in an ample time with a bold angle when there is a risk of collision with approaching vessel. If there is no bearing change with the approaching vessel, the danger of a collision is involved. Two basic principles for collision avoidance rules are starboard hand rule and priority rule in accordance with maneuverability. The vessel which has the other approaching vessel on her starboard side is the give-way vessel, and it should turn the key to starboard side, as a result of which both vessels are to pass port-to-port. It is called the starboard hand rule. The vessel which has better maneuverability than the other should keep out of the way of the other. For example, a power-driven vessel should be kept out of the way of the vessel not under command due to engine breakdown or anchored vessel. It is obvious that the power-driven vessel is capable of avoiding the other hampered vessel more easily than the other vessel.

III. Special Rules in Korea

517. The Korean government enacted a local rule for safe navigation within the trade port area. The Korean Act for Vessel's Entering and Leaving Port (KAVELP) has the nature of a special law in relation to the KMA. The rules in KAVELP prevail over rules in the KMSA. When a vessel entering a trade port meets a vessel departing the port, the former should give-way to the latter regardless of rules in accordance with the KMSA (Article 14). The Vessel entering or leaving the fairway in the trade port shall be kept out of the way of the vessel navigating in the fairway (Article 13(1)(i)). The vessel in the fairway shall navigate on the starboard side of the fairway when there is a risk of meeting another vessel in the fairway (Article 13(1)(iii). Small vessels such as barges, boats, and tugboats which are navigating within the port limit of the trade port shall not impede the way of another vessel (Article 17). Navigation rules in the trade port are interpreted as being applicable regardless of visibility.

518. The Korean government established a Special Area for Traffic Safety in Pusan, Inchon, and Yeosu (Article 10). The vessel within that area shall follow the designated lane. There exist two designated lanes such as the entering lane and the leaving lane. The vessel entering the port shall navigate by using the entering lane, and the vessel leaving the port shall navigate by using the leaving lane (Presidential Decree Article 7).

519. The provisions in the KMSA or the KAVELP impose an obligation upon foreign navigators to observe the navigation rules when they sail within the Korean territorial waters or trade port areas and upon Korean navigators to observe the navigation rules wherever they sail (KMSA Article 3).

§5. Liability

I. Tort Liability

520. When a collision occurs and damages subsequently result, if it is the result of the master's or crew's acts against the obligation imposed upon them, the master or crew should be held liable in tort to victims of the collision. According to the Korean Civil Code, the owner of a vessel as an employer of the master or crew should be held vicariously liable for the damages. Both the employer and the master or crews are jointly and severally liable for the damages. The claimants usually try to get indemnification from the owner. In return, the owners are entitled to make a recourse claim against the master or crew who committed tort. However, it is a Korean practice that the owners do not try to seek recourse claims against the master or crew.

II. Damages

521. Under the KCC, the general rule of mutually committed tort was changed into proportional liability in case of physical damages. Therefore, the victims cannot claim more than one defendant's share of liability (Article 879(2)). This rule originates from the 1910 Collision Convention[100] Article 4.[101] Even though Korea was not a party to the 1910 Collision Convention, the Korean government adopted it in the KCC.

522. However, damages caused by personal injury or loss of life are not subject to Article 879(2). Both parties involved in the collision are jointly and severally liable for the loss of life or personal injury caused by the collision.

---

100. International Convention for the Unification of Certain Rules of Law Relating to Collision between Vessels, 1910.

101. If two or more vessels are in fault, the liability of each vessel shall be in proportion to the degree of the faults respectively committed.

III. Apportionment of Liability

523. The extent of the liability of a vessel as the defendant depends on the fault ratio, which contributed to the collision damages. The fault ratio in the civil case is decided by the court proceeding. Korea does not operate an admiralty court, unlike China, Singapore, or the U.K. The case involved in the collision has been dealt with by the average judge without specialty on the collision. In order to get expertise, the court invites a special advisor for collision and gets an explanation of the collision circumstances or the apportionment of liability. The expert who has master's experience with legal background is designated as the special advisor for the judge by the Korean Supreme Court. While the special advisor for the judge is called upon by the judge at the court proceeding, the expert on the collision submits its opinion on the cause of the collision and the apportionment of liability by the request of one party to the lawsuit. The latter is adopted as an evidence, but the former does not have such power as the evidence. However, the judge presiding the case may be heavily affected by the special advisor's expert opinion because he is in a more objective position than the expert for one party.

524. In a collision case named as the Ida, the Pusan District Court case *1998.2.1. Docket No. 97gahap7786*, the court decided that the Tugboat Seorin was the give-way vessel while M/V Ida was the stand-on vessel because the Tugboat Seorin had the approaching M/V Ida on her starboard side. Under the circumstance that both vessels did not make a lookout properly, the court imposed 60% liability on the Tugboat Seorin and 40% on M/V Ida.

525. In the Korean Supreme Court case *2011.1.13. Docket No. 2009chu220*, the barge Pos No. 5000 at anchor did not turn the light to represent that the vessel was anchored, as a result of which the passing fishing vessel named as Shinsung collided with the barge. The Central KMST decided that the collision occurred partly because the general power-driven vessel Shinsung did not make a sharp lookout and did not find the barge and partly because the barge did not turn on the light to show its presence. It proportioned that Shinsung contributed to the collision of 55% and the barge Pos of 45%. The master of the Shinsung raised the revocation action to the Korean Supreme Court to cancel the decision of the KMST to reprimand him. The court rejected the appeal, saying that the KMST's decision was correct and rightful.

526. In the Inchon District Court case of limitation proceeding *2013.5.21. Docket No. 2011gahap17126,* M/V CS Crane and M/V Fuping Yuan collided under the restricted visibility off Inchon port in Korea. M/V CS Crane was navigating at a speed ranging from 12 knots to 6 knots for six minutes just before the collision, whereas M/V Fuping Yuan was at a speed of 2 knots. The court criticized the high speed of M/V CS Crane and imposed a 75% fault ratio upon M/V CS Crane and 25% upon M/V Fuping Yuan.

527. In the Seoul Southern District Court case *2013.6.5. Docket No. 2012gahap7046*, M/V NCC Qassim collided with M/V JL Braver in sight of one another. In the first stage, the latter overtook the former, and an overtaking situation was formed. However, at the later stage, the former increased the speed, and thus, the former and the latter navigated side by side. The court decided that the overtaking rule could not be applicable because the later stage, the former was overtaking the latter. And thus, the ordinary seamanship principle should be applied to the case. The court apportioned the 60% fault ratio to M/V JL Brave because the intrusion of the vessel between M/V NCC Qassim and the third-party vessel was the main cause of the collision.

§6. Time Bar

528. If the claimant does not bring a lawsuit within two years after the accident occurred, it can no longer claim against the owner of the vessel which caused the collision damages (Article 881). The two-year time-bar period is shorter than that in the general tort law in the Civil Code. According to the Civil Code Article 766, the time-bar period is ten years from the date when the tortfeasor committed tort.[102] In this respect, the time-bar provision in the collision section functions as protecting the owner's interest.

§7. KMST

I. Function of KMST

529. As we *see* above, damages' compensation is calculated based on the fault ratio (blame ratio) of the parties involved in the collision (Article 879). Therefore, the fault ratio is very important under the Korean law. In practice, the fault ratio is virtually determined by the decision of the KMST.

530. The KMST functions as an administrative agency to find out the cause of marine accidents such as collision, fire, grounding, deaths of crews, etc. Furthermore, it has another function as an agency imposing a penalty on the holder of a maritime officer's license. This function is authorized to the KMST from the Korean government which issues licenses for masters, navigational officers, and pilots. The tribunal renders two major decisions: one for cause of accident and the other for admonishing the license holders who committed wrongdoing. The cause of the collision in the KMST's decision may affect the extent of party's compensation against the other party. Therefore, parties try to get good results from the KMST. If the owner of the vessel was not satisfied with the result of the Central KMST, it made an appeal to the Korean Supreme Court to change the cause of the accident (to The Daejon High Court as of 2015 due to the revision of the KMST Act in 2014). In

102. The victim's claim will be time-barred if three years passes from the moment when it came to know the fact that it sustained damages and the identity of the tortfeasor under Art. 766.

these proceedings, the Korean Supreme Court decided several times that the decision on the cause of the accident by the KMST was not subject to the court's canceling proceeding of the governmental action of the KMST to impose upon the holder of the navigation license. The decision for the cause of the accident is not related to the right or obligation of the people. The decision of the KMST without such right and obligation is not subject to the court's cancelation proceeding against the governmental action.

531. The cause of accident decided by the KMST has an authority even on the civil and criminal proceedings. The KMST Act provides that the KMST is allowed to fix a contributed portion of each party involved in the causation of the accident (Article 4(2)).[103] The fault ratio decided in the KMST is separate and distinctive from judgments by civil courts, and thus, the civil courts are not obliged to follow the fault ratio decided by the KMST. However, the judges in the civil courts show a general tendency to rely on the decisions rendered by the KMST, including the fault ratio. Nevertheless, there are several cases that which the civil court decided the fault ratio differently from those decided by the KMST.

532. The KMST operates four district tribunals at Incheon, Pusan, Mokpo, and Donghae. The Central KMST is located in Seoul (<www.kmst.go.kr>). If there is any doubt on the decision rendered by the district tribunals, the persons involved in the case are entitled to make an appeal. If the person before the second instance tribunal is not satisfied with the decision rendered by the Central Tribunal, he has a right to make an appeal to the Korean Supreme Court (Daejon High Court as of 2015).

II. Guideline for the KMST's Umpire Regarding the Apportionment of Collision Liability

533. Since 1999, the KMST has rendered decisions on the contributing ratio of vessel fault to the accident involved in collision according to the KMST Act Article 4(2). Even though the ratio was based on administrative proceedings, the civil courts showed a tendency to rely on it. Stimulated by the increasing reliance of the parties on the contributing ratio rendered by it, the KMST sought the uniform application of it throughout the KMST's local tribunals and set a guideline on the basic collision cases as followings:

AA. A basic situation is that both vessels did not take any action before the collision. From the basic ratio, the umpire is allowed to increase or decrease the ratio appropriately according to the action taken by each vessel. Fault of navigators which did not contribute to the collisions should not be assessed in the contributing ratio.

---

103. KMST Art. 4(2) In finding out the cause of the accident, KMST can state the contributing fault ratio of each person or parties in case that a marine accident involves in more than two person or parties.

BB. Collision in sight of one another
- (1) At the crossing situation; give-way vessel 65%: Stand-on vessel 35%.
- (2) At the head-on situation; both vessels 50%.
- (3) At the overtaking situation; overtaking vessel as a give-way vessel 80%: Overtaken vessel as a stand-on vessel 20%.
- (4) At the collision between vessels with different manoeuverabilities; vessel not under command 10%: power-driven vessel 90%.

CC. Collision in restricted visibility
- (1) At collision in the restricted visibility: both vessels 50% DD. Collision in any condition of visibility

DD. Collision in any condition of visibility.
- (1) At the collision in the narrow channel;

  A vessel keeping as near to the outer limit of the channel which lies on her starboard side 15%: Approaching vessel from the opposite course 85%;

  When two vessels are approaching correctly, but a vessel turns the key toward the other vessel at surprise; the turned vessel 100%.
- (1) At the collision in the Traffic Separation Scheme; same as the above.

EE. Ordinary Seamanship case;
- (1) Anchored vessel not sounded warning signal 5%: power-driven vessel 95%.
- (2) Vessel moored at shore 0%.

534. In the *M/V Tae young Sun* collision case, the Central KMST, 2000-3 (May 10, 2000) case rendered that M/V Taeyoung Sun as a general power-driven vessel should keep out of the way of the fishing boat Daeo, which was engaged in the fishing and thus M/V Taeyoung Sun should be apportioned to have 80% of contributing ratio. In Gwangju District Court case *2002.11.15 Docket No. 2000GaHap5758*, the court accepted the decision of the Central KMST and apportioned the 80% fault ratio to M/V Taeyoung Sun.

535. In the collision case between *M/V Morning Express* and *M/V Pos Bravery*, the Central KMST apportioned the contributing ratio as 50%: 50%. However, in the Seoul Central District Court case *2008.10.24 Docket No. 2000gahap15313*, the court decided differently from that of the KMST by imposing a 65% fault ratio upon the M/V Pos Bravery and 35% upon the M/V Morning Express. The difference came from the different applications of the law. The Central KMST applied the ordinary seamanship principle to the case because a vessel did not set on course, and thus, the crossing rule could not be applied (COLREG 15); but, the court applied the crossing situation rule to the case because the vessel was on course and decided that the M/V Morning Express was in the status as the stand-on vessel.

536. In the recent collision case between *M/V Duqm* and *Fortune Miracle*, the latter vessel was navigating following the fairway to the north. M/V Duqm just left the berth and was turning. It finally entered the left side of the fairway. Fortune Miracle also mistakenly entered into the left side of the fairway. The Central KMST rendered that the vessel entering the fairway should avoid the vessel following the fairway in accordance with Article 13(1). It apportioned the contributing ratio as 60%:40% in favor of Fortune Miracle. In the Kwangju High Court case *2018.8.10. Docket No. 2017na15873*, the court maintained the fault ratio just as the Central KMST. Whether the vessel entering the fairway from outside has a duty to keep clear of the other side of the fairway or not was raised. If not, the cause of collision was incurred by Fortune Miracle's entering into the other side of the fairway.

537. When the special committee made the guideline, they took into consideration the extent of the culpability of each vessel when it acted or did not act against its duty imposed in the provisions of the COLREG. It also referred to case materials in relation to the apportionment of liability rendered by the civil courts.[104] The KMST started to apply the guideline to the collision case as of January 1, 2007.

104. The writer published several articles on the apportionment of liability in case of the collision; In Hyeon, Kim, *Maritime Treatises* (2003), 806; In Hyeon, Kim, The Relationship between the KMST's Decision and the Apportionment of Liability In Case of the collision, Bup Jo 562 (2003): 91.

Chapter 14. Marine Pollution

§1. General

I. Necessity for Special Treatment

538. Generally speaking, oil pollution is a kind of tort. Victims who sustain damages resulting from pollution have a right to claim compensation from the wrongdoer based on the cause of action in tort.

539. Oil pollution damages have several different aspects from general pollution damages. Victims who suffer damages caused by oil pollution usually do not enter into insurance arrangements. Victims as plaintiffs do not have easy access to prove the negligence of the shipowner as the defendant. If general maritime law applies to the case, the owner of the vessel can limit its liability, and thus, the victims cannot be fully compensated to restore their livelihood. Taking into consideration this special circumstance, the special laws to protect victims were made internationally or domestically.

II. CLC and Bunker Convention

540. Two main sources of oil pollution by ship are crude oil and bunker. Crude oil becomes the source of oil pollution when it is discharged to the sea by an oil tanker laden with the oil as the cargo. Bunker is a kind of fuel required for a vessel to propel. Almost all ocean-going vessels use bunker as a fuel. When a general cargo vessel goes aground and leaks the bunker to the sea, oil pollution occurs.

541. International maritime community made the CLC and the IOPC FUND regimes in order to regulate compensation caused by the oil pollution from oil tankers. In addition, the Bunker Convention regulating pollution compensation caused by bunker oil took effect in 2008.

542. Korea is a contracting state to the 1992 CLC, the 1992 IOPC FUND Convention and the Bunker Convention. In addition, it became a state party to the Supplementary Fund to the 1992 IOPC FUND Convention in 2010. Korea enacted a domestic law called the Korean Oil Pollution Compensation Act (KOPCA) in 1992. It was revised in 2003 in accordance with the revision of the 1992 CLC and the IOPC FUND Convention for increasing the limitation amount of tanker owners and the IOPC FUND. Once again, it was revised in 2009 to implement the Bunker Convention and the Supplementary Fund Protocol.

III. Pollution Cases in Korea

543. The Sea Prince accident in 1995 and the Hebei Spirit accident in 2007 are recorded as the two major oil pollution cases in Korea. Except for these two accidents, Korea has experienced dozens of oil pollution cases since Korea's ratification of the IOPC FUND Convention in 2010.

§2. Oil Pollution from Oil Tanker

I. Definition

544. The oil pollution from an oil tanker is applicable only for oil pollution caused by crude oil or bunker from oil tankers other than general cargo vessels. The bunker oil pollution from general cargo vessels had been regulated by tort law in the Civil Code; however, since 2010, it has also been governed by the Bunker Convention and the KOPCA.

II. Source of Law

545. Korea is a contracting state of both the 1992 CLC and the 1992 IOPC FUND Convention.[105] In addition, Korea has a separate national law named as the KOPCA. Most of the provisions in the KOPCA are identical to those of the 1992 CLC and the FUND Convention. However, there are several differences between the 1992 CLC and the KOPCA.

III. Geographical Scope of Application

546. The KOPCA shall apply exclusively to pollution damages and to preventive measures to prevent or minimize such damages caused in the territorial seas and in the EEZ in Korea.

IV. Strict Liability

547. Under the KOPCA, the registered owner is strictly liable for oil pollution damages (KOPCA Article 4(1); CLC Article 3(1)). By imposing strict liability upon the registered owner, the claimant is not required to prove that the damages were caused by the fault of the servant or agent of the shipowner.

548. Under the KOPCA Article 4(4), the Korean-registered bareboat charterer is held liable jointly and severally with the registered owner. The Korean government

105. Korea is the third largest contributor for the 1992 FUND.

tries to secure compensation fully by imposing liability upon the bareboat charterer, in addition to the owner, unlike the 1992 CLC.[106]

549. The CLC adopts a so-called channeling system, which means that only the registered owner of the tanker is liable for oil pollution damages. Even though the vessel is operated by the bareboat charterer, the responsible party to the victims caused by the oil pollution is the registered owner other than the bareboat charterer or the master of the vessel who commits tort. The victims are not allowed to raise a lawsuit against charterers, master of the vessel, pilots or classification societies. The registered owner of the oil tanker who paid the damages is entitled to make a recourse claim against the responsible party who contributed to the damage only if the party acted with intention or recklessly. The registered owner of the oil tanker is the person to prepare for financial security for the victims caused by the oil pollution. Unlike the CLC, the bareboat charterer is the responsible party with the registered owner under the KOPCA.

V. Compulsory Insurance and Direct Action

550. In order to protect victims resulting from oil pollution accidents, the KOPCA requires the registered owner of tankers and the bareboat charterer to provide liability insurance or other financial security. This insurance is a kind of compulsory liability insurance (KOPCA Article 14; CLC Article 7(1)).[107] By prohibiting vessels without compulsory insurance from entering Korean ports, the above legal scheme is implemented effectively (KOPCA Article 14(4) and (5)).

551. Victims are entitled to invoke a direct action against the liability insurer of the vessel (KOPCA Article 16; CLC Article 7(8)). Even though the victims do not have any contractual relation with the insurer, the victims come to have the legal right to claim insurance proceeds against the insurer by the operation of the law. It is a very useful tool to protect the victims when the owner of the oil tanker, who is liable for pollution damages, goes bankrupt. The victims also have another cause of action against the liability insurer pursuant to Article 724(2) of the KCC.

552. The most noticeable difference between the 1992 CLC and the KOPCA is the threshold tonnage for compulsory insurance. Under the KOPCA, the vessel carrying more than 200 tons of oil in bulk should have compulsory liability insurance, whereas, under the 1992 CLC, a vessel carrying more than 2,000 tons of oil in bulk should have it. The Korean government lowered the threshold tonnage from 2,000 tons down to 200 tons in order to protect the victims caused by oil pollution.

---

106. A practitioner argues that the provision should be amended because it treats Korean bareboat charterer unfavorably as opposed to the case in the IOPC FUND. Jong Hyun, Choi, *Opinion on the revision of Korean Oil Pollution Compensation Act*, Journal of KMLA, 28(1) (2006.4.): 118.

107. The KOPCA Art. 14 says that vessel carrying more than 200 tons of oil in bulk shall be required to maintain insurance of other financial security, the vessel include Korean-flagged vessel and foreign-flagged vessel as well.

553. Furthermore, the victims have a legal right to pursue claims against the 1992 FUND in the Korean court pursuant to the FUND Conventions (KOPCA Article 23). In the recent major oil pollution case of *M/T Hebei Spirit* in 2007, the victims brought a lawsuit against the 1992 IOPC FUND in a Korean court.

VI. Shipowner's Right to Limit Its Liability

554. The registered shipowner is entitled to limit its liability (KOPCA Article 6(1); CLC Article 5(1)). The limitation level is identical to that of the CLC. These figures are higher than that of the general 1976 LLMC for the purpose of protecting the victims caused by the oil pollution. The liability of the registered owner is limited only to that of oil pollution caused by the crude oil as the cargo on board the tanker and caused by the bunker from the oil tanker. Where an oil tanker collides with a certain berth at the port as a result of which the oil was leaked, the damages of the owner of the berth are not included in the liability under the KOPCA. Only the damages sustained by the victim due to oil pollution fall within the category of liability under the KOPCA. Because the oil pollution damages are treated as being separate and independent from other claims, the victims who resulted from oil pollution are protected with higher compensation as opposed to the claimant under the KCC (or general LLMC).

555. The owner of an oil tanker is entitled to limit its liability to an amount calculated as follows: (a) 4,510,000 SDR for a ship not exceeding 5,000 units of tonnage; (b) for a ship with a tonnage in excess thereof for each additional unit of tonnage, 631 SDR in addition to the amount mentioned in (a); provided, however, that this aggregate amount shall not in any event exceed 89,770,000 SDR.

556. The owners shall not be entitled to limit their liability if it is proved that the pollution damage resulted from its personal act or omission, committed with the intent to cause such damages, or recklessly and with the knowledge that such damages would probably result (reckless behavior) (KOPCA Article 6(1): CLC Article 5(2)). The claimant's proving the above is not easy, and thus, there is no reported case that the owner's limitation right was broken under the KOPCA. In the above *Hebei Spirit* case, the limitation court admitted the registered owner of the vessel to avail of the limitation of the liability because the claimant did not prove that the damages were caused by the owner's intentional act or reckless behavior.

VII. Time Bar

557. The owner enjoys a benefit of a shorter period of time bar of three years after the damages incurred (Article 11) as opposed to the time bar of ten years after the tort was committed under the Korean Civil Code Article 766(2)

VIII. Maritime Lien Allowed to the Claimants

558. The KOPCA Article 43 allows the claimants who suffered from oil pollution to exercise maritime lien against the vessel which caused the damages. This maritime lien is inferior to the general maritime lien stipulated in the KCC Article 777. It is not stipulated in the CLC. Under Korean law, the maritime lien is regarded as a means of counterbalance against the shipowner's right to limit its liability. Therefore, it appears that the KOPCA intends to give the victims a kind of protective measure against the registered owner, who is entitled to limit its liability.[108] However, now that the registered owner should maintain a compulsory liability insurance or financial security for the victims, the presence of KOPCA Article 43 seems redundant, except that the registered owner does not provide such insurance.

IX. Separate Procedural Rules for Limitation

559. When the registered owner tries to invoke the right to limit its liability, it should apply for limitation procedure in a separate court from the court which deals with merits of the case. For this purpose, Korea has an act called the Shipowner's Limitation of Liability Procedural Act (SLLPA).

560. The KOPCA has several special procedural provisions for the shipowner to invoke its right to limit liability. The court for limitation procedure should order the applicant to deposit the limitation amount in the court within fourteen days if the court admits that the application for the commencement of the limitation procedure is reasonable (Article 35(1)).

X. Provision on IOPC FUND

561. Korea is a state party to the 1992 IOPC FUND and the Supplementary FUND. The KOPCA has several provisions to implement the IOPC FUND system. The victims have a right to receive compensation from the IOPC FUND in accordance with the Fund Convention (Article 21). The 1992 IOPC FUND is an eligible defendant pursuant to the KOPCA Article 22 in Korea. The 1992 IOPC FUND is entitled to participate in the limitation procedure in Korea (KOPCA Article 36).

562. Any person who receives in total quantities exceeding 150,000 tons per year in a Korean port should pay a contribution to the IOPC FUND (KOPCA Article 31(1)).

563. According to IOPC FUND Convention, the FUND has an obligation to pay compensation to the victims where: (i) the registered owner's liability was limited, and thus, there is gap between the damaged amount sustained by the victims and

108. In Hyeon Kim, *supra*, 314.

legally payable amount; (ii) the responsible registered owner is financially incapable of meeting his obligations in full to pay the damages for the victims; (iii) no liability for the damage arises under the 1992 CLC such as the responsible party for damages is not found (Article 4(1)). 1992 FUND's maximum available compensation amount is 230,000,000 SDR and that of the Supplementary FUND is 750,000,000 SDR.

XI. Special Act for M/T Hebei Spirit Oil Pollution Accident

564. The worst oil pollution accident in Korean history occurred on the west coast of Korea on December 7, 2007. About 10,500 tons of crude oil escaped from the Hebei Spirit into the sea.[109] The Hebei Spirit at anchor was collided by the tug and barges under the control of Samsung Heavy Industry Co., Ltd. At the initial stage, the total damage was thought to easily exceed the maximum amount payable by the 1992 IOPC FUND. The owner of the Hebei Sprit is entitled to limit its liability up to KRW 12 million. The 1992 FUND is liable for up to KRW 32 million.[110] According to the 1992 FUND, the total damages will range from KRW 53 million to KRW 57 million. Therefore, there is a huge gap between the actual damages and the expected compensation amount.

565. The Korean government passed the Special Act for compensating victims fully and promptly in March 2008 and it became effective as of June 15, 2008. The Special Act aims at empowering victims to receive full amount of damages over the limitation amount of the 1992 FUND from the Korean government (Article 9(1)(2)). Under the Special Act, the recoverable amount is to be decided by the assessment of the IOPC FUND's damage surveyors (Article 8(2)). Victims are entitled to receive advance payment from the Korean government in exchange for the recourse right against the FUND (Article 8(1)(2)(3)). Victims can request the government for a loan for the amount fixed in advance if they have not received any offer of compensation from the shipowner's P&I Club and the 1992 FUND within six months from the date of submission of their claims pursuant to Article 8(5) and (6). The Korean government will compensate the remainder between the assessed amounts by the FUND and actually paid by the P&I Club and the FUND (Article 9), which means that the victims are treated as if there was no limitation scheme in the case, and thus, the victims can be compensated fully without any limitation to payable amount.

566. Now that the total claims may easily exceed the limitation amount of the 1992 FUND in the Hebei Spirit oil pollution accident, the Korean government tried to have a more secure legal system with full compensation scheme for victims than the current system. Since then, Korea ratified the Supplementary Fund in 2010 and

109. The Hebei Spirit was at anchor when the tug-barge collided. The Hebei Spirit argued that it did not breach duty of care to prevent the collision.
110. 92 FUND/EXC. 41/9/Add2.

it seems that the special law is no longer required in the future oil pollution accident in Korea. Victims in Korea will be fully compensated by the IOPC FUND regimes, including the Supplementary Fund. However, there are several proposals to establish an additional compensation regime for the purpose of shortening compensation duration.[111, 112]

567. The Hebei Spirit oil spill case was concluded through the limitation of liability proceedings. The Seosan Branch of the Daejeon District Court ruled that out of the 4 trillion KRW (127,000 claims) in damage claims, only 432.9 billion KRW was eligible for compensation. Of this amount, the Hebei Spirit shipowner limited their liability to 186.8 billion KRW. The IOPC FUND was responsible for compensation of up to 321 billion KRW (including the amount to be paid by the shipowner). The additional 111.9 billion KRW beyond the 321 billion KRW was covered by the South Korean government under a special law. Some of the recipients of the compensation raised objections to the distribution table. The case was finally concluded on August 30, 2019, when the Supreme Court made a ruling on the re-appeal.

§3. Bunker Oil Pollution

I. Definition

568. Motor vessels propelled by engine need bunker oil as a fuel. When a vessel is grounded on the rock at sea, the bunker at the bottom tank may be discharged and become the source of oil pollution. Until 2009, no special legal regime was introduced, and thus, general commercial law and civil law were applicable for the case. In order to protect victims caused by bunker oil pollution, a new approach different from general civil law principle was required. The new approach includes strict liability imposed upon the owner of the vessel and implementing compulsory insurance.

II. Source of Law

569. The CLC and IOPC FUND Convention deal with only oil pollution from oil tankers. In order to cope with oil pollution from bunker from the general cargo

111. In Hyeon Kim & Se Ryoun Choi, *Canadian Oil Pollution Compensation Fund Regime and its Implication for Korea,* Journal of KMLA 32-2 (2010): 167.
112. Samsung Heavy Industry Co., Ltd who was mainly liable for the accident successfully applied for the ship owner's limitation of liability and its liability was limited to KRW 5.6 billion. However, the owner of Hebei Spirit and IOPC FUND jointly brought about lawsuit against Samsung Heavy Industry before the Ningbo Maritime Court in China in 2010. As a result, two different limitation proceedings will eventually compete in both Korea and China. If both Korea and China are contracting states to 1976 LLMC, Korea will be admitted as a sole forum for the limitation proceeding according to 1976 LLMC Art. 13(1). The proceeding before the Ningbo Maritime Court was rejected by the court due to lack of the jurisdiction. The court regarded that the Korean court had more substantial relation with the cases than China.

vessel, the international maritime community made the Bunker Convention. It came into force on November 21, 2008. Korea ratified it in 2009 (hereinafter "2009 KOPCA"). The Korean government revised the KOPCA in 2009 in order to implement the Bunker Convention in Korea.

III. Strict Liability

570. As in the case of oil pollution from oil tanker, the owner in case of oil pollution from bunker is also strictly liable for pollution damages (Article 43). By imposing strict liability on the registered shipowner (2009 KOPCA Article 43(1); the Bunker Convention Article 3(1)), the victim's heavy burden to prove the presence of the wrongdoer's fault is lifted, and thus, the victim will be in a favorable position in the litigation as opposed to the general tort case.

571. Unlike CLC, the Bunker Convention could not adopt the so-called channeling system. Therefore, the registered owner is not the sole responsible party to the oil pollution damages. The bareboat charterer or time charterer or manager or operator of the vessel can be an obligor to pay compensation for the damages against the oil pollution victims (Article 1(iii), Article 3(1)). However, the KOPCA applies for the same rule as the oil tanker, and thus, the registered owner and bareboat charterers are only responsible parties to the pollution damages (Article 43, Article 5(4)).

IV. Limitation of Liability

572. The most noticeable difference between the 1992 CLC and the Bunker Convention is that the latter does not have a free-standing limitation mechanism for the owner (Bunker Convention Article 6). The convention just connects the limitation mechanism with the LLMC or domestic law. As a result, the protection of victims caused by bunker oil pollution is not fully satisfactory.

573. There was confusion in Korea for a year on whether the removal expenses of the oil pollution from the general cargo vessel were part of damages subject to the limitation of the shipowner like that in the case of the oil tanker.

In the Pusan High Court case *2012.10.29. Docket No. 2012ra61*, an oil pollution removal company requested payment for the removal of oil pollution to the shipowner. The owner applied for the shipowner's limitation of liability under the KOPCA. The court accepted the application, saying that the shipowner has the right to invoke the limitation of the liability against claims for the removal expenses caused by the bunker oil from the general cargo vessel pursuant to Article 45 of the KOPCA. Soon after the above decision, the Korean government admitted that Article 45 had been misstated against the Bunker Convention and revised Article 45 once again in 2013. Under the current Article 45 of the KOPCA, it is very clear that the removal expenses of oil pollution from the general cargo vessel are not subject to the limitation.

574. For example, let's say that, as the consequence of the collision accident: (i) the opposing vessel's ten crew died; (ii) the opposing vessel's cargo was damaged; and (iii) the fishermen's cultivating fishes perished by the leaked bunker oil. In this case, three parties, such as crews' family (USD 3 million), cargo interests (USD 4 million) and fishermen (USD 7 million), may have claims against the owner. If we have a special and distinctive limitation mechanism for the victims caused by oil pollution as in the 1992 CLC, the fishermen will be only the sole claimant who is eligible for obtaining limitation fund (e.g., USD 7 million) set by the 1992 CLC or the KOPCA because it is set up for the purpose of compensating victims caused by the oil pollution. However, under the current Bunker oil pollution case, the fisherman should be treated just as a claimant among three claimants in relation to the distribution of the limitation fund (USD 7 million). Accordingly, the portion of the fisherman to be allocated (USD 3.5 million) is lower than that of the otherwise CLC case (USD 7 million).

575. The new KOPCA states that the minimum amount of insurance for the owner to provide is based on the limitation amount for only property damages rather than for the property damage plus death and personal injury damage (2009 KOPCA Article 48(3)). However, the Japanese OPCA requires the owner to provide liability insurance with a minimum insurance amount calculated based on the property damages plus death and personal injury damages in the limitation amount (Japanese OPCA Article 39-5(3)).[113] Japan increased the global limitation amount by adopting the 1996 protocol to the 1976 LLMC in 2005. However, Korea still remains the country applying a limitation amount of 1976 LLMC in the KCC. Accordingly, under KOPCA, the guaranteed insurance amount is relatively too low as compared with that of the Japanese OPCA. It appears that now that many Korean-flagged vessels are engaged in entering a Japanese port, the Korean owners may inevitably buy insurance guaranteeing the higher amount which the Japanese OPCA requires.

V. Compulsory Insurance and Direct Action

576. The registered owner of a ship having a gross tonnage greater than 1,000 registered in Korea shall be required to maintain liability insurance or other financial security (2009 KOPCA Article 47(1); Bunker Convention Article 7(1)). By the operation of the law, the victim has a right of direct action (2009 KOPCA Articles 49 and 16; Bunker Convention Article 7(10)) against the liability insurer, which means that it can claim the insurance proceeds for the damage against the insurer of the wrongdoer. As a result, the victims can be protected from bunker oil pollution damages. Under the current civil law and commercial law regime, the victims cannot be protected if the owner does not have enough assets for compensation.

113. Because damage to the person will be occurred in the accident of the general cargo vessel, the limitation fund may be required to be established in the death and personal injury damage claims as well as property damage claims. However, Southampton on Shipping Law says that the convention does not cover the damage to the death and personal damages but covers the damage to the property and thus the available limits are, at most, one-third of the total limitation fund. Institute of Maritime Law, Southampton on *Shipping Law*, Informa (2008), 272.

577. Under the basic principle of the insurance law, the victim does not have any legal relationship with the insurer because it is not one of the parties in the insurance contract. In order to protect the victims, the KCC allows the victim to claim damages against the insurer directly (Article 724(2)).[114] The KOPCA also introduced a direct action provision (Article 16) based on the 1992 CLC (Article 7(8)). The provision is different from that of the KCC in that the insurer cannot invoke the so-called pay-to-be-paid rule. There is a room for the P&I insurer to invoke the pay-to-be-paid rule against the victims under KCC Article 724(2).[115] However, the KOPCA Article 16(1), like the 1992 CLC, does not allow it. The 2009 KOPCA has a *mutatis mutandis* provision on direct action in case of bunker oil pollution.

578. The new KOPCA adopts 1,000 tons as the threshold tonnage for compulsory insurance in line with the Bunker Convention. (KOPCA Article 42-4 Article 1)).[116] It appears that the threshold tonnage is too high under Korean law. According to the statistics, there is a strong tendency that the Korean-flagged small vessels do not have liability insurance,[117] and thus, there is a possibility that the victims cannot be fully protected.

VI. No Additional Compensation Scheme

579. Unlike oil pollution from an oil tanker, there is no additional mechanism by way of compensation from the fund contributed by the oil receiver, which means that the victims of bunker oil pollution are not protected fully as opposed to the case of oil pollution from oil tanker.

VII. Maritime Lien

580. The claimant has a maritime lien upon the vessel involved in the accident, its accessory, and freight unpaid (2009 KOPCA Article 51(1)). However, this maritime lien has the lowest priority than that stipulated in the KCC Article 777 (2009 KOPCA Article 51(2)).

114. Japanese Commercial Code does not have identical provisions.

115. In Hyeon Kim, *supra*, 344.

116. Japanese OPCA requires vessel over 100 tons to have compulsory insurance contract (Japanese OPCA Art. 39-4(1).

117. The following three cases involving small oil tankers No. 3 Osung (786 tons) in 1997, Kyungwon (144 tons) in 2003, and No. 7 Kwangmin (139 tons) in 2005 were the cases in which the IOPC FUND paid compensation for the victims based on the fact that the shipowner does not maintain liability insurance. Therefore, it can be inferred that the several general cargo vessel under 1000 tons does not have liability insurance in Korea.

§4. Other Oil Pollution

581. The CLC or KOPCA is applicable for oil pollution caused by persistent crude oil. Accordingly, if the oil pollution accident occurs due to the pollution caused by the non-persistent oil or Liquefied Natural Gas (LNG), the compensation should be based on general tort law principle in the Korean Civil Code or the limitation of liability scheme in the KCC.

582. Korea neither has ratified the International Convention on Liability and Compensation for Damage in connection with the Carriage of Hazardous and Noxious Substances by Sea, 1996 (HNS Convention) nor has a domestic law to implement the same.

583. There was a totally different kind of oil pollution. In the case of the M/T Uisan accident, oil was leaked from an oil refinery facility after it was hit by M/T Uisan on January 31, 2014. Because the oil pollution came not from a vessel but from an oil refinery facility at shore, the KOPCA was not applicable. Instead, tort law in the Korean Civil Code was applicable to the case. The owner of the oil refinery facility was not allowed to invoke global limitation of the liability.

Chapter 15. The Arrest of Ships

§1. General

584. Korea is not a party to the Arrest Conventions. Therefore, only Korean domestic laws are applicable for the arrest of ships. Ships are arrested by way of four different types of arrest in Korea: prejudgment attachment, attachment based on maritime lien or mortgage, and arrest for executing wining judgment.

§2. Prejudgment Attachment

585. In order for the claimant to secure its claims in an earlier stage of disputes, the Korean law allows the claimant to apply for prejudgment attachment in accordance with the Korean Civil Execution Act (KCEA) Article 279. According to the Korean law, if the debtor hands over its property to a third party, the claimant cannot execute the property of the debtor even though it won the lawsuit against the debtor in merit. The possible claimants are entitled to apply for arresting a ship to secure its claims even before it wins the lawsuit in merit, according to the KCEA Article 276. Korea is known as one of the countries which allow the claimant to arrest the ship owned by the obligor very easily.

586. For successful prejudgment attachment, the claimant should: (i) establish the existence of an enforceable right against the debtor, and (ii) show that the provisional remedy is necessary for securing the execution of a subsequent judgment in merit.

587. The claimant may obtain a prejudgment attachment of a vessel owned by the debtor (such as shipowner). In this case, any vessel which belongs to the debtor, even any other assets which belong to the debtor, in addition to the vessel involved in the accident, is also subject to the attachment by the claimant. In contrast, the claimant based on the maritime lien is allowed to arrest only the vessel which caused the claim.

588. Furthermore, the claimant is allowed to apply for the prejudgment attachment against any property of the debtor with any kind of claim, not limited to the maritime-related claim. For example, claimant A as the shipper is eligible for arresting a vessel owned by the debtor with the cargo damages claim against the debtor as the shipowner. In addition, it is also allowed to arrest another vessel owned by the debtor with the personal injury claims at shore against the debtor.

589. An application may be made to the court having jurisdiction over the location of the vessel or to the court having jurisdiction on the merits of the case. If an application for prejudgment attachment is made, the court reviews the application and, if it intends to grant the application, the court orders the claimant to provide counter security. In case of a vessel, the amount of counter security may be about 10% of the claims amount. Counter security may be provided with a bond. As soon as the counter security is provided, the court issues the decision ordering to allow the prejudgment attachment on the vessel as requested by the claimant.

590. The attachment is recorded on the ship record book, which prevents the debtor from changing the ownership of the vessel, and as a result, the owner of the vessel is not able to sell the vessel to others, that is, maintaining status quo.

591. In order for the claimant to sell the vessel, a winning judgment is further required in the subsequent lawsuit for the merit. In order for the shipowner to release the arrested vessel, it should deposit "cash" equivalent to the claim amount to the court (Civil Execution Act, Article 299(1)).

592. Because the prejudgment attachment order alone would not effectively detain the vessel physically in Korea, an application for the maintenance and preservation order is usually made in a case where the vessel is not a Korean vessel. The shipowner may raise an objection to the attachment order. The shipowner may seek the cancelation of enforcing the prejudgment attachment order by paying the court cash deposit equivalent to the claim amount.

§3. Arrest by Claimant as Security Holder

593. The claimant is also entitled to arrest the vessel as a mortgagee. Similar to a prejudgment attachment, the claimant is not required to have a winning judgment. It has the power to arrest the vessel and apply for judicial sale through the application to the court, verifying that it is the mortgagee and the mortgagor has not paid the money by the due date. This is also applicable to all kinds of mortgage situations, not only mortgages on the vessel.

594. The court gives the decision for the arrestor to sell the vessel and an order for the vessel to be stayed at the designated port upon receiving the application for the arrest, and the arrestor provides requirements such as the existence of the security right.

§4. Attachment such as Maritime Lien

595. The other type of arrest is the arrest by way of a maritime lien. The KCC allows the claimant with maritime claims to arrest the vessel involved in the accident for auction sale in accordance with the KCC Article 777. Even though the obligor is not the owner of the vessel, the claimant is entitled to arrest the vessel. It is a big difference from the arrest by way of prejudgment attachment. In the latter, the property subject to prejudgment attachment should be owned by the obligor.

596. The maritime lien is allowed without a lawsuit in merit, which is the same as the prejudgment attachment and mortgage situation. It does not need to record the presence of the maritime lien on the ship record book, which is different from the prejudgment attachment and mortgage. The maritime lien holder is allowed to arrest only the relevant vessel, which is the same as a mortgage situation and different from the prejudgment attachment and winning judgment case.

597. The maritime lien holder is still entitled to exercise its right against the vessel even though the vessel's ownership title has changed to another person from the debtor.

598. Just like the arrest by the claimant with a winning judgment, the claimant is not required to provide any bonds for the benefit of the debtor because it is the security holder. In order for it to release its vessel under the judicial sale process, the shipowner should apply for cancelation or temporary stoppage of the process with another lawsuit to argue that the process is wrong, depositing cash equivalent to the claim amount.

599. The claims which give rise to maritime lien are listed in the KCC Article 777.[118] These claims are relevant to the Korean-registered vessels. When a foreign vessel is the subject of the arrest based on maritime lien, the claims which trigger maritime lien should be determined by reference to the law of the vessel's flag country in accordance with the KPIL.

600. A maritime lien holder or a mortgagee of a vessel may request the commencement of an auction sale of the vessel, and the court would order the vessel to remain at the place where the vessel is attached (KCEA Articles 269 and 176).

601. The court having jurisdiction over the place where the vessel is located at the time of the attachment has jurisdiction (KCEA Article 173). The claimant may submit an application for the commencement of auction procedure to the court having jurisdiction. The auction costs should be paid in advance by the applicant. A decision granting the commencement of an auction sale of a vessel may be obtained on the day of making the application for the same or on the following day.

§5. Arrest by Claimant with Winning Judgment

602. The claimant is also allowed to arrest and sell the vessel after it obtains a winning judgment from the court. The cargo claimant may bring a lawsuit against the carrier before a Korean court. Only after it obtains a winning judgment does it become entitled to apply for the document of executing the wining judgment. The claimant with such document goes to the bailiff in order to arrest the vessel of the debtor and to sell it in the auction sale to satisfy its claim. The claimant with the winning judgment has the power to sell the debtor's property which is the major difference from that of the prejudgment attachment.

118. Please refer to Ch. 2.

603. The claimant is not required to provide any bond for the benefit of the debtor because it has a winning judgment. In order for the shipowner to release its vessel under the judicial sale process, it should apply for cancelation or temporary stoppage of the process with another lawsuit to argue that the process is wrong, depositing cash equivalent to the claim amount.

§6. Korean Law and Arrest Convention

604. Korea is neither a contracting party to the 1952 Arrest Convention nor to the 1999 Arrest Convention. In addition, Korea does not reflect the convention in Korean domestic law.

605. Under Korean law, a claimant can obtain security for its claim by way of prejudgment attachment against another vessel which the debtor owns in addition to the vessel itself which brought about the debt. However, the claimants cannot apply for the arrest of the vessel which does not belong to the debtor. However, under the 1999 Arrest Convention, the claimants are entitled to apply for the arrest of the vessel which does not belong to the debtor (Article 3(2)).

606. The claimants are entitled to apply for prejudgment attachment based on any kind of claims not limited to maritime claims against the obligor, such as the carrier or the owner, according to Korean law. However, the claimants are entitled to apply it only with the maritime claims related to the numerated maritime businesses according to the Arrest Convention.

607. There is a provision in the KCC to the effect that the vessel ready for sailing should be allowed neither to the prejudgment attachment arrest nor to the arrest unless the claim stems from the preparation for the sailing. However, the provision is not effective in practice in Korea.

Chapter 16. Carriage of Passengers

§1. General

I. Definition

608. A contract for the carriage of passenger at sea is that the carrier undertakes to carry a passenger from a departing port to an arrival port by ship at sea and that the passenger agrees to pay remuneration for the carriage to the carrier (Article 817).

II. Practice in Korea

609. Inland carriage does not fall into the Maritime Law section in the KCC. The carriages of passengers: (i) among ports in mainland Korea, (ii) between ports in mainland Korea and several islands in Korea, and (iii) between ports in Korea and ports in neighboring countries such as Japan, China, and Russia are subject to the Maritime Law section in the KCC.

610. Several Korean passenger shipping companies run the business of carrying passengers between Korea and Japan, China and Northeastern Russia. They use not the cruise vessel but the car-ferry vessel. They carry passengers and cargo together on board one vessel. There is neither an owner nor a carrier for the cruise vessel in Korea. Korean government pursues raising number of tourists through cruise vessels visiting Korean ports.

§2. Liability of the Carrier

611. Because there is no effective International Convention on the Civil Liability of the Carriage of Passenger, regulating legal relationship between the carrier and passenger are totally left to the domestic law. Korea is not a party to any international convention for the carriage of passengers at sea.

612. The KCC has several provisions on the carriage of passengers at sea. Party autonomy prevails over the provisions in the KCC except in the case of passenger's death or personal injury case. General terms in the passenger ticket play as evidence to verify the presence of contract for the carriage of passenger.

613. The legal regimes in the contract for carriage of passenger in the KCC are divided into three different parts: (i) passenger's death or personal injury case, (ii) luggage of passengers entrusted to the carrier, and (iii) luggage of passengers not entrusted to the carrier.

614. For the passenger's death or personal injury case, the same provisions in the contract for carriage of passenger in land in the KCC are applicable, *mutatis mutandis* to the case (Article 826(1)). Accordingly, the carrier's liability is based on the presumed fault liability (Article 148). Unless the carrier proves that it or its servant did exercise due diligence for the carriage, the carrier is liable for the death or personal injury of the passenger. The carrier has a duty to make the ship seaworthy (Articles 826(1) and 794(1)). The agreement to derogate from the carrier's obligation and liability is null and void (Articles 826(1) and 799(1)).

615. For the luggage of passengers entrusted to the carrier, several provisions of the common carriage of goods in the KCC are applicable, *mutatis mutandis* to the case (Article 826(2)). The carrier's liability is based on the presumed fault liability (Article 795(1)). The carrier has duty to make ship seaworthy. The carrier has right to invoke the package limitation in accordance with the KCC Article 797. The agreement to derogate from the carrier's these obligations and liability is null and void (Articles 826(2) and 799(1)).

616. For the luggage of passengers not entrusted to the carrier, the provisions in the carriage of passenger in land are applicable to the case (Article 826(3)). According to the KCC Article 150, the carrier is not liable for the damages of the luggage not entrusted to it if there is no fault of the carrier or its servant, which means unless the passenger proves that the damages were caused by the fault of the carrier or its servant, the carrier is not liable for the damages. It is a big difference from the case of the entrusted luggage case.

§3. Carrier's Limitation of Liability

617. The KCC allows the carrier of the passenger to invoke the global limitation. In the 2007 revision of the KCC, the Korean government introduced the global limitation provision in the 1996 Protocol to the 1976 LLMC in respect of the passenger to the KCC. The carrier's maximum amount of global limitation is calculated based on 175,000 SDR multiplied by the maximum allowable number of passengers for the relevant vessel (The KCC Article 770(1)). However, the KCC does not adopt the limitation scheme for the carrier based on each passenger.[119] Under the current Korean law, the carrier can invoke the limitation based on each passenger by way of individual agreement in the contract for the carriage of passenger unless it is against the compulsory provision in the KCC.

618. Therefore, it can be said that the carrier for passenger ship is not fully protected because it is not allowed to limit its liability per passenger in a normal accident case as opposed to a big accident such as total loss of the vessel. There is a call for adopting limitation of liability scheme per passenger like the Athens Convention relating to the carriage of passengers and their luggage by sea in 1974. The

119. According to Protocol to Amend the Athens Convention Relating to the Carriage of Passengers and Their Luggage by Sea (1990) (1990 Athens Convention) the carrier's liability for the death of or personal injury to a passenger shall in no case exceed 175,000 SDR per carriage (Protocol Art. II, Athens Convention Art. 7(1)).

1974 Athens Convention came into force on April 28, 1987. The carrier is entitled to limit its liability to 46,666 SDR under the 1974 Athens Convention. This figure is too law, and thus, it is desirable for the Korean government to adopt 175,000 SDR as the limitation amount, the same as the 1990 Protocol to Athens Convention.[120]

619. The KCC does not impose upon the carrier to buy liability insurance to cover compensation against the death or loss of lives of passengers. However, it is a usual manner in Korea that the carrier of passenger boat enters into the liability insurance with a kind of P&I club in Korea. The insurance amount to be paid by the Korean Shipping Association per passenger as the liability insurer is about USD 300,000 (about an equal amount to 175,000 SDR).

620. On April 16, 2014, the tragic ferry (The Sewol) accident occurred on the south coast of the Korean Peninsula. The ferry capsized due to the lack of stability. About 300 innocent passengers died as a result of the accident. The Sewol was a car-ferry (vehicular ferry), and thus, at the time of the accident, the cars, containers, and passengers were on board. Chunghaejin as the carrier is liable for the loss of cargo and death of passengers due to breach of contract for the carriage and tort. Unless the Chunghaejin proves that it exercised reasonable care for the carriage, it is liable for the damages in accordance with the KCC Articles 794, 825 and 148.

621. Passenger claims became a major issue soon after the accident. According to the KCC, the passenger carrier does not have any right to limit its liability per passenger. However, it has a right to limit its liability in accordance with the general terms. According to the general terms between Chunghaejin and passenger, Chunghajin's liability is limited to KRW 350 million (about USD 300,000). About 300 passengers on board the vessel died or are still missing. Therefore, the carrier's total liability against the passenger is limited to KRW 300 million x KRW 350 million = KRW 105 billion (about USD 100 million).[121]

120. The 2002 Athens Convention increased the limitation amount to 400,000 SDR per passenger.
121. For details, In Hyeon Kim, *The Sewol Accident and Its Legal Implication*, 45-2 HKLJ 554 (2015).

Part III. Other Transport

Chapter 1. Transport by Road and Rail

§1. GENERAL

I. Definition

622. Transportation by road and rail is regulated in the same section of the KCC. The title of the section in the KCC is the transportation in land. It can be defined as the contract for carriage of goods or passenger by road or rail. The carrier undertakes to transport goods or passengers from departing place to arrival place and, in turn, the shipper promises to pay charges to the carrier.

623. The parties in the contract for carriage of goods in land are the carrier and the shipper. The consignor is the person who sends the goods to the consignee. The consignee is the person who is entitled to receive the goods. The consignor is not necessarily the shipper who enters into contract for the carriage with the carrier.

II. Practice in Korea

624. Geographically, Korea is located in the Korean Peninsula, which connects to the Asian continent. Therefore, theoretically, there is a high possibility that the goods may be transported by road or by rail from Korea to neighboring countries such as China, Russia, and even European countries. However, in reality, the Korean Peninsula is divided into South Korea and North Korea. Because there is no diplomatic relation between South and North Korea, the use of road or rail by the other side is not permitted. As a result of the above political and geographical circumstances, transportation by road and rail is not engaged in the international movement of logistics.

625. Korean Railway Company, supported by the government subsidy, operates transportation by rail. The governing law for transportation by rail in Korea is not different from that for transportation by road. The KCC is the governing law for both transport by road and by rail.

§2. SOURCE OF LAW

I. KCC

626. The governing law for the carriage of goods by road and rail is Chapter 9 (land transportation) in Book II of the KCC. If there is no provision in the section, relevant provisions in the Korean Civil Code will be applicable. The provisions in Chapter 9 play as the basic rules for the various contracts for the carriage such as the contract for the goods by sea.

627. Because the KCC has special provisions on the maritime transport in Book V and air transport in Book VI, the provisions in Chapter 9 of Book II is applicable only for the land transport.

II. International Convention

628. There is no international convention for the carriage of goods or passengers by road and road covering East-Asian countries. Convention on the Contract for the International Carriage of Goods by Road (Geneva, May 19, 1956) (CMR) is limited to the European countries.

§3. CARRIER'S OBLIGATION AND LIABILITY

I. Carriage of Goods

629. The carrier is liable for the cargo damages unless it proves that it or its servant or agent was not negligent in exercising due diligence to receive, load, carry, keep, care for, discharge, or deliver the goods (The KCC Article 135). There is no legal regime for the carrier to invoke the limitation of liability in the land carriage. There is no compulsory provision to the effect that the carrier is not allowed to derogate its obligation and liability, unlike maritime transportation section in the KCC. Therefore, the carrier can make arrangement to limit its liability with the shipper by mutual agreement. According to a standard general term of a Korean land transportation company, the carrier's liability is limited to KRW 500,000 (approximately USD 400) per package.

630. The damages recoverable by the shipper or consignee from the carrier are limited to the price of goods at the place where the goods were delivered or were to be delivered (Article 137). The provision aims at early settlement of claim between parties and protecting the carrier from unexpected claims. Consequential damage is excluded from the recoverable damages from the carrier.

II. Carriage of Passengers

631. The KCC has several provisions on the carriage of passenger. The carrier's fault is presumed, and thus, if the carrier cannot verify that it exercised due care for the carriage of passenger, it is liable for the loss of life or personal injury of the passenger (Article 148). Article 148 is also applicable to the luggage entrusted to the carrier (Article 149(1)). However, the carrier is not liable for cargo damages unless the shipper proves that the damages were caused by the negligence of the carrier or its servant in case of luggage not entrusted to the carrier (Article 150).

§4. The Legal Status of the Consignee

632. Without the consignee's right to receive goods at the delivery place, the purpose of the contract for carriage of goods in land may not be accomplished satisfactorily. However, because the consignee is not a party to the contract, it does not have any right to request the delivery of the goods to the carrier. The KCC solves the dilemma by empowering the consignee as the person who is eligible to request or receive the goods at the delivery place. When the goods arrive at the delivery place, the consignee has the same right as the shipper (consignor) in accordance with the KCC Article 140(1). When the consignee requests the delivery of the goods to the carrier after the goods arrive at the delivery place, the right of the consignee prevails over that of the shipper (Article 140(2)).

633. The consignee has obligation to pay freight and other expenses incurred during the carriage against the carrier, after it receives the goods (Article 141). The shipper (consignee) has obligation to pay freight to the carrier. However, there is need to impose the duty to pay freight upon the consignee. The KCC imposes the duty upon the consignee only after it receives the goods. Therefore, before the shipper receives goods, it does not have any obligation to pay freight. The consignee is liable for the freight jointly and severally against the carrier with the shipper after it receives goods.

§5. Transport Document

634. The carrier should issue the B/L for land transportation upon the request of the shipper (Article 128). It can be said that it is an equivalent to the B/L in maritime transportation in Book V. Therefore, the same legal principle and rules as for the B/L are applicable for the B/L for land transportation. The holder of the B/L for land transportation has, on the one hand, benefit of the same evidentiary effect (Article 131) as that in the B/L and is, on the other hand, regarded to possess the goods because it is a kind of document of title (Article 133). The carrier should hand over the goods in exchange for the B/L for land transportation.

§6. Time Bar

635. The time-bar period for the claimant to make claims against the carrier is one year after the goods are delivered (Articles 147, 121). It functions to protect the carrier. Taking into consideration that the time-bar period for general commercial activities is five years, the time-bar period for claims against the carrier is very short, which functions to protect the carrier.

636. According to the Korean Supreme Court, the time-bar provision in Articles 121 and 147 has a characteristic of prescription period in the Civil Code, and thus, the shortening of the period is allowed, but the extension of the period is not allowed.[122] The nine-months time-bar provision was decided as being valid. In this respect, the interpretation of time-bar provision between Article 121 in land transportation and Article 814 in maritime transportation is sharply contrasted. In the Civil Code, the time-bar provision aims at partly protecting the obligor by not allowing the obligee to extend the time-bar period by agreement but allowing shortening of the period. However, the time-bar provision in the maritime law section aims at partly protecting the obligee, such as the shipper or holder of the B/L, by not allowing to make an agreement to shorten the fixed period of time bar but allowing to extend the time-bar period by agreement.

637. In a Korean Supreme Court case *2009.8.20. Docket No. 2008da58978*, an F/F as the carrier issued a B/L to the shipper with a time bar clause for nine months. The court rendered when the accident occurred within the land transport area, the time-bar clause for nine months was valid because not Article 814 but Article 121 was applicable for the case.

638. When an accident occurs in the land leg in case of multimodal transportation, the law regulating the land leg is applicable according to Article 816 in the KCC. When the transferable document is issued, the holder of the document may not know the fact that the time-bar period is nine months rather than one year in the document issued by the carrier. In this case, the claimant is the holder of the B/L. Therefore, there is a necessity to protect the obligee, such as the holder of the B/L in land transportation. The author has an opinion that Article 121, in this case, should be interpreted the same as the time-bar provision in Article 814. In this case, the agreement should be decided as null and void. The interpretation of the Korean Supreme Court is doubtful.

122. There are two different kinds of time bar: Prescription period and Limitation period. In the prescription period, the right to sue and the cause of action itself are deprived of the claimant together. In the limitation period, the right to sue is only deprived of the claimant. Korea only has a time bar in terms of the prescription period. But it has two different kinds. One is that the suspension or interruption is allowed and the other is that it is not allowed. Time-bar provision in the KCC Art. 814 is an example of the latter and the KCC Art. 121 is one example of the former.

§7. Cause of Action

639. Korea is a country to allow a claimant to raise a lawsuit with the cause of action based on either the breach of the contract or in tort (Korean Supreme Court case *1980.11.11. Docket No. 80da1812*; *1983.3.22. Docket No. 92daka1533*). Accordingly, the claimant can raise another lawsuit based on the cause of action in tort even after it failed a lawsuit for the cargo damages against the carrier. When the claim is based on the cause of action in tort, it is subject to the time bar, ranging from three years to ten years (The Civil Code Article 766). However, when the claim is based on the cause of action with the breach of contract, it is subject to the time bar with one-year period (Articles 121 and 147).[123]

640. The reader should be very cautious about the difference between the law applicable in the land transportation and that in the maritime transportation. According to the maritime law section in the KCC, the liability of the carrier is applicable for the cases with the cause of action based either on the breach of contract or in tort (Article 798(1)). As a result, the carrier is entitled to invoke the limitation of liability even when the claimant makes a claim based on the cause of action in tort.

§8. Inland Navigation

641. Korea does not have international canals used for transportation. Several rivers and lakes are enclosed by the land. Therefore, legal disputes involved in inland transportation rarely occur. The transportation by use of boats in rivers or lakes is governed by the general provision in the land transportation of the KCC. According to Article 125, the carriage of goods or passenger in land, river or lake, or in port is subject to Chapter 9 (transportation) in Book II (Business Activities) of the KCC. Chapter 9 for transportation has no limitation scheme, and thus, the carrier for carriage in a lake or river does not have any right to limit its liability, while the carrier for carriage at sea enjoys the right to limit its liability.

123. The burden of proof to verify the presence of the negligence is imposed upon the claimant when it raises a lawsuit based on the cause of action in tort. However, the burden of proof is upon the defendant when the lawsuit is based on the breach of the contract.

Chapter 2. Air Transportation

§1. General

642. In air transportation, the carrier undertakes to transport goods or passengers from a departure place to an arrival place by airplane, and the shipper promises to pay remuneration for the carriage to the carrier.

643. Korea has two international airline companies: Korean Airlines Company and Asiana Airlines Company. These companies are engaged in the domestic and international air transportation. Most foreign international airline companies carry out business in Korea.

§2. Source of Law for International Carriage

I. International Convention

644. Korea ratified the 1955 Hague Protocol to the Warsaw Convention in 1967,[124] and thus, the Protocol played as the governing law for the air transportation involved in Korea according to the Korean Constitution.[125] In 2007, Korea ratified the Montreal Convention which supersedes the Warsaw Convention and the amended convention in case of the international passenger transportation between the contracting states of the Montreal Convention (Article 55). Accordingly, the Montreal Convention and the Hague Protocol to the Warsaw Convention, in some cases, are the governing laws in relation to the legal issues involved in air transportation when the Korean law is applicable. However, both conventions do not apply to the pure domestic carriage in Korea and the carriage between Korea as the contracting state of the Montreal Convention and other non-contracting states to the convention.

II. Draft Proposal and New Law in the KCC

645. Although both the Warsaw Convention and the Montreal Convention are parts of Korean law because Korea ratified them, they are applicable for neither domestic air transportation nor transportation between Korean airport and airports of foreign countries which are not party to either of the international conventions. Therefore, it can be said that there are no governing law in Korea for the above case. The Korean government understood this vacuum in the governing law and launched a program to draft the so-called Air Transportation Law section in the KCC. It was completed in 2009. The draft was passed by the Korean Parliament on May 23, 2011, effective as of November 24, 2011.

---

124. Korea does not ratify 1929 Warsaw Convention but only the 1955 Hague Protocol to the Warsaw Convention.
125. Korean Supreme Court case *1986.7.22. Docket No. 82daka1372.*

646. The Draft was modeled on the Montreal Convention. It was inserted as Book VI of the KCC as "Air Transportation Law Section" (hereinafter "New Law"). It has three chapters. The first chapter is on the general. The second chapter deals with international air transportation. The third chapter addresses the carrier's liability on the victims on earth caused by the airplane's crash.

647. The Second Chapter (Air Transportation) is divided by three sections. The first section is General. The second and the third sections are dealing with the international air transportation of passenger and goods respectively. These sections are core provisions dealing with the obligation and liability of the carrier. The fourth section addresses the transportation document.

648. The first section (The General) has several provisions applicable for both the carriage of passenger and the carriage of cargo. The time-bar period of the carrier's liability against the passenger or shipper is two years (Article 902), regardless of the cause of action from the date the passenger or the cargo's arrival at the destination, from the date on which the aircraft ought to have arrived, or from the date on which the carriage stopped, whichever is the latest one.[126] The actual carrier is jointly and severally liable for the damages with the contractual carrier (Article 900). The provisions of the carrier's liability in this chapter are applicable regardless of the cause of action based on the breach of contract or in tort (Article 899).[127] The servant or agent or actual carrier is entitled to invoke the same limitation and defenses as the carrier (Articles 899 and 900).[128] The carrier is not allowed to derogate from its liability by special agreement (Article 903).[129]

649. Like the Montreal Convention, the carrier is liable for damage sustained in case of death or bodily injury of a passenger upon condition only that the accident took place on board the aircraft or in the course of any of the operations of embarking or disembarking during the carriage (Article 904). It is a kind of strict liability. For damages not exceeding 113,100 SDR for each passenger, the carrier shall not be able to exclude or limit its liability. However, the carrier shall not be liable for damages exceeding 113,100 SDR if it proves: (i) that such damage was not due to the negligence or other wrongful act or omission of the carrier or its servants or agents; or (ii) such damage was solely due to the negligence or other wrongful act or omission of a third party (Article 905).[130] The carrier does not have a right to limit its liability.

650. The carrier is liable for damages caused by the delay to the passenger in the carriage unless it proves that it and its servants or agent exercised all measures that could reasonably be required to avoid the damage or it was impossible for it or

126. Montreal Convention Art. 35(1).
127. Montreal Convention Art. 29.
128. Montreal Convention Arts. 30 & 43.
129. Montreal Convention Art. 26.
130. Montreal Convention Arts. 17(1) & 21(1)(2).

them to take such measures. However, the liability of the carrier to each passenger is limited to 4,694 SDR but to 1,000 SDR in case of domestic carriage (Article 907).[131]

651. The carrier is strictly liable for the damages sustained in case of destruction or loss of, or damage to, checked baggage upon condition only that the event which caused the above took place on board the aircraft or during any period within the checked baggage was in the charge of the carrier. However, the carrier is not liable if and to the extent that the damage resulted from the inherent defect, quality or vice of the baggage. The liability of the carrier is limited to 1,131 SDR for each passenger (Articles 908(1)) and 910(1)).[132] However, the carrier is not liable for the damages to the unchecked baggage unless the passenger proves that the damage was caused by the carrier's fault or that of its servant or agents. The maximum liability of the carrier is 1,131 SDR for each passenger (Articles 908(2) and 910(1)).[133]

652. Regarding the carrier's liability for the loss or damage to the cargo during the carriage of goods by air, the New Law is based on strict liability. However, the scope of items it could escape from liability is very narrow. The items are as follows: the fact that the loss or damages were caused by a latent defect, quality, or vice of that cargo, defective packing of that cargo performed by a person other than the carrier or its servants or agents, an act of war or an armed conflict, an act of public authority carried out in connection with the entry, exit, or transit of the cargo (Article 913). The carrier is always entitled to limit its liability to 19 SDR per kg (Article 915) or 15 SDR per kg in case of domestic carriage.[134]

653. The carrier is also liable for the damages caused by delay. The liability is based on the presumed fault liability. The carrier is liable for the cargo damages during the carriage unless it proves that it or its servant or agent did exercise all measures that could reasonably be required to avoid the damages (Article 914). The Carrier is always entitled to limit its liability to 19 SDR per kg or 15 SDR per kg in case of domestic carriage (Article 915).[135]

654. The fourth section regulates transport document. The shipper shall be deemed to have guaranteed to the carrier the accuracy and completeness of the written remarks in the air waybill or the particular of the cargo or the statement of the cargo furnished by it (Article 928(1)). The shipper shall indemnify the carrier against all damage suffered by it by reason of the inaccuracy and incompleteness (Article 928(2)).[136]

655. The air waybill or the cargo receipt is prima facie evidence of the conclusion of the contract, of the acceptance of the cargo and of the conditions of carriage

131. Montreal Convention Arts. 19 & 22(1).
132. Montreal Convention Arts. 17(2) & 22(2).
133. Montreal Convention Arts. 17(2) & 22(2).
134. Montreal Convention Arts. 18 & 22(3).
135. Montreal Convention Arts. 19 & 22(3).
136. Montreal Convention Art. 10.

mentioned therein (Article 929(1)). Any statements in the air waybill, dimensions and packing of the cargo, as well as those relating to the number of packages, are prima facie evidence of the facts stated (Article 929(2)); Those relating to the quantity, volume and condition of the cargo do not constitute evidence against the carrier except so far as they both have been, and are stated in the air waybill or the cargo receipt to have been, checked by it in the presence of the consignor, or relate to the apparent condition of the cargo (Article 929(3)).[137]

656. Air waybill is not a negotiable document. The holder of the air waybill does not obtain the right to demand the cargo against the carrier. The holder of the bill is presumably regarded as the consignee. It is entitled to demand the cargo because it is the consignee. The consignee has the right to demand the delivery of the cargo against the carrier by the operation of the law under the KCC Article 918. The carrier is not required to deliver the cargo to the consignee in exchange for the air waybill.

657. The third chapter (Liability to the Third Party on the Surface) addresses the liability issue of the carrier to the third party on the surface. The New Law of the KCC is modeled on the liability of the carrier stipulated in the 1952 Rome Convention and 1978 Rome Convention. The carrier which caused damages to the third party on the surface by dropping of the aircraft or materials from the aircraft is absolutely liable for the damage (Article 930) but it is allowed to limit its liability (Article 932).[138]

III. General Terms

658. Unless the agreement in the contract for carriage of passenger or cargo by air does not violate the compulsory provision (Article 902), the agreement is valid. According to Korean Airline Co, Ltd, the carrier's liability in case of carriage of passenger is based on the Hague Protocol and the Montreal Convention.

§3. Source of Law for Domestic Carriage

659. The KCC did not have any provision regarding air transportation. However, the Korean government adopted new provisions on air transportation as of May 2011. Therefore, the KCC Book VI is the governing law for domestic air transportation.

137. Montreal Convention Art. 11.
138. Rome Convention Art. 11.3.

Chapter 3. Multimodal Transportation

§1. General

I. Definition

660. In multimodal transportation, a carrier undertakes to transport a carriage of goods from a departing place to an arrival place by use of at least two different modes of transportation, and in turn, the shipper promises to pay the freight for reward to the carrier. A carrier should undertake to transport whole coverage of the carriage. Even though the carrier makes another subcontract for the carriage with the other carrier (actual carrier), the party to the contract of multimodal transportation is the multimodal carrier. For example, an exporter in Korea wants to export goods to an importer in Washington DC, U.S. There are two ways: first, it makes a contract for the carriage of goods to Washington DC with one carrier; second, it makes two different contracts for the carriage with the ocean carrier and subsequently with the railroad carrier. The first arrangement of contract is called the multimodal or combined transportation contract.

II. Practice in Korea

661. Korea is one of the countries that is heavily dependent on foreign trade. Especially Japan, China, and the U.S. are three important trading partners with Korea. Exporting and importing goods to and from these countries are necessarily transported by ship or airplane. Because the Korean *Peninsula* has been divided into the Demilitarized Zone (DMZ), trains from South Korea cannot pass the North Korea, and thus, transportation by railroad is undeveloped in Korea. Owing to the relatively cheap cost, transportation by ship is the most widely used means of transportation for goods to and from Korea.

662. Several liner companies, such as the Hanjin Shipping Co., Ltd and the Hyundai Shipping Co., Ltd, have expanded their business by undertaking transportation covering maritime and, in addition, rail or road carriage since the 1990s. In this case, the liner companies become the contractual carrier and act as actual carrier in the sea leg, but it will make another contract for the carriage with the rail load carrier, which becomes the actual carrier. The liner company will be held liable for the cargo damages, even though the accident occurs at the land leg because it is the contractual carrier.

663. The other type of multimodal transportation can be easily found in conjunction with the F/F. There is no restriction for the F/F to act as the contractual carrier. Because the F/F does not possess or operate the vessel for the carriage, it makes subcontract for the carriage with the ocean carrier and railroad carrier, respectively. In this context, the F/F is the contractual carrier, and the ocean and railroad carriers are the actual carriers. The financial stability of the F/F as the contractual carrier is very low. Therefore, cargo interests usually raise a lawsuit against the actual carrier (ocean carrier) rather than the contractual carrier (the F/F).

664. Among several combinations of transport modes, land-sea combination is widely engaged in Korea. Nowadays, sea-air combination is gaining popularity. Commodities from China to the U.S. are transported by way of combined transport of sea-air combination. A cargo from Shanghai is shifted to Inchon by a car-ferry vessel, and it is dispatched to Inchon International Air Port. It is transported by air plane to the destination in the U.S.

§2. Source of Law

I. Article 816 in the KCC

665. The Korean government inserted a provision on multimodal transportation when it was revised in 2007. The provision addresses only the case of multimodal transportation in which the maritime carriage is necessarily engaged. The KCC Article 816 says that the carrier is liable for the cargo damages in accordance with the law applicable for the place where the accident occurred; however, in the case of concealed damages, the carrier is liable for the cargo damages in accordance with the law applicable for the place where the longest coverage is involved. Article 816 does not apply for multimodal transportation involved in air and road transportation. In order to fill up this deficiency, the Korean government tries to enact laws regulating general multimodal transportation.

II. Multimodal Transport B/L

666. In practice, the International Federation of Freight Forwarders Association (FIATA) or KIFFA bills of lading are widely used in multimodal transportation. Instead of issuing a written contract for the multimodal transportation, the carrier issues the above B/L. Under the current Korean law, the maritime law section in the KCC Chapter V is applicable for damages which occurred at sea leg while the land law section in the KCC Chapter II is applicable for damages which occurred at land leg. There is a limitation regime in maritime transportation, and thus, the carrier can reduce its liability. In this respect, the victims are not protected fully.

667. In the recent Korean Supreme Court case *2009.8.20. Docket No. 2008da58978*, the court reconfirmed that the nine-months time-bar provision in the FIATA B/L is null and void if the accident occurred at the sea leg because the one-year time-bar provision in the KCC Article 814 is compulsorily applicable for the purpose of protecting the consignee or the holder of the B/L.[139] Furthermore, the

139. The Korean Supreme Court case *1997.11.28. Docket No. 97da28490.*

court rendered that the one-year time-bar provision in the B/L was valid if the accident occurred at the land leg because the carrier was entitled to reduce the time-bar period in Articles 147 and 121 according to the Civil Code Article 184(2).

§3. Draft of Multimodal Transport Law

I. Background

668. Because the newly inserted Article 816 did not fully cover multimodal transportation, there was a call to insert a new legal system in the KCC. The Korean Ministry of Justice launched a program to draft a new private law governing multimodal transportation. The committee was formulated in April 2010 and started to draft the multimodal transportation law.

II. Draft of Multimodal Transportation Law

669. The Draft of New Multimodal Transport Provisions (hereinafter "the Draft"), which will be inserted in Book II of the KCC, contains the following provisions.

670. First, the Draft is applicable for multimodal transportation. Only when the case which a carrier undertakes to transport goods by more than two modes of transportation and, in addition, more than two different laws are applicable, the case is subject to the application of the Draft (Article 150–2). Under these special circumstances as pursuant to Korean law, land transportation is very simply stipulated. Under the KCC, transportation by rail is regulated in the same way as by road. Therefore, if a contract contains multimodal transportation combined both by rail and truck, only one law is applicable, and thus, the Draft is not applicable to the case.

671. Second, the network liability system is adopted where the place which the accident occurred is ascertained. The carrier is liable for the cargo damages in accordance with the law, which would have been applicable if a separate contract was made for the leg where the accident occurred (Draft Article 150–5(1)). If the accident occurred at the land leg, the law for land leg under the KCC is applicable to the case. The burden of proof to ascertain where the accident occurred is imposed upon the carrier. Even if there is a limitation of liability regimes in maritime and air transportation, there is no such regime in land transportation in the KCC.

672. Third, the limited network liability system is adopted where the place in which the accident occurred is not ascertained. The carrier is liable for the cargo damages in accordance with the law applicable to the leg, which is the longest among more than two legs of transportation in terms of transport distance (Draft Article 150–5(2)). Accordingly, if the distance of transportation by sea is longer than that by air, the law applicable for sea transportation, that is, the maritime law section of the KCC, is applicable to the case.

673. However, where the place which the accident occurred is not ascertained, the Draft has several modifications from this basic principle in the area of limitation of liability, time bar and notice period. For example, the provisions in the land law do not address the limitation of liability of the carrier. The limitation of the carrier in air transportation is 19 SDR as opposed to 2 SDR in maritime transportation. Where the contract for transportation involves air leg, and if the distance for the sea leg is longer than that for the air leg, the difference in limitation amount is too large. To alleviate the imbalance, the Draft has a provision to fix the limitation amount without leaving it to the law applicable in the separate leg. The carrier's liability is limited to 666.67 SDR per package or 2 SDR per kg, whichever is higher. However, in case the air leg is the longest in terms of the transport distance, the limitation amount for the carrier to invoke is 8.33 SDR per kg (Draft Article 150–6(1)). The carrier is prohibited from derogating this limitation amount due to the obligatory provision in the Draft (Article 150–10).

674. The servant or agent and actual carrier are entitled to invoke the benefit of the carrier, such as the package limitation, when the claimant claims against them with the cause of action in tort based on the laws regulating each leg of transportation (Draft Article 150–5 & 150–9).

675. Fourth, the applicable law designated by Article 150–5(1) and (2) is not allowed to contract out. If the parties in the contract make an agreement to apply law different from the law designated in accordance with Article 150–4, the agreement is null and void. For example, where the land and air leg are combined and the accident occurred at the air leg, the air transportation law is applicable for the case. In this case, if the parties agree that the land law is applicable to the case before the accident, the agreement is null and void. This provision is applicable only when Korean law is the governing law.

§4. Comprehensive Logistics Contract

676. Comprehensive logistics contracts are now being implemented in Korea. A comprehensive logistics contract refers to an agreement where a single merchant takes responsibility for handling the entire logistics flow from the exporter's factory to the importer's factory. In the past, separate contracts were made for each stage, such as packaging, labeling, customs clearance, stevedoring, warehousing, and transportation, with different merchants. Now, all these tasks are contracted with a single merchant, making it more convenient for the exporter, who only needs to enter into one contract instead of multiple contracts. This type of contract is known as a comprehensive logistics contract.

677. The Korean Supreme Court has also recognized such comprehensive logistics contracts for the first time (Supreme Court Judgment 2019Da213009, dated July

10, 2019) (Kim In-Hyun, Baek Ji-Soo, "Distinction Between Comprehensive Logistics Contracts and Multimodal Transport," Commercial Case Studies Vol. 33 No. 1, March 1, 2020, p. 47 et seq.). However, since there are no specific provisions in the Commercial Act regarding these contracts, the court applied Article 816 of the Commercial Act, which relates to multimodal transport.

678. In the *Jeju Samdasoo* case, Samdasoo entered into a comprehensive logistics contract to transport its products from Jeju Island to Seoul. When the first contractor abandoned the contract, a second contractor was hired. Samdasoo then filed a claim against the first contractor for the costs incurred during this process. The Supreme Court: (i) recognized the contract as a comprehensive logistics contract, (ii) applied Article 816 of the Commercial Act, which pertains to multimodal transport, and (iii) applied the one-year statute of limitations based on the long-distance land transportation law, as per Article 816(2).

However, Article 816 deals with transportation, whereas this case involves a breach of contract, so the application of Article 816 of the Commercial Act is not appropriate. There is a need for the enactment of new legislation.

Part IV. Marine Insurance

Chapter 1. Introduction

§1. General

679. As a whole, three different kinds of marine insurance exist in Korea: Hull insurance, cargo insurance, and P&I insurance. Under hull insurance and P&I insurance, the shipowner has an insurable interest in a vessel, and thus, it is eligible for the insured. Under cargo insurance, the cargo owner has an insurable interest in a cargo, and it is eligible for the insured.

680. In cargo insurance and hull insurance, the insurer is usually a Korean company. However, in P&I insurance, foreign P&I clubs are dominant in Korea. Foreign insurance companies and foreign P&I clubs freely operate business in Korea. There are sixteen Korean non-life insurance companies which are eligible for underwriting marine insurance as of July 2016, such as Hyundai Marine & Fire Insurance Co., Ltd and Samsung Fire & Marine Insurance Co., Ltd. These insurance companies underwrite hull insurance and cargo insurance as well. The Korea Shipping Association (KSA) provides hull insurance for its members.

681. As far as the P&I Insurance is concerned, foreign P&I clubs such as the U.K. P&I club, Britannia P&I club, Gard P&I club, and Japan P&I club dominate the Korean P&I insurance market. Major foreign P&I clubs maintain their correspondents in Korea. They sometimes play a substantial role as a claim handler for the benefit of their members in a claim dispute. Many P&I insurance brokers exist in Korea.

682. The Korea P&I club, which started its operation in 2000, are expanding its business. The Korea P&I club's business is limited to domestic interests partly because it is still not a member of the International Group of P&I clubs. Most members of the Korean P&I club are Korean shipowners. The KSA provides P&I insurance services for its members. Members of KSA are limited to the vessel owners who operate vessels mainly within Korean territorial seas. KSA provides the owners of Korean coastal tankers with liability insurance, which is required pursuant to KOPCA. The KSA provides hull insurance in addition to liability insurance for its members.

§2. Source of Law

I. The KCC

683. The KCC has a section for marine insurance as a part of insurance law. Unlike China and Japan, marine insurance is stipulated as a part of insurance law rather than maritime law. Unlike the U.K., Australia, and Canada, Korea does not have a separate and distinctive marine insurance act.

684. The name of Book IV in the KCC is Insurance. Book IV has three chapters: Chapter 1 is general introduction, Chapter 2 is non-life (or property) insurance and Chapter 3 is life insurance. Section 4 marine insurance is included in Chapter 2.

685. Insurance is divided into two parts: the one is non-life (property) insurance and the other is life insurance. Marine insurance law is a part of property insurance. Property insurance is the insurance under which the insurer is to indemnify the loss or damages of the insured (Article 665). According to Article 693, the insurer has an obligation to indemnify the loss of the insured caused by an accident in relation to marine adventure. Hull insurance and cargo insurance are two major specified insurance stipulated in the KCC. Although P&I insurance has become an essential insurance for Korean shipowners in practice, the KCC does not have any provisions on the P&I insurance. However, it is understood that it is a kind of liability insurance regulated by the KCC.

686. The insurance contract enters between the insurer and the insured. While the insurer is a legal person, such as a business entity, the insured may be a natural person. The natural person may not have expertise in insurance. The general terms follow the insurance contract. The general terms are prepared by the insurer, and the insured does not have a chance to amend the contents in the general terms. Accordingly, there is a necessity to protect the insured. The KCC Article 663 serves for this purpose. According to first part of Article 663, the agreement between the insurer and the insured is null and void if it makes the insured less favored than the KCC. However, it is not applicable for the case of marine insurance and reinsurance.

687. Nonetheless, the Korean Supreme Court ruled that the small fishing vessel's owner was in a disadvantageous position to the knowledge of insurance as opposed to the insurer, and thus, the first part of Article 663 should be applied. The court decided an agreement between the insurer and the owner of the fishing boat as the insured was null and void. In conclusion, it can be said the insurer in marine insurance is allowed to enter into the agreement, which puts the insured in a less advantageous position than the KCC, except a marine insurance involved in a fishing boat. In other words, provisions in the KCC marine insurance law section function as default rules.

688. Under the KCC, the insurer is not liable for the insurance accident if the accident is caused by an intentional act or gross negligence (Article 659).[140] However, the insurer is not liable for any loss attributable to the willful misconduct of the insured under MIA Article 55(2). Therefore, it can be said that the insured is more protected under the 1906 MIA than under the KCC because the insured is not able to receive the insurance proceeds if the accident occurs due to its gross negligence under the KCC but otherwise under the 1906 MIA.

689. Under the KCC, the insurer obtains the recourse claims from the insured against the person who is responsible for the loss automatically at the same time when it pays the insurance proceeds to the insured because it is subrogated to all rights of the insured (Article 682(2)). The right is given automatically to the insurer by the operation of the law. No further arrangement is required. Accordingly, the insurer for cargo insurance is allowed to bring about a lawsuit against the carrier who is responsible for cargo damage. On the other hand, even though the insurer who had paid the insurance proceeds to the insured obtained the recourse right and subrogated all the rights of the insured under 1906 MIA Article 79(1), it should raise the lawsuit in the name of the insured in order to exercise the recourse claim under the English law. Therefore, the assignment of the right is required for the insurer to get a recourse claim successfully under the English law, which is not required under the Korean law.

II. Act for Regulating General Terms

690. Korea has an Act for regulating General Terms. General terms are issued soon after the insurance contract is entered into. Therefore, the Act is applicable for the general terms in the insurance contract. The insurer has a duty to explain the material facts in the relevant insurance to the insured. The KCC has a provision (Article 638ter) similar to that of the Act. In the Korean Supreme Court case *1998.11.27. Docket No. 98da32564*, the court decided that the insured were availed of both provisions. According to Article 3(4) of the ACT, the insurer is prohibited from arguing that the agreement should be applied to the case unless it is explained to the insurer when the insurance contract was made. For example, when the insurer argues that the insured breached the warranty in the general terms of the relevant insurance contract, the courts accept the argument of the insured that the insurer did not give an explanation of the content and effect of the warranty when the insurance contract was made, and thus, the insurer was not allowed to invoke the effect of the breach of the warranty.

140. The KSA's general clause for P&I insurance says that it will not pay insurance proceed if the insurance accident is caused by the intentional act of the insured, which means that the insurer should pay the insurance proceed even if the accident is resulted from the gross negligence of the insured.

III. 1906 MIA

691. The 1906 Marine Insurance Act (hereinafter "1906 MIA") becomes a governing law by party's agreement. Even though both the insured and insurer are Korean nationalities or Korean entities, many insurance contracts have a provision that the case will be governed by English law. The Korean Supreme Court rendered several times that English governing law was valid.[141] When English law is decided as the governing law, the 1906 MIA becomes a relevant law. The 1906 MIA does not have a mandatory provision, and thus, all provisions are default rules. Therefore, the party's agreement against the provisions in the 1906 MIA is valid and prevails over provisions in the 1906 MIA. Provisions in the ITC (Hull) or ICC, which contradict the 1906 MIA, are effectively applied to the case.

692. Where the insurance contract has a foreign factor and the lawsuit was brought before the Korean court, the judge should consult with the KIPL to designate governing law. The KIPL also adopts the principle of party autonomy. The parties in the insurance contract are free to select the governing law of their free will. Based on the party autonomy principle, the agreement of the English governing law is valid under the Korean law. However, in the Korean Supreme Court cases *2001.7.27. Docket No. 99da55533 and 2010.9.9. Docket No. 2009da105383,* the court took a different position from the previous precedents by applying Korean law to the case regardless of the presence of the English governing law clause.

693. Whether the Korean law should be the governing law in case both parties are Koreans, regardless of the presence of English governing law clause or not, has been in dispute. In the Seoul High Court case *2012.10.25 Docket No. 2012na7207*, the court decided that if there was no foreign factor involved in the relevant case, the Korean law should be the governing law regardless of the presence of different agreement on the governing law pursuant to the KIPL Article 25(4) because the Act for regulating General Terms are regarded as a mandatory rule.[142] However, the court decided that the case was involved in several foreign factors, and thus, the above Korean Act as a mandatory rule was not applicable. The judgment was affirmed by the Korean Supreme Court case *2015.3.20. Docket No. 2012da118846.*

---

141. The Korean Supreme Court cases *1977.1.11. Docket No. 71da2116; 1991.5.14. Docket No. 90daka25314; 1996.3.8. Docket No. 95da28779; 2005.11.25. Docket No. 59528.*

142. The KIPL Article 25 (party Autonomy)

> (1) The contract is governed by the law designated explicitly and implicitly. The implicit designation is admitted only if it is reasonable taking into consideration all circumstances.
>
> (4) The mandatory provision in the relevant country should be applied even if parties select the law of different country as the governing law, in case that all factors are related to the country except the governing law.

Chapter 2. Hull and Cargo Insurance

§1. General

I. Definition

694. Shipowner or the cargo owner as the insured makes an insurance contract with the insurer to the effect that if the subject matter (vessel or cargo) becomes loss or damaged, the insurer pays insurance proceeds to the insured, and in return, the insured pays insurance premium to the insurer. Under the KCC, the hull insurance and cargo insurance fall within the non-life insurance.

695. The shipowner usually experiences a marine accident which results in the total loss of its vessel. The shipowner seeks for the countermeasure to protect its interest in its vessel. It enters into a hull insurance contract with the insurer. Article 695(1) refers to hull insurance by saying, "when the vessel is the subject of the insurance." Cargo insurance is the insurance for which the importer or exporter enters into a contract with the insurer to be indemnified for its loss during sea transportation from the insurer. Article 695 refers to cargo insurance by saying "when the cargo is the subject of the insurance."

II. Function

696. Hull insurance functions as a means for the owner to alleviate the risks that it may face during the operation of the vessel. Cargo insurance has a function to help the cargo owner recover the loss of cargo during its transit. The main purpose for the insured, such as the owner of the vessel or cargo, to enter into the insurance contract is to obtain the insurance proceed to get indemnification of its loss from the insurer while the vessel or cargo is at sea.

697. The insured can avoid undesirably prolonged lawsuit against the carrier or other vessel's owner by entering into a marine insurance contract. Without entering into the marine insurance contract, the insured in cargo insurance should raise a lawsuit against the carrier for the cargo damages, and the insured in hull insurance as well should raise a lawsuit against the opposite vessel's owner in a collision case, if they deny the responsibility. Immediately after the insurance accident occurs, the insured is able to receive the insurance proceeds. Thereafter, the insurer puts in the shoes of the insured, and thus, it makes the recourse or subrogated claims against the third parties, such as the carrier or the opposite vessel's owner, who are liable for the loss of damages against the insured (Article 682).

§2. The KCC

698. The KCC has a compulsory provision to the effect that the provisions in the insurance sections should not be derogated by the party's agreement. According to Article 663, any agreement to put the insured into a detrimental position compared with the provisions in the KCC Book III will be null and void. It aims at protecting the insured. However, the proviso of Article 663 says that it is not applicable for reinsurance and marine insurance or similar insurance. Therefore, parties in the marine insurance are free to enter into an agreement different from the insurance provisions in the KCC. Time-bar period for the insured to claim the insured proceeds against the insurer is two years from the accident date under the KCC (Article 662). Where parties enter into an agreement having a one-year time-bar clause, the agreement is null and void. However, it is valid and enforceable in case of marine insurance. However, the Korean Supreme Court held that the marine insurance involved in small fishing boats falls within the application of Article 663 (*1996.12.20. Docket No. 96da23818*). Therefore, the above agreement is null and void.

699. The marine insurance section in the KCC deals with hull insurance and cargo insurance as well. Because they are a type of non-life (property) insurance, the general provision in the non-life insurance is applicable. Article 659 is a good example stipulated in the general provision section. Therefore, if the insurance accident occurs due to the intent or gross negligence of the insured, the insurer is exempted from liability (Article 659).[143] General average contribution and salvage award are covered by marine insurance (Article 694, 694*bis*).

700. If the insured's vessel was under unseaworthy condition when the vessel left a port in case of voyage policy and it contributed to the accident, the insurer is exempted from liability (Article 706(1)). In contrast, unseaworthy condition is stipulated as a type of warranty under the 1906 MIA. The proof of causation between the unseaworthy condition and the accident is required for the insurer to deny liability under the KCC, whereas it is not required under the 1906 MIA. There is no provision on warranty under the KCC.

Furthermore, there is no provision for the case of time policy in Article 706 of the KCC. According to ITC (Hull) and 1906 MIA Article 39(5), the hull insurer is exempted from liability if the insured has privity to the vessel's unseaworthy condition. According to the Korean Supreme Court, this provision is valid under the English governing law clause.[144]

701. Deviation is one of the causes to allow the insurer to be exempted from liability according to Article 701bis. Even if the deviation does not cause the accident, the insurer is exempted, which is a departure from general principle of the Korean law, which requires causation for liability. The insertion of the provision in the 1991 KCC was affected by the same provision in the 1906 MIA.

---

143. In the life insurance, only if the insurance accident occurs due to the intentional act of the insured, the insurer is exempted from liability.

144. Korean Supreme Court cases *1977.1.11. Docket No. 71da2116*; *2005.11.25 Docket No. 2002da59528*.

702. The KCC has a very detailed provision on the abandonment of Articles 710–718. The insured who suffered heavy damages on the vessel or cargo as the subject matter of the insurance is allowed to abandon the subject matter in order to treat it as a total loss. One of the conditions to trigger the abandonment is that the expected repair expenses exceed the price of the vessel after it is repaired (Article 710). The insured's notifying the insurer of its intention to abandonment endows the insured to right to demand the insurance proceed as if there was a total loss of the subject matter (Article 710). The insurer obtains the right of the insured on the abandoned subject matter. There is a dispute on whether the insurer is bound to have an obligation on the abandoned subject matter at the same time when it obtained the right to it. Court case has not been reported yet on the issue.

703. The Korean Supreme Court rendered several marine insurance cases since 1961, when Korea enacted the KCC. Most of the precedents by the court in marine insurance cases are governed by English law. The courts addressed the legal meaning of provisions in the 1906 MIA, such as warranty, seaworthiness and privity under the time policy. The Korean Supreme Court showed a tendency to follow and respect the judgments of the U.K. courts.

§3. Insurance Policy Circulated in Korea

I. General

704. All provisions in the marine insurance section are non-mandatory, and thus, parties are free to make different agreements from provisions in the marine insurance section of the KCC. Accordingly, general terms issued by the insurer after the insurance contract was entered into play as applicable rules with the KCC in case the parties selected the Korean law as the governing law.

705. In almost all marine insurance contracts in Korea, the insurer issues general terms as a part of an agreement for the contract. In case of cargo insurance, the general terms are shown on the back side of the cargo insurance policy. In case of hull insurance, a separate booklet containing general terms is issued, apart from the hull insurance policy. The main contents of the general terms are listed on the front page of the policy. There is an argument that the general terms in the hull insurance should not be regarded as the adhesion contract, taking into consideration that the insured has a chance to select the content of general terms from standard marine insurance terms such as ITC Hull.

706. When the insurance accident occurs and the insured applies for the insurance proceeds, the insurer rejects the application on the ground that the accident falls within the scope of exempted items in the insurance contract, evidenced by the general terms. The insured argues against the validity of the general terms on the ground that it did not know the presence of the particular general terms or the insurer did not give an explanation of the meaning of the special clause, and therefore, the insurer cannot invoke the exemption of liability based on the general terms. The validity of the general terms often goes to the court.

707. In addition to the KCC, the Act for Regulating Standard Terms is applicable to the case.[145] However, the application of the Act is very limited in accordance with Article 15, which allows general terms circulated internationally not to be applied to the Act.

708. In the Korean Supreme Court case *1996.4.12. Docket No. 96da4893,* the court rendered to the effect that the clause in the general terms is basically valid as a part of contract, but if the disputed matter is material[146] and the insurer did not explain the meaning of the clause to the insured before entering into contract, the insurer cannot claim the validity of the clause in accordance with Act for Regulating Standard Terms Article 3(4).

II. Hull Insurance

A. *In Case of Foreign Law Jurisdiction Clause*

709. There are sixteen marine and fire insurance companies in Korea. When they enter into a hull insurance contract with the Korean shipowner as the insured, the ITC (Hull) is incorporated in the insurance policy with the Korean jurisdiction clause but the English governing law clause. They provide the insured with the Korean version of the policy. However, the ITC (Hull) written in English is issued with the official policy.

710. The Korean Supreme Court has maintained for several years that the English governing law clause is valid even though the Korean insurance company and Korean insured enter into the insurance contract. The typical clause says that this insurance is subject to English law and practice. For example, the insured raised lawsuits against the validity of the warranty under the English law before the Korean Supreme Court, arguing that a warranty under the English law does not require causation, and it is different from that of Korean law. However, this argument has always failed. Minority scholars argue that the governing law clause should be decided differently because it is against the Korean public policy pursuant to the KIPL.

145. The general clauses in both policy and rule book are regarded as general clauses, and thus, they should be subject to Act on regulating Standard Terms. As far as the marine insurance policy or rule books are related to the international trade, the Act is applicable only in some limited extent. As a result of this limitation to the application, the principle of freedom of contract maintains.

146. The Korean Supreme Court rendered that the meaning and effect of the warranty are a material fact imposing the duty to explain upon the insurer (*2010.9.9. Docket No. 2009da105383*).

711. In Pusan District Court case *2008.10.30. Docket No. 2007 gahap20269*, the owner of the Korean vessel entered into the hull insurance contract with the Korean hull insurer. 1983 ITC (Hull) with English governing law clause was incorporated into the policy. Hull and machinery were written as the subject matter insured in the hull insurance policy. The sand hose of the vessel burst and the owner of the vessel wasted repair expenses. The owner applied to the insurer for the insurance proceeds. The insurer argued that the hose at issue is only a separate part of sand recovery machine, and thus, it is neither the hull nor the machinery. The court supported the insurer's argument on the grounds that the sand hose was not listed as part of the machinery on the survey report made after the insurance contract was made.[147]

B. In Case of Korean Governing Law Clause

712. Two mutual insurance organizations such as the KSA and the Korean Fishery Cooperation Partnership provide Korean small shipowners with hull insurance. The policy is based on the ITC (Hull). However, there are several modifications. One of the noticeable differences from the original ITC (Hull) is the presence of the Korean governing law clause. It is the result of the effort of the KSA to meet the small-size shipowner's demand and the Korean Supreme Court's judgment.

713. In the small-sized shipowner case, the insured is a private person rather than a company, which means that the insured does not have expertise in marine insurance, especially in English marine insurance law.

714. There is a famous Korean Supreme Court case (*1996.12.20. Docket No. 96da23818*) in which the court rendered that Article 663 should not apply in case of a small fishing boat owner because he was not regarded as a sophisticated merchant. Therefore, agreements between the insurer and a small shipowner in the policy were decided as being null and void because it was against Article 663 in the KCC. The initiative taken by mutual insurance to follow the Korean Supreme Court's judgment seems very pertinent and reasonable.

III. Cargo Insurance

715. ICC(A), ICC(B), and ICC(C) prevail in the Korean cargo insurance market. These policies maintain the English governing law clause. An insurance policy having a Korean governing clause is rarely found in Korea. Even in the case that both insured and insurer are Korean private persons or legal entities, an English governing law clause is inserted in the cargo insurance policy. This tendency reflects the international aspect of cargo insurance. Even though domestic parties are involved in the contract, the policy may affect the third-party importer in the foreign country. As a result, the widespread English governing law clause is required to be maintained even in Korea.

---

147. For details, In Hyeon Kim, *Korean Maritime Law Update: 2008*, 40-3 JMLC 445 (July 2009).

716. The Korean Supreme Court maintains a different position on the scope of application of the English governing law clause. The typical provisions are as followings: (i) All questions of liability under this policy are to be governed by the law and custom of England, or (ii) This insurance is understood and agreed to be subject to English law and practice only as to liability for and settlement of any and all claims. Unlike the hull insurance policy in the ITC (hull), the court interprets the meaning of the English governing clause in a narrow manner, saying that the English law governs the liability and settlement issues and other matters such as formation of contract are left to the general principle of the law.

IV. Korean Supreme Court's Cases

717. Most Korean Supreme Court cases are related to the cases governed by the English governing law clauses. The Korean Supreme Court follows interpretations made by the U.K. courts on the 1906 MIA when it dealt with cases involved in marine insurance law with the English governing law clause. Every attempt for the insured to nullify the clause has been failed. Since the Korean Supreme Court decided the English governing law cause as valid in the Korean Supreme Court case *1977.1.11 Docket No. 71da2116*, the court has maintained the original position as of today.[148]

718. However, the Korean Supreme Court seems to find out the detour by adopting the policy to apply the Act for regulating General Terms to the case with the English governing law clause. In the Korean Supreme Court case *2001.7.27 Docket No, 99da55533*, the effect of the breach of the warranty was at issue under the ICC clause. If the court applied the English law, the insurer was exempted from liability. However, the court applied the Korean Act to regulate general terms to the case even though the case had the English governing law clause. As a result of applying the Act, the insurer should pay the insurance proceeds because it did not explain the content of the warranty and its effect on the insured, and thus, it was not allowed to invoke the effect of the breach of the warranty stipulated in the 1906 MIA. The court did not give an explanation as to why it applied the Korean law even if the case has the English governing clause and the court admitted its validity. In the Korean Supreme Court case *2010.9.9.Docket No. 2009 da105388,* the court under the 1983 ITC (Hull) with English governing law clause once again rendered the same decision on the warranty issue as it did in the above case.

719. Warranty is very peculiar from the perspective of the Korean law. The Korean law requires the presence of the causation between wrongdoer's act and damages in order that the aggrieved party is allowed to have compensation from the wrongdoer or the breaching party. If the insured does not keep warranty, the insurer is exempted from liability, even though the act of the insured against warranty did

148. Korean Supreme Court cases *1991.5.14. Docket No. 90daka25314; 1996.3.8. Docket No. 95da28779; 2005.11.25. Docket No. 2002da59528.*

not cause the damages. This different legal effect of warranty in 1906 MIA invited many marine insurance law disputes in Korea.

720. In the Korean Supreme Court case *1996.10.11 Docket No. 94da60332*, the court rendered that the warranty is valid under the English law and it should follow the interpretation of the U.K. court when the governing law is the English law. Since then, the court has not changed its position. Nevertheless, several scholars and judges expressed their negative opinions on the validity of warranty that it is too harsh for the insured because the insured, especially a private individual, does not understand the meaning of warranty under the English law.

721. There is no precedent addressing the validity of the warranty under the Korean governing law clause. Because the Korea P&I club and the KSA's rules include warranty provisions with the Korean governing law clause, Korean courts are expected to decide the validity of warranty based on the Korean law in the near future. The KCC does not provide any provision on warranty, and thus, it is up to the court's interpretation.

722. The revision committee for the KCC has a serious discussion on the insertion of the warranty into the KCC. There was a preliminary decision that the definition of the warranty and validity may be inserted in a provision. The committee agreed that the harshness of the effect in case the warranty is breached should be alleviated. The causal linkage between the breach of the warranty and the accident was suggested as a possible solution.

723. According to the English marine insurance law, seaworthiness is a kind of implied warranty in the voyage policy, and thus, the insurer is exonerated from its liability when the accident occurs even without the causal linkage with the breach of seaworthiness warranty (Article 39(1)). It is different from the KCC's seaworthiness provision, which requires causation (The KCC Article 706). The KCC does not specifically state seaworthiness obligation of the insured in the time policy, unlike the Chinese Maritime Code. However, the privity of the insured on the fact that the vessel was sailed under unseaworthy condition is the requirement for the insurer to be exempted from the time policy (1906 MIA Article 39(5)). The Korean Supreme Court rendered several decisions regarding the privity of the insured in the time policy.[149]

724. The theory of utmost good faith is adopted in the KCC Article 651. However, the scope of the application is different from that of the 1906 MIA Article 17. Before or at the beginning of entering into the insurance contract the insured is required to notify the material fact regarding the insurance to the insurer. The breach of the duty qualifies the insurer to cancel the insurance. On the other hand, the duty of utmost good faith in the 1906 MIA Article 17 imposed upon the insured should be kept during the whole period of the insurance contract, which has not been

149. The Korean Supreme Court cases *2002.6.28. Docket No. 2000da21062; 2005.11.10. Docket No. 2003da31299.*

adopted in the KCC. In the Korean Supreme Court case *2005.3.25. Docket No. 2004da22711*, the court rendered that the insured was in breach of the utmost good faith under the 1906 MIA Article 17 and did not allow the insured to receive the insurance proceed when the insured reported the price of the insurance subject twice as much as it was. The duty is imposed upon only the insured under the Korean law as opposed to upon both the insurer and the insured as well under the English law.

Chapter 3. Protection and Indemnity Insurance

§1. General

I. Definition and Function

725. Shipowners tried to alleviate all kinds of liability or expenses involved in the operation of its vessel. Hull insurance served only part of this need. Liability of the shipowner as the carrier for the cargo damage, oil pollution damages and liability against the damaged vessel's owner caused by the collisions are those risks which cannot be indemnified by the hull insurer.

726. In order to indemnify these kinds of liability of the owner, the owners of the vessels established P&I Insurance in 1855.[150] By entering into a P&I club as a kind of mutual insurance, the owner obtains two legal statuses. One is as the insurer, and the other is as the insured.

727. The P&I Insurance is regarded as a mutual insurance and liability insurance in Korea. The shipowner becomes a member of the club by entering into the club and gets the status of the insured as well. Only when the insured acts as the insurer as well in an insurance, the insurance falls within the definition of mutual insurance. Mutual insurance does not aim at maximization of the profit, which differentiates it from general business insurance. Even though mutual insurance has different characteristics from general business insurance, the Korean Supreme Court upheld that the KCC is applicable *mutatis mutandis* to the mutual insurance case.

728. The P&I club as the insurer promises to indemnify the insured when the insured pays the liability to the victim. Furthermore, the victim has a direct action against the insurer pursuant to the KCC Article 724(2). Without waiting until the insured as the debtor pays the liability to it, the victim is allowed to demand the insurance proceed directly to the insurer. This kind of insurance falls within the definition of liability insurance under the KCC. Because the legal nature of the P&I insurance is a kind of liability insurance the provisions for the liability insurance under the KCC are applicable *mutatis mutandis* to the relevant case.

729. According to liability insurance theory, the insurer has an obligation to pay any damages which the assured is likely to pay as a result of occurrences which are defined in the insurance cover. In turn, the insured promises to pay calls to the insured. According to indemnity insurance theory, the insurer has an obligation to reimburse or indemnify the insured only to the extent that the insured has incurred and discharged its liability. The insurer's duty to indemnify does not arise until the insured has paid damages to the third party. The concept of indemnity insurance exists in the U.K. and U.S. However, only the concept of liability insurance exists under the KCC.

150. Hazelwood, *P&I Clubs LAW AND PRACTICE*, 1994, LLP, 8.2. *Ibid.*, 99.

II. Practice in Korea

730. It is a long tradition in Korea that almost all Korean shipowners enter into a foreign P&I Club, such as U.K. P&I, Britannia P&I, Steamship Mutual P&I, Guard P&I, and Japan P&I. However, this tradition was broken when the Korean P&I club initiated its operation in 2000. Because the Korea P&I club is not a member of the International Group of the P&I clubs, the international credibility of the Korea P&I club is not so high, and thus, it does not attract many foreign shipowners. The main members of the Korean P&I club are medium-sized Korean shipowners. However, the Korea P&I club gained members gradually.

§2. The KCC

I. Legal Nature of P&I Insurance

731. Hull insurance and cargo insurance are not compulsory but voluntary. However, P&I insurance is operated based on both voluntary and compulsory insurance as well. The owners of oil tankers are required to buy liability insurance or similar arrangements for the victims caused by oil pollution (the KOPCA Article 15). The owners of general cargo vessels are also required to prepare for compensation to protect the victims caused by fuel oil pollution (the KOPCA Article 47). Every shipowner is required to prepare a compensation scheme enough to discharge its liability for its crew on board in case of loss of life or injury (the Korean Seamen's Act Article 98).

732. The KCC does not have any provision on the P&I insurance. However, the P&I insurance has two legal natures: one is mutual insurance and the other is liability insurance as well. Therefore, the provisions of liability insurance in the KCC are applicable *mutatis mutandis* to the legal relationship in the P&I insurance.

733. One of the issues regarding P&I insurance is the validity of the clause of "pay-to-be-paid" rule in Korea. Most P&I insurance contracts are governed by the English law through the insurance arrangement between Korean shipowners and the U.K.-based P&I clubs. There is no doubt that the pay-to-be-paid rule is valid under the English law between the insurer and the claimant based on the U.K. House of Lords judgment.[151] According to the House of Lords, when the victims seek insurance proceed directly to the insurer rather than the shipowner, the pay-to-be-paid clause works. The pay-to-be-paid rule clause says that the liability of the insurer is not brought about until the insured pays the damages to the claimant. Therefore, there is no liability for the insurer to pay the victims. The U.K. House of Lords upheld the validity of the clause.

734. However, when the owner enters into a P&I insurance contract with the Korea P&I club, the governing law is the Korean law, and thus, the validity of the

151. The Fanti and The Padre Island, [1990] 2 Lloyd's Reports, 191; Steven Hazelwood, *supra,* 329.

pay-to-be-paid rule will depend on the KCC because the governing law is the Korean law. The KCC allows the third-party victims to bring about direct action against the insurer according to KCC Article 724(2). The insurer may invoke the same defense as the insured can invoke against the third-party victims. However, there is no provision in the KCC on whether the insurer may invoke the same defense as the insurer can invoke against the insured. There are split views on the validity of the rule in Korea. One view is that the provision regarding direct action is a compulsory provision because it was invented in order to protect innocent third-party victims without any restriction. As a result, the rule is not valid, and the insured are able to receive the insurance proceeds from the insurer.[152] The other view is that the nature of the P&I insurance is the indemnity insurance rather than the liability insurance. Therefore, the third-party victims do not have any right against the insurer until the insured pays damages to the victims and subsequently sustains a loss, which triggers the liability of the insurer to pay the insurance amount to the insured. According to this view, the insurer is allowed to raise the same defense against the victims as the insurer can invoke against the insured.

§3. Insurance Policy Circulated in Korea: P&I Insurance

I. General Situation in Korea

735. Foreign P&I insurance clubs had completely dominated in Korea until the Korea P&I club started its operation in 2001. The KSA (<www.haewoon.or.kr>) also has played a great role since its inception of P&I insurance for focusing on vessels navigating the Korean coasts in 1998.[153]

II. Foreign P&I Club

736. The Britannia and Steamship Mutual clubs are two major P&I clubs operated in the U.K., which the Korean ocean-going shipowner selects. They provide the English law jurisdiction and English governing law clause. The Gard P&I club and the Japan P&I club also attract some Korean shipowners. The Gard P&I club provides the Norway jurisdiction and Norway governing law clause, and the Japan P&I club provides the Japan jurisdiction and Japanese governing law clause, respectively.

152. In a Seoul District Court case *2002.7.5. Docket No. 2001 gahap 3698*, the court decided that the pay-to-be-paid clause in the Hull Insurance agreement is valid only between the insured and the insurer, and that it is not valid to the third-party victims because they are not the party to the agreement. However, the liability insurer was not mutual insurer such as the P&I club but the business insurer.

153. The KSA started its service as the Hull Insurer for the member of the association as early as 1958.

III. The Korea P&I Club

737. The Korea P&I club started its operation as late as 2001. The Korean government had a great role in establishing the national P&I club. The Korea P&I club was born by the Special Act on the Korean P&I Club. Because the foreign P&I club preoccupied the P&I insurance market in Korea, the Korea P&I club started from a disadvantageous status. Nowadays, it has gained popularity domestically and abroad as well.

738. The general clauses of the Korea P&I club are based on that of foreign P&I clubs. However, there are several different provisions in the general clauses. The most distinguished difference is the way of dispute resolution and governing law clause. According to Articles 47 and 48, the dispute on the insurance should be resolved by the KCAB in Seoul, and the governing law is the Korean law. Korea does not have a distinct and separate maritime arbitration, unlike Japan, China and the U.K. However, the KCA has a special committee for maritime cases.

739. The KSA provides P&I insurance coverage for its members. Most members of the KSA are the owners of Korean-flagged vessels which navigate within Korean waters and neighboring Japanese and Chinese waters. The covered risks include oil pollution damages, cargo claims and one-fourth of collision liability. Its policy is based on the U.K.-based P&I club's rules. The most notable difference is the dispute resolution procedure and governing law clause. The KSA P&I rules says that the dispute on the insurance should be solved by the Korean Commercial Arbitration situated at Seoul with the Korean governing law.

740. The KSA revised two controversial clauses such as the warranty clause and the pay-to-be-paid rule clause in 2012. Newly revised clause on the warranty requires a causal linkage between the breach of the warranty and the accident in order for the insurer to be exempted from the liability to pay insurance proceeds.[154] It followed general principle of the Korean law requiring causation to impose liability upon the wrongdoer in tort cases and aimed at protecting the insured. The new P&I insurance general clauses also alleviated the requirement for the insurer to pay the insurance proceeds against the victims. The KSA as the liability insurer will not apply the pay-to-be-paid rule in case the accident occurs in a mandatory liability situation, such as oil pollution, crew compensation, and wreck removal. Nevertheless, the KSA is entitled to invoke the pay-to-be-paid rule against the owner of the damaged cargo (or the insurer) in case of cargo claims.[155]

154. For details, In Hyeon Kim, *Warranty and the Pay-to-be-Paid Rule in Korea*, 43-4 JMLC 572 (October 2013).
155. For details, *ibid.*, 573.

Selected Bibliography

Articles

In Hyeon Kim. 'An Introduction to Korean Law Governing Carriage of Goods by Sea'. *Journal of Maritime Law and Commerce* 36, No. 4 (October 2005).

In Hyeon Kim. 'Korean Maritime Law Update: 2004'. *Journal of Maritime Law and Commerce* 36, No. 2 (July 2005).

In Hyeon Kim. 'Korean Maritime Law Update: 2006'. *Journal of Maritime Law and Commerce* 38, No. 2 (July 2007).

In Hyeon Kim. 'Korean Maritime Law Update: 2007'. *Journal of Maritime Law and Commerce* 39, No. 2 (July 2008).

In Hyeon Kim. 'Korean Maritime Law Update: 2008'. *Journal of Maritime Law and Commerce* 40, No. 2 (July 2009).

In Hyeon Kim. 'Korean Maritime Law Update: 2009'. *Journal of Maritime Law and Commerce* 41, No. 2 (July 2010).

In Hyeon Kim. 'Korean Maritime Law Update: 2010'. *Journal of Maritime Law and Commerce* 42, No. 2 (July 2011).

In Hyeon Kim. 'Korean Maritime Law Update: 2011–2012'. *Journal of Maritime Law and Commerce* 44, No. 2 (July 2013).

In Hyeon Kim. 'Warranty and the Pay-to-be-Paid Rule in Korea', *Journal of Maritime Law and Commerce* 43, No. 4 (July 2012).

In Hyeon Kim. Mari *Maritime Law*. Seoul: Bubmoonsa, 2007 (Written in Korean).

In Hyeon Kim & Jong Hyun Choi. 'Korean Maritime Law Update: 2005'. *Journal of Maritime Law and Commerce* 37, No. 2 (July 2006).

Jae Du Shim. *English Marine Transportation Law*. Seoul: Kilansa, 1997 (Written in Korean).

Jong Hyun Choi. *Maritime Law*. Seoul: Parkyounsa, 2009 (Written in Korean).

Lee Sik Chai. *An Introduction to Korean Maritime Law*. Seoul: Korea University Press, 1999 (Written in English).

Sung Kyun Lee. *Maritime Law* in details. Seoul: KMI, 2010 (Written in Korean).

Books

Aleka Mandaraka-Sheppard. *Modern Maritime Law*. London: Routledge-Cavendish, 2007.

Boris Soyer. *Warranties in Marine Insurance*. London: Cavendish Publishing, 2006.

Burdick Brittin. *International Law for Seagoing Officers*. Annapolis, Maryland: Naval Institute Press, 1986.

Selected Bibliography

Christopher Hill. *Maritime Law*. London: LLP, 2003.

David Robertson, Steven Friedell & Michael Sturley. *Admiralty and Maritime Law in the United States.* Durham, North Carolina: Carolina Academic Press, 2001.

Felix Wh Chan, Jimmy JM NG & Bobby KY Wong. *Shipping and Logistics Law - Principles and Practice in Hong Kong*. Hong Kong: Hong Kong University Press, 2002.

Francesco Berlingieri. *Berlingieri on Arrest of Ships*. London: Informa, 2006.

Gorton et al. *Shipbroking and Chartering Practice*. London: Informa, 2009.

Grant Gilmore & Charles Black. *The Law of Admiralty*. Mineola, New York: The Foundation Press, 1975.

Howard Bennett. *The Law of Marine Insurance*. New York: Oxford University Press, 2006.

Institute of Maritime Law. *Southampton on Shipping Law*. London: Informa, 2008.

John Wilson. *Carriage of Goods by Sea.* London: Pearson, 2010.

Julian Cooke et al. *Voyage Charters*. London: Informa, 2007.

Leo D'arcy, Carole Murray & Barbara Cleave. *Schmitthoff's Export Trade, The Law and Practice of International Trade.* London: Thomson Sweet & Maxwell, 2005.

Lindy Johnson. *Coastal State Regulation of International Shipping*. Dobbs Ferry, New York: Oceana Publications, Inc. 2004.

Malcolm Clarke. *Contracts of Carriage by Air*. London: LLP, 2002.

Martin Davies. (ed.). *Jurisdiction and Forum Selection in International Maritime Law.* The Hague: Kluwer Law International, 2005.

Nicholas Healy & Joseph Sweeney. *The Law of Marine Collision*. Centreville, Maryland: Cornell Maritime Press, 1998.

Sir Alan Abraham Mocatta. *Scrutton on Charterparties and Bills of Lading*. London Sweet & Maxwell, 1984.

Steven Hazelwood. *P&I Clubs Law and Practice*. London: LLP, 1994.

Susan Hodges. *Law of Marine Insurance*. London: Cavendish Publishing, 1996.

Terence Coghlin et al. *Time Charters*. London: Informa, 2008.

Thor Falkanger, Hans Jacob Bull & Lasse Brautaset. *Introduction to Maritime Law—The Scandinavian Perspective.* Oslo: Tano Aschehoug, 1998.

William Tetley. *International Maritime and Admiralty Law*. Montreal: Yvon Blais, 2002.

William Tetley. *Marine Cargo Claims*. Canada: Thomson Carswell, 2008.

Table of Cases

The numbers here refer to paragraph numbers

Table of Cases

Index

The numbers here refer to paragraph numbers

Index

Index

www.ingramcontent.com/pod-product-compliance
Ingram Content Group UK Ltd.
Pitfield, Milton Keynes, MK11 3LW, UK
UKHW020142290926
15471UKWH00004B/644

9 789403 52459